Sex in the Heartland

Sex in the Heartland

~

Beth Bailey

10/00

Harvard University Press

Cambridge, Massachusetts, and London, England

1999

Library of Congress Cataloging-in-Publication Data
Bailey, Beth L., 1957–
  Sex in the heartland / Beth Bailey.
    p. cm.
  Includes bibliographical references (p.) and index.
  ISBN 0-674-80278-0 (alk. paper)
  1. Sex customs—Middle West—History—20th century. 2. Sex
ethics—Middle West—History—20th century. I. Title.
HQ18.M53B35 1999
306.7'0977—dc21   99-21754

For David

Contents

Introduction

1 Before the Revolution   **13**

2 Sex and the Therapeutic Culture   **45**

3 Responsible Sex   **75**

4 Prescribing the Pill   **105**

5 Revolutionary Intent   **136**

6 Sex as a Weapon   **154**

7 Sex and Liberation   **175**

8 Remaking Sex   **200**

Epilogue   **216**

Abbreviations   **221**

Notes   **223**

Credits   **251**

Acknowledgments   **253**

Index   **257**

There is a great crowded bluff
in Lawrence Kansas
that looks a long way
into the astonished heart
of America.

—*Lawrence Ferlinghetti*

Sex in the Heartland

Introduction

Television current events programs often walk a fine line between chronicling trends and creating them, and the producers of the popular TV show *Open End* were probably doing both when they scheduled a show entitled "The Sexual Revolution in America." It was 1963. John F. Kennedy was president. Going steady was the fad in high school. Female college students had curfews; many student handbooks included some reference to setting sexual "standards." The Pill had been available as a contraceptive for almost three years, but few doctors would prescribe it to unmarried women. People married young: more than half the women who got married that year were under the age of 21. Homosexuality was officially designated a mental illness by the American Psychiatric Association. In fact, a televised discussion of sex was beyond the limits of acceptability: panicked by the explosive topic, the New York station responsible for *Open End* canceled the sexual revolution show and withdrew it from national distribution.[1] What sexual revolution?

In hindsight, the sexual climate of the early 1960s appears repressed and repressive. Most of the events we identify with the sexual revolution lay in the future, and in the early fall of 1963 no one imagined the tumultuous years to come. Nonetheless, well before the "Summer of Love" or the gay liberation movement or even the bestselling sex manual *The Joy of Sex,* Americans were already talking about sexual revolution. They looked to *Playboy* magazine and its imitators, to the sexual claims of self-defined outsiders like the Beat poets, to skyrocketing rates of juvenile delinquency,

1

to the statistics offered a decade earlier in Alfred Kinsey's studies of human sexuality. Fifty percent of American women had had premarital intercourse. Thirty-seven percent of American men had participated in some sort of homosexual activity. Revolution. To most Americans in 1963, when combined with "sex," the word "revolution" signaled danger.

From the early 1960s on, Americans used a metaphor of revolution to make sense of changes in the nation's sexual landscape. "Revolution" provided the framework for understanding conflicts over sex; "revolution" was the context within which change occurred. Because of this overarching context, many Americans amplified the importance of what they might otherwise have understood as minor events or as results of long-term, gradual trends. The Pill, men with long hair, and student protests against curfews on college campuses all took on a significance as part of "the sexual revolution" that each lacked on its own. In a climate of revolution, it seemed that a great deal was at stake.

Those who watched this "revolution" with varying degrees of alarm were not all wrong in seeing it as such. Things were changing, and by the late 1960s there were many in America who embraced revolution, sexual and otherwise. But in the eyes of the nation the metaphor of revolution lent coherence to impulses that were, in fact, often in tension with one another. Young women's insistence that they were responsible enough not to need curfews at college was quite different from the politics of pleasure celebrated by parts of the 1960s "counterculture," for example, and the monogamous sexual relationship of an unmarried couple was not quite the same thing as "free love." In subsuming a diverse set of changes under the term "revolution," Americans conflated changes that had very different origins, intentions, and outcomes.

We have inherited the term "sexual revolution" from those who first coined it in the 1960s, and in adopting their phrase we have perpetuated some of the confusions of that era. We continue to hear echoes of danger in the word "revolution." We continue to conflate very different impulses and outcomes. This received language of revolution has made it much more difficult for us to understand and discuss the roles and meanings of sex in contemporary America.

In order to make sense of "the sexual revolution," we need to sort out its various strands. They do not all have to stand—or fall—together. Too many of those who raise their voices in current debates about sex in our society see in the sexual revolution only the excesses and extremes of a violent and difficult era. In a simpler time one might have said they risked throwing the baby out with the bath water. By offering a history of America's recent struggles over sex, showing what people were rebelling against and why and how things changed, I hope to make possible more complex judgments about the various legacies of revolution. Yes, some of it was excessive, and some of it was bad. But a great deal of it was good and necessary, and those portions made our society more just and perhaps even more moral.

Of course, good and bad, when it comes to sex in contemporary America, are not universal concepts. For those who believe homosexuality is a sin and premarital intercourse a moral crime, this book offers no common ground. But those who see the sexual revolution as the triumph of irresponsible and exploitative sexuality over decent, morally grounded, and responsible sexual behavior may discover new and useful perspectives in this history. And those who claim the radical nature of the revolution may be surprised by just how deep-seated and *mainstream* the origins of many of those revolutionary changes really were.

—

Despite the way it is often portrayed in contemporary diatribes and debates, the sexual revolution was not created by a set of radicals on the fringe of American society and then imposed on the rest of the nation. It was forged in America's heartland as well, shaped not only by committed revolutionaries but by people who had absolutely no intention of abetting a revolution in sex. Adding the heartland to our stories of the sexual revolution changes its meaning: this revolution was thoroughly *of* America.

For that reason, this book is not about the cosmopolitan enclaves and radical gatherings on the east and west coasts. It is also not the tale of larger-than-life actors—Hefner, Kinsey, Pincus, et al.—who too often stand in for the sexual revolution in our histories. These "heroes of the revolution" and its most committed activists are indeed critical actors. America's sexual revolution would have looked much different without *Playboy*, the Kinsey reports, or the Pill; it might not have happened in any recognizable form without the Summer of Love or the Stonewall Inn rebellion (which helped to coalesce a gay liberation movement) or the flood of writings that poured out of the radical communities in New York and California.

However, if the challenges to America's sexual codes had taken place only in the streets of Greenwich Village and the Haight-Ashbury, there would have been no revolution. The noise and ferment of the late 1960s and early 1970s would have been just another episode in which a small but highly visible group—like the bohemians of the early twentieth century or the Beats of more recent provenance—rejected the mores of a society its members found stifling. They might have claimed influence and importance greatly disproportionate to their numbers, but they would not have constituted a revolution.

To go beyond the usual suspects and demonstrate how widespread and fundamental were the changes we call the sexual revolution, where better to look than Kansas? Thanks to *The Wizard of Oz,* Kansas is the state that most consistently represents the antithesis of bicoastal sophistication. It is the ultimate provincial place, the ultimate not–New York. "Toto, I have a feeling we're not in Kansas anymore," Dorothy says as she opens her eyes to the Technicolor world of Oz. As Paul Nathanson puts it in *Over the Rainbow: The Wizard of Oz as a Secular Myth of America,* "Kansas lies precisely at the geographical center of the country: it is midway between East and West, North and South. This region symbolically transcends time, space, history, and geography. It is (to use a metaphor from *The Wizard*) the eye of the storm, the calm center around which national life swirls. This landscape belongs to none of the major sources of power."[2] Kansas is the quintessential heartland state.

It was in the town of Lawrence that the battles of the sexual revolution were most widely engaged and most visible to the citizens of the rest of Kansas. Lawrence is home to the University of Kansas, which, like other major state universities, has been an engine of change in its state and region for much of the twentieth century. Throughout its history, Lawrence has often been somewhat out of step with much of the rest of the state.

Lawrence, however, is very much a part of Kansas. While the town's economy is largely dependent on the university, the university is funded by the state legislature at the taxpayers' pleasure and filled with the sons and daughters of the state's voters. Even though some of the town's residents have wished it possible at times, Lawrence could never ignore the state to which it belongs. And despite the centrality of the university, the town of Lawrence has always been much more than KU. Town-gown conflicts have a long history in Lawrence, as do tensions among the various other groups that make up the population. Many of Lawrence's people have not "belonged" to the university, and in the decades following World War II these citizens ranged from members of the prosperous business community to farm families on the town's outskirts to a large number of people who had not completed a high school education, much less attended college. While Lawrence is not a "typical" Kansas town, facts of geography, population, politics, economy, and culture link it firmly to Kansas, and to the rest of America's heartland.[3]

Lawrence's sexual revolution is not representative of America's experience, but that is not because it lies in the heartland. Lawrence's revolution is specific to itself—as were the revolutions lived in San Francisco, New York, Atlanta, Ann Arbor, and Albuquerque. Different parts of the revolution flourished in different places. Lawrence, for example, never developed the large-scale singles-bar scene that was so important in some of the nation's big cities. It never had a gay bathhouse culture or a district full of adult bookstores and theaters showing X-rated films. And neither did the towns and suburbs and even urban neighborhoods in which the vast majority of Americans lived. Throughout America, people were affected by what was happening on a national scale, whether structural changes that touched their lives directly or simply awareness of geographically distant events through the omnipresent mass media. Nonetheless, these national events played themselves out on the local level in ways profoundly influenced by the specifics of local situations. While a study of one place does not provide a representative model of "the revolution," it does move us past policies and polemics to the texture of change in Americans' lives. By looking beyond the famous personalities, the rhetoric of national organizations, and the constructions of the media to the experiences of one midwestern university town embedded in an increasingly potent national culture, we can learn much about the social and cultural changes we call the sexual revolution.

—

To claim the sexual revolution for the heartland as well as for the radical fringes matters because our notions about what the sexual revolution was—the stories we tell, the histories we make—are tools in our continuing negotiations over the shape of our society.[4] Portraying the sexual revolution as the product of a few extremists, somehow unattached to the world the rest of us lived in, is a political act. Such portrayals obscure the true sources of social change and often work to marginalize and discredit these past challenges to the sexual status quo. This version of the sexual revolution is also historically inaccurate.[4] The set of changes we call the sexual revolution was thoroughly part of American culture, born of widely shared values and beliefs and of major transformations in the structure of American society. For while the revolution was built of purposeful assertions and acts, often on the part of self-proclaimed outsiders, it was possible because of the recasting of American society during and after World War II.

6

In those years the nationalizing forces of the federal government, the market, consumer society, the mass media, and large institutions, both public and private, undermined the ability of local elites to control the boundaries of their communities. The opportunities for mobility—both social and geographic—presented by a strong economy, by universal high school education and the explosion of attendance at colleges and universities, and by new legal protections of civil rights, changed the face of America. Radio, television, and Hollywood films offered people knowledge of a wider world, and that knowledge sometimes challenged local beliefs and local hierarchies. The increasing power and presence of national institutions and national culture upset "traditional" ways—be it Jim Crow or sexual mores—and created openings for contestation and change.

The emerging national culture was not an outside force imposed on authentic, local cultures. It was created as a national project, as who we are became determined less by our geographic communities and more by other sorts of identities. Lawrence's people were residents of Kansas, but that was only one facet of more complex identities derived, at least partially, from cultural categories and institutions of national scope. Medical doctors, professors, university administrators, public health officials—all had professional identities that transcended the local, and all claimed authority to act or speak based on professional credentials that were nationally constituted and recognized. The people of Lawrence participated in national professional societies and in local branches of national organizations. None of these organizations—the American Medical Association, the American Civil Liberties Union, Zero Population Growth, Campus Crusade for Christ, the Episcopal Church, Students for a Democratic Society, the Minutemen—was born in Lawrence, but all were active there.

University and high school students also claimed identities that transcended the local—as members of the nationally validated category of "youth." They understood their actions within a national framework, formed local branches of national organizations, and corresponded with their peers about the issues of the day. Lawrence's African-American population situated itself in relation to struggles for civil rights or for Black

Power that were definitely not centered in this small town. And virtually all of Lawrence's citizens were immersed in national culture as communicated by the mass media. Just like people throughout the country, they watched television and saw movies and read *Time* or *Newsweek* or the *Ladies' Home Journal.* This was not a foreign "national" culture. It was *their* culture.

In the sexual revolution, both those who fought for change and those who opposed it acted in local arenas but drew on identities, understandings, and institutions that were defined nationally. Change was introduced in a set of locally negotiated actions by Kansans—and Iowans and North Carolinians and, yes, Californians and New Yorkers—who were full participants in the national postwar culture.

—

In sorting out the impulses and movements commonly conflated into "the sexual revolution," it is crucial to recognize how many challenges to America's sexual status quo were not made in the name of revolution. Many of them, in fact, seemed to have nothing to do with sex. The fundamental and large-scale transformations that reduced local cultural autonomy and isolation certainly did not originate in a desire for sexual revolution, but neither did a host of changes that are more clearly associated with shifting sexual mores and behavior. Some of the most important elements of the sexual revolution were unintended consequences of actions with quite different goals.

The birth control pill, to a great degree, made possible the (hetero)sexual revolution. Yet those who developed oral contraceptives did not intend their work to promote what the majority of Americans at the time called "promiscuity." Doctors generally refused to prescribe the Pill to women who were not married; the Supreme Court did not rule this practice unconstitutional until 1972. It was largely because of widespread concern about the "population explosion" and through the public health community's involvement with Lyndon Johnson's Great Society that the Pill became more generally available. Those who acted in such capacities were not promoting sexual freedom or championing women's right to control their own bodies.

On college campuses, too, the sexual revolution took root in spaces not intended for its growth. College students often found allies among administrators when they challenged curfews for women and other aspects of the *in loco parentis* system that provided (limited) institutional controls on sexual behavior. Few of these administrators accepted doctrines of sexual freedom. Some supported liberalization of rules as a way to develop responsibility and maturity among students. Many deans of women believed parietals violated the principle of equality between the sexes. Other administrators, especially provosts, presidents, and members of boards of trustees or regents, became increasingly aware that *in loco parentis* was a potential legal nightmare, with the limits of universities' responsibility and liability undefined. By the time large numbers of students phrased their attacks in revolutionary terms, this system of sexual controls had already been weakened.

Even those who attempted to police the boundaries of acceptable sexual behavior made progressive change possible—though usually not intentionally. In the years during and after World War II, many "sexually deviate" behaviors, including homosexuality, were redefined as mental illnesses, deserving treatment, rather than misconduct, deserving punishment. This shift affected institutional policies, and so had real impact on men's and women's lives. Being forced to undergo "treatment" was arguably as bad as or worse than being summarily dismissed from job or school, and this redefinition may have seemed little more than semantic to some of the men and women labeled sick instead of sinful. Nonetheless, the institutional move from punishment to treatment complicated lines of authority within the institutions and forced some of those who implemented the policies to confront what they saw as logical inconsistencies in such definitions. While defining homosexuality as mental illness did not foster sexual freedom, the concomitant changes in policy worked to undermine the authority of those who implemented the rules. That loss of authority would have long-term and profound effects.

The sexual revolution was not completely dependent on any of the above: the Pill was not the only means of preventing pregnancy; one could have sex before an 11:00 curfew quite as well as after; the turn to psychology as a means of managing transgressive sexuality may have stifled not only individual lives but also the options of liberation movements. Nonetheless, these developments and others like them helped to shape the sexual revolution. Even though these strands of revolution were largely unintended consequences of other efforts, they were critical parts of the whole.

By the late 1960s these nonrevolutionary origins were largely eclipsed by purposeful claims and radical acts. Young people adopted the Pill as a tool of revolution. College students no longer appealed for greater freedom by arguing that they were "responsible," but simply demanded freedom. Gay men and lesbians actively rejected the paradigms of sin and mental illness and created a public culture of liberation. A very visible portion of America's youth were fighting for a revolution in sex, and a great many Americans, in more limited fashion, lived out the opportunities their battles made possible. Those who pursued revolution, however, did not share a single vision. While the disparate efforts of those who wanted very different sorts of change took on greater weight in society because they were all "part" of "the" revolution, these revolutionaries often were at odds with one another.

Some of them sought to challenge the values and norms of a repressive society they often called "Amerika." Capitalizing on the sexual chaos and fears of the nation, political-cultural revolutionaries attempted to use sex as a weapon against "straight" society. In their own lives, some members of America's counterculture practiced a Dionysian and polymorphous sexuality that completely rejected mainstream concerns about "respectability." John Sinclair, manager of the rock group MC5, proclaimed in his "Total Assault on the Culture" manifesto: "Our position is that all people must be free to fuck freely, whenever and wherever they want to."[5] Other countercultural seekers believed they had to remake love and reclaim sex to create a new and viable community, and they experimented with sex as with other forms of community organization. Still others celebrated sex as a "natural" act that symbolized an alternative to materialism, capitalism, or the military-industrial complex. In these different ways, members of America's growing counterculture used sex as a tool of revolution.

The movements for women's liberation and gay liberation that gained force at the cusp of the 1970s overlapped with America's countercultural and hip communities. There is no way to fully untangle these strands, and conflicts over sex and gender among members of these intertwined movements profoundly affected the "revolution" as a whole. The concept of liberation, however, distinguishes these movements from the larger counterculture. By the late 1960s many Americans considered sexual orientation and sexuality crucial aspects of an individual's identity. Sexual identities, so constructed, were a critical component of "liberation" struggles, which were public and avowedly political. Among those who fought for gay liberation, some men and women pursued what was essentially a civil rights agenda. However, many women saw lesbianism as a sexual *and* political identity assumed in defiance against patriarchal oppression, and gay men sought to forge a public gay culture in which sexuality played a prominent role.

The women's liberation movement, like the gay liberation movement, ranged from supporters of a NOW-type equal rights agenda to those who questioned the fundamental organization of society. However, unlike members of the gay liberation movement, which defined sex as a liberating force, many feminists believed sex was the key element in their oppression. Women demanded "the right to control our own bodies." They, along with male allies, fought to reform rape laws. They analyzed the ways in which women's sexuality was appropriated and devalued in a patriarchal or misogynist culture. At the same time, many women claimed the right to sexual freedom and/or sexual pleasure. "The Myth of the Vaginal Orgasm" ranks right up there with *The Feminine Mystique* in many women's personal histories. Across America, women—alone or with other women—took mirrors and looked, for the first time, at their own sexual organs. While some feminists saw the differences between women and men as culturally constructed, others found pride and power in claims of an essential difference between the sexes, a difference that many believed was rooted in women's biological—and sexual-reproductive—nature.

Yet another strand of this revolution appears modest compared to the counterculture and the liberation movements but is perhaps the most revolutionary of all. During the late 1960s and early 1970s many young people began to rethink the role of gender in relation to sex. In coed dorms, college students declared that they were trying to escape the "sexual role-playing" of dating relationships. Men and women explored the possibilities of friendship. Androgyny was in. And an increasing number of young men and women began to live together "without benefit of matrimony," not as an affirmation of free love or revolution, but in a *de facto* rejection of the sexual double standard. Despite the lack of state or religious sanction, most of these couples looked more like young marrieds than like wild-eyed revolutionaries. The revolution they sought was in the meaning of sex, and their battles were over gender roles, not sexual freedom.

The sexual revolution was not a simple, two-sided contest between the proponents of freedom and the forces of repression. Even those who actively supported the "revolution" had radically different concepts of what it was and what it should accomplish. Those who actively opposed it varied as well. Parents who worried about their daughters' "safety"; public health officials who feared a potential explosion of venereal disease; fundamentalist preachers who called down the wrath of God on fornicators and homo-sexuals; and the many women (especially working-class women and women of color) who believed women's liberation, including its sexual components, was not in touch with their realities—these did not form a coherent movement.

Yet the diverse revolutionaries and their fellow travelers in sexual revolt were rebelling against a coherent set of sexual norms, a coherent sexual culture. In order to evaluate their revolution and its legacies, we must recognize that sexual culture. It was not a world of responsible sexual behavior, governed by moral standards. It was not a world in which the young were chaste until marriage, despite public insistence that they be so. What people did in private was quite often radically different from what they admitted to in public. Young people were not sexually pure; rather, most engaged in a series of sexual skirmishes. "Nice girls" said no; boys kept pushing. Women were supposed to be virgins when they married, though about half of American women were not. Furthermore, virginity was not an absolute state; it was frequently no more than "technical," true according to the letter, not the spirit, of the law. So long as there was no vaginal penetration, a whole variety of other sexual acts, including oral sex, didn't count.

As presented to the nation's youth in everything from advertisements to advice columns, the line that separated healthy masculinity from sexual aggression was a fine one. Girls faced a similar dilemma: Where was the line between "respectability" and frigidity? Between sexually attractive and cheap? The sexual double standard was a powerful force, even in monoga-mous and committed relationships, and decisions about sex often were made as much from fear as from moral principles. The fears were many: fear of pregnancy, fear of being discovered, fear of losing one's boyfriend, fear of losing one's "reputation." In 1968 a young woman discovered to be living with her boyfriend in a monogamous relationship was branded a "whore" in newspapers throughout the nation (see Chapter 8). And the risks attached to homosexual relationships were even greater.

In fundamental ways, the sexual revolution combated this ugliness and hypocrisy. But it also called into question what many Americans be-lieved were timeless truths and traditional values. Subjected to vehement attacks from self-styled revolutionaries of many stripes, these Americans fought back. In general, the sexual revolution came about less through pitched battles and overt cultural warfare than through negotiation and compromise, for there was significant common ground between various strands of the two "sides." Nonetheless, the confrontations over sex were emotional and hard fought, the victories often ambiguous. Decades later we are still fighting about sex and its legitimate expression, those battles complicated by the scourge of AIDS, by the problems of teenage pregnancy and motherhood, by emerging medical technologies that offer new possibilities and new questions about ethics and morality. At this point the full outcome of the sexual revolution is as yet unclear. But as we try to understand the meaning of the revolution and its legacy, it helps to untangle the threads, rejecting the conflation of disparate impulses into a singular revolution and acknowledging that the conflicts were rarely so simple as the metaphor of revolution suggests.

1

Before the Revolution

World War II came to Lawrence as it did to the rest of America: in degrees of anger and horror and shock. Throughout the evening of December 7, 1941, the Lawrence *Journal World* reported, people stood in the cold in front of the newspaper office windows to read war dispatches the staff posted as they came over the wire. Most people surely gathered around radios in warm rooms, talking in tense voices about the future, for nine out of ten of Lawrence's families had radios.[1] Yet there is something in the portrait of people gathered together before the lighted windows. Perhaps they didn't want to be alone at this difficult moment, and sought in public space a form of community that radio, tying us ever more closely together in our separate homes, could not sustain. In this time of crisis, Lawrence, like towns and cities across America, had already begun negotiating the new boundaries of public life.

The *Journal World* stayed connected with the AP wire until ten o'clock that Sunday night, even though it usually had no Sunday wire service at all. Maintaining the wire connection was a minor act, but it symbolizes a whole constellation of connections that would transform America during the war and in the years that followed. During World War II and then the Cold War era, the federal government came to play an increasingly central role in American life. The total mobilization for the war against the Axis powers, followed by postwar social policies that sent millions of veterans to college on the G.I. Bill, linked the nation with high-speed interstate highways, and helped to create a national middle-class culture that encompassed an unprecedented majority of the nation's citizens, touched the lives of virtually all of America's people.

Such actions changed the country's cultural geography, creating new arenas of possibility and new spaces for contestation and change. It was in these new spaces, these cracks and fissures, that America's sexual revolution would emerge, an unintended byproduct of acts and policies and decisions that had little or nothing to do with sex. The seeds of the sexual revolution took root long before American youth demanded revolution; they were planted in ground prepared by the disruptions and transformations of a previous generation's war.

In Lawrence, Kansas, as elsewhere, World War II had a profound effect. Compared with the devastation of much of the rest of the globe, America's cities and towns were physically untouched but in less visible ways they were fundamentally changed. As America mobilized for war, national goals often conflicted with "the way we do it here," and though local ways often triumphed (as with the race issue in military training camps in the South), the needs of the wartime state frequently challenged local autonomy and local custom. Most of these challenges were unintentional, byproducts of the nation's concerted attempt to win the war. Nonetheless, they sometimes undermined existing social hierarchies and weakened the power of local elites. In spaces created by federal action, other Americans contested the status quo, whether by demanding civil rights or by defying definitions of "respectability" that had worked to separate social classes. As Americans fought enemies abroad, they also struggled with one another for control of their rapidly changing communities.

The clearest of the challenges to established patterns of authority was structural. During the war, building on FDR's New Deal, the federal government expanded its role and its reach. As federal authorities administered the draft and military training, oversaw defense industries, and attempted to manage the homefront war, the federal government became a greater presence in the daily lives of Americans and in the civic and economic lives of their towns and cities. In this process, the government often interrupted local practices and created new sites of power and authority.

It was not that the government was avowedly or inherently progressive, especially about sex. Some of the institutions created or reconstituted during the war—such as the public health departments charged with treating wartime outbreaks of venereal disease—aggressively attempted to control sexual behavior deemed dangerous to the body politic and thus to the war effort. It is hard to view their actions as anything but repressive, even if the officials involved largely avoided mentioning sexual morality and spoke instead of health or of winning the war. Nonetheless, institutions such as public health departments and public universities (increasingly funded by the federal government) were critical parts of the nationalizing process. They tied local communities and their citizens more closely to an increasingly powerful national culture, and they interrupted the continuity of local patterns and local prejudices alike. Even though these institutions were often quite conservative in their positions on sex, the sexual revolution of the following decades would not have been possible without their nationalizing force.

The government's more interventionist stance during the war also set a precedent that would prove crucial to the postwar sexual revolution. Limited successes in establishing national standards for local acts, whether in dealing with the question of race in military training camps, managing industry's war production, or developing ways to motivate people on the homefront, would lead some Americans to look to the federal government for support in their struggles for equal rights after the war. Though governmental action on civil rights was slow and uneven, by the time the self-described sexual revolution had emerged, many citizens saw the federal government as a powerful and appropriate guarantor of rights. Many who sought a sexual revolution were revolutionary in their politics as well and rejected government as either tool or ally. But crucial battles of the sexual revolution—questions about birth control and abortion, obscenity standards and free speech, the issue of discrimination on the basis of gender and, eventually, sexual orientation—were played out in Congress, the executive branch, and the Supreme Court.

Another critical challenge to the established order during World War II came from a conjunction of federal actions and market forces. The experience of the war unsettled local cultures. In the United States people moved in unprecedented numbers: more than 12 million men and women served in the armed forces; more than 15 million civilians moved to another county or another state, most for defense-related work.[2] The fact that people who had never traveled more than a hundred miles from their homes moved across the country or across the world, where they lived in close proximity to people from vastly different backgrounds, fundamentally altered the nation's cultural landscape.

The American people had always been mobile, but this vast internal migration was qualitatively different: it transpired under the rubric of national purpose and the mandate of the war emergency, and many of those who moved spent their time in large-scale institutions or organizations supervised, directly or indirectly, by the U.S. government. Perhaps most important, during the war more Americans than in any previous era found themselves in close and enforced contact with others not like themselves. Even during the years when immigrants flowed into America, on New York City's Lower East Side, one of the most crowded places on earth, people had managed to live with others of their own nationality or ethnicity—even with others from the same village of origin or extended family. The war forced individuals loose from all these connections: family, region, ethnicity, religion, even class. (Race was frequently an exception here, for the army separated men into "white" and "Negro" units. But African-American units were forged from southern rural black men and northern urban black men, trained in the Midwest and shipped to Europe. The units may have been segregated, but they weren't homogeneous, and the experience certainly disrupted prewar patterns of life.) The war also forced into motion many from families that stretched back generations in one place and had the economic security to stay put. The war was like someone shaking one of those snow-filled paperweights: flakes flew in all directions and settled where they dropped.

At the end of the war, people didn't always land where they'd started out. Even those who went back home, settled down, married the girl or boy next door, for better or worse carried something of their faraway experiences with them. In countless minor arguments and adjustments over dinner tables or in the workplace, their new ideas and new ways unsettled local knowledge. Though the culture of the postwar years is suffused with conformism and materialism and a desire for stability, one can also see a people negotiating the cultural dislocations of war and its aftermath. As the awareness of different ways of life precipitated by the war destabilized local certainties, whether about some small point of etiquette or about unexamined prejudices, local ground became more fertile for change to take root. Both sexual mores and the role of sex in America's public life would be part of what changed.

The social and economic changes that came about as America emerged from the war with unprecedented prosperity and international influence greatly enlarged America's civil society. To put it bluntly, more people were included in American society after the war than before. Different sorts of people began to count—to be visible in the American landscape, to have a voice. From today's standpoint, in a society that debates the meaning of multiculturalism and attempts to celebrate diversity, the culture of the postwar years seems repressively homogeneous. It was an avowedly white, middle-class culture, assimilative in intent (at least to a certain point), with penalties for those who did not conform. Nonetheless, this process of assimilation—universal high school education, for example—drew people from radically different backgrounds into what was defined as the national "American" culture.[3] Women, African Americans, Native Americans, Asian Americans, Hispanics, and others who had served the country during the war were now laying claim to their place in civilian society. Their participation was changing the face of America.

This process was not always smoothly accomplished; the clashes over racial integration are the obvious example. But one could also think of the millions of urban (often ethnic) and rural people who met in the postwar suburbs, or of a national media that crossed all sorts of lines: the ethnic humor of "[I Remember] Mama," and "The Goldbergs," and "Life with Riley," Nat King Cole's controversial prime-time show, and the Ed Sullivan Show, featuring performers like Bo Diddley and Elvis Presley—all were seen in the small towns of the Midwest and the rural South, as well as in the nation's big cities, from gold coasts to ghettos. In the new space created by television, as well as in classrooms and offices and factories and PTAs and homes throughout America, people had to contend with different mores and customs, with different definitions of respectability, and with sexualized images of popular culture and advertising, produced on a national scale for a national audience. Because of economic and technological developments that drew more and more Americans into a national culture, the boundaries of regions and towns—and of class and race—became more permeable than ever before.

Thus the nationalizing forces of World War II and its aftermath, even as they had nothing directly to do with sex, created openings for the direct challenges to the established order posed by the sexual revolution. The major cultural and structural changes stemming from the war would, to a great extent, determine the shape of that revolution. As such, the conflicts over cultural authority and control during and after World War II can be seen as the opening battles of the sexual revolution.

Sex itself was also a critically important issue during the war. Issues of sex—and its governance—were virtually omnipresent in wartime America. The marriage rate skyrocketed: Were those marriages appropriate? What rules should govern the behavior of couples separated "for the duration"? What about the problem of "Victory Girls," who seemed to confuse promiscuity with patriotism? How could the federal government guarantee a "wholesome" environment in training camps? How might venereal disease—the common companion of war's dislocations—best be controlled? How could homosexuals be detected and barred from military service so as not to pose a "threat" to other men? How could towns maintain a "clean and wholesome" environment when inundated by war workers or servicemen and their need for recreation?[4] These were not questions to debate at leisure, but pressing issues made more so by the high stakes of the war. In discussing sex Americans debated not only issues of sexual morality but also the relative power of the state and of local elites, the meaning of gender and of social class, questions of individual rights and freedoms in relation to some concept of the public good, the boundaries of public life, and the nature of community. Like their counterparts all over America, the people of Lawrence, Kansas, struggled with the problems posed by wartime sex.

—

One of the most exciting things that happened in Lawrence in 1940, as the nation moved closer to war, was a movie about another war. During the Civil War era Lawrence—located only forty miles from free-state Kansas's border with slaveholding Missouri—had been a center of abolitionist sentiment. On August 21, 1863, the Confederate officer William Clarke Quantrill led 450 men in a surprise attack on the town of 3,000. When the rebels rode out of Lawrence, 150 people lay dead and much of the town smoldered in near ruin. Republic Pictures' dramatic version of the bloody raid, starring John Wayne and Walter Pigeon, premiered in Lawrence in April 1940. No one theater was large enough to accommodate the crowds—with tickets going for a record-breaking 75¢ each—so *Dark Command* opened at all three of Lawrence's theaters simultaneously. Two lucky students from the University of Kansas were chosen to escort the stars to the premiere.[5]

What the visitors from Hollywood found was a town bearing no resemblance to the Kansas of *The Wizard of Oz*, which had premiered in Hollywood the previous year. Unlike the gray, dusty, and windswept plains from which the tornado plucked Dorothy and Toto, Lawrence was a lush, green town on the banks of a river locals called the Kaw. It was as hilly as the western plains were flat. The university, called KU for short, occupied the town's highest point, commonly referred to as the Hill or Mount Oread. A piece of college wisdom, passed down through student generations, was that you could tell a senior from a freshman by the size of her calf muscles—the climb up to campus was a steep one. Past KU, down the hill, was the town's other major public institution: Haskell Institute, which enrolled fewer than a thousand high school and vocational students, the majority of them Cherokee, Choctow, and Sioux. The town's main street, Massachusetts, was lined with shops that served not only the town and the university but also the farms of Douglas County. Churches significantly outnumbered restaurants in those days. Gracious mansions lined the elm-shaded streets west of the neat town center. Lawrence's poor concentrated in humbler neighborhoods on the floodplain that lay along the river and close to the railroad tracks (the Santa Fe line) that linked Lawrence to the rest of the nation.

Fewer than 15,000 people lived in Lawrence in 1940, though KU and Haskell students added significantly to that number from September through May. Mainly because of the university, Lawrence had a large professional class. Almost a third of its adult residents had attended or graduated from college at a time when the national figure was about 16 percent. But 47 percent of adult men had a grade school education or less, so that a graph of social class in Lawrence resembled a two-humped camel much more than a bell curve.[6] The missing middle had significant implications for politics and public policy.

In terms of race, Lawrence was fairly homogeneous. About 90 percent of its population claimed European ancestry, but because of the town's abolitionist legacy it also had a substantial and long-standing African-American community.[7] Lawrence's twentieth-century record on race relations did not compare well with its free-state history. KU accepted "Negro" students but segregated nonacademic facilities and too often tolerated discriminatory treatment in the classroom. Many downtown businesses relied on old Jim Crow, applied to African Americans and Native Americans as well. Still, for that era and that region, Lawrence was relatively progressive in its race relations and social policies, and was regarded with some suspicion by much of the rest of the state.

At the brink of war, Lawrence was still very much the same town that had opened its airport just ten days before the stock market crashed. In 1929 town leaders saw Lawrence as a progressive, modern place, just on the verge of really taking off. A paved highway had linked Lawrence to Topeka in 1927, and visionaries had dreams of a coast-to-coast highway that would pass right through Lawrence.

The Depression had interrupted such plans. As wheat prices plummeted from 99¢ a bushel in 1929 to 33¢ a bushel in 1932 and dust storms swept the plains, the vast acreages of western Kansas were devastated. So too was the economy of the state. The state legislature reduced the operating budget for the University of Kansas precipitously during the first half of the 1930s. Enrollment fell, as did employment, and faculty salaries were gradually reduced by 25 percent. Twelve percent fewer of Lawrence's families owned homes in 1940 than in 1930. But federal money kept Lawrence afloat, despite the Republican-leaning city government's reservations about the New Deal. And the university regained its pre-Crash enrollment by 1936. While the state of Kansas lost more than 100,000 people in the 1930s, Lawrence's population grew by almost 5 percent.[8] Lawrence suffered in the Great Depression, but not as badly as many communities. At the end of the decade, Lawrence remained stalled in its quest for economic "progress," but the desire for growth persisted.

With the outbreak of war, some of the town's leaders saw an opportunity. Lawrence's Chamber of Commerce formed a defense planning committee, chaired by Frank Stockton, the dean of KU's business school. This committee's goal was to attract war industry. By March 1942, it announced success: "a major war industry to our very doorstep," in Stockton's words. The Sunflower Ordnance Works for manufacturing smokeless powder was to be built on an 8,000-acre site outside Lawrence. A plant spokesman estimated that construction would require up to 28,000 workers—almost double Lawrence's population. "Construction workers will descend on Lawrence like locusts," he predicted.[9]

Those who courted the ordnance works were well aware of the problems it would bring. At the same time, there was more than a bit of hubris in their writings. They seemed certain they could control the forces of change. Sounding like Progressive era reformers, they emphasized the importance of wholesome recreation, efficiency, civic responsibility, and, above all else, planning. The *Journal World,* in an editorial shortly after the plans for the munitions plant were announced, stressed the importance of control. By planning for growth, the editors argued, "we can avoid the mistakes of other towns which did not start to plan until it was too late." Their concerns were not simply about overtaxed infrastructure or infectious disease, but also about sexual conduct. "In our planning we all must remember the great importance of keeping Lawrence a clean and wholesome city," they wrote, heralding a theme that was to be reiterated frequently during the war years.[10]

What were they worried about? Lawrence's civic leaders foresaw a flood of single men into their community. Some of the construction workers and ordnance factory workers would be drawn from their own community, but there weren't enough men in the Lawrence area to fill the plant's needs, especially as a large number would be serving in the armed forces. (Douglas County sent 3,335 men to war; 102 of them died.) Women would make up much of the shortfall—at one point, 60 percent of the ordnance works' operating personnel were female—but the plant would also attract many male workers, who, the town's business leaders imagined (not altogether without reason), would be rough, working-class men without the steadying influences of family or long-term community ties. Housing would be tight and trailer camps would materialize.[11]

The men would pump money into the local economy—but what would they spend their money on? Women and drink, according to stereotype. But except for beer, Lawrence was dry; neither the passage nor the repeal of national prohibition had much significance for this town's public life.[12] And women—that presented problems, too. The town's daughters? No. Prostitutes? Before the war, if prostitutes operated in Lawrence (and at least a few probably did, because of the university), they did so covertly enough that most citizens believed there were none. The upstanding citizens of Lawrence talked about the "fleshpots" of Kansas City or Topeka. When the *Journal World* editors advised planning for wholesomeness, they were quite serious. Large numbers of men with money in their pockets spelled not only economic recovery but also trouble.

The *Journal World,* which was closely allied with the town's business interests, ran another editorial about the munitions plant in late April 1942.[13] This piece, "Munitions Plant—Good or Evil?" began as a fairly careful weighing of interests, noting that the plant was "controversial." Universities and war production plants may both provide economic sustenance, the editor noted, but they are not interchangeable in their effects. "Defense workers do a good job well, but they insist upon their fun, too," he wrote. "Sedate townspeople who think college students are the *plus ultra* [sic] of wickedness and sin will have an unpleasant awakening. Bootleggers will probably blossom like dandelions. It is stupidity to believe that such boom-time sidelines as gambling and prostitution can be kept away from Lawrence. No longer will it be the cultural little city on the Kaw. Reno may gaze with envious eyes upon her midwestern prototype."

An exaggeration, surely, but here the editorial seems to spin out of control, exposing, in what was probably meant as humor, both the class subtext of these fears and also fault lines among the town's elite. As the university becomes little more than a "sideline," imagine the consequences: "The better clothing stores may begin to show only the newest things in denim overalls and workmen's brogans. That would be hell. And what of the sensitive seekers after culture who inhabit Mt. Oread? What will be their fate in this maelstrom of howling proletariat aces? They will either hole up on the Hill and . . . devote entire lifetimes to the pursuit of purity, or they will mingle with the crude newscomers [sic], and by so doing will lose their inbred polish and deep-seated culture." "Ah, well," the editor concluded, "progress necessitates far-reaching changes."

The Sunflower Ordnance Works, which produced rocket propellent powder and the powder used for Long Tom guns that fired 95-pound shells, never quite reached the proportions imagined in 1942, though with a peak employment of 12,000 workers, operating on twenty-four-hour shifts, it was the largest rocket powder plant in the world.[14] And it did have a profound effect on the small but ambitious town of Lawrence. By early 1943 twenty-six new bars crowded together in the small downtown district.

Bars were a boomtown business, and licensing requirements were relatively lax: licenses cost $50, and applicants had to be at least 21 years old, resident of Kansas for at least one year, resident of Douglas County for at least six months, and with no convictions for crimes involving moral turpitude in the past two years. Even so, licensees were often fronts for the real entrepreneurs: a 40-year old "aunt" stood in for the true owner of the Wonder Bar, which occupied a prominent position at Lawrence's major downtown intersection. In addition to a name with an oddly Germanic resonance, the Wonder Bar had only one toilet for both sexes and illegal venetian blinds, which screened the activities of its patrons from passersby. In the case of the Wonder Bar, the blinds hid illegal gambling. In other bars the blinds hid dancing, which was strictly prohibited in such establishments.

These "dirty-windowed dispensaries," as the *Journal World* called them, served only beer, for Douglas County was still dry to the extent that all hard liquor was forbidden. But plenty of the men got drunk on beer or bootleg whiskey, brawled and cursed, met women who were also looking for a good time, danced, necked, staggered out onto public streets. The highly sexualized atmosphere of these bars, spilling out into what had been polite, if not staid, downtown streets, alarmed many old Lawrence residents—and attracted others. Even more suspect establishments grew up on the outskirts of town, where marginal and disreputable businesses had traditionally clustered. Eleven new "outlying taverns" competed with the downtown "beer emporiums" for the dollars that war workers suddenly had in plenty. Dancing was allowed at these taverns—places with names like "Dine-a-Mite" and the "Teepee"—but the sheriff made the rounds on weekend nights to make sure things didn't get out of hand.[15]

Most of Lawrence's upstanding citizens believed that public drinking and illicit sex went hand-in-hand. Some of Lawrence's citizens were outraged: in late 1943 the Kansas River Baptist Convention publicly called on government officials to "ban the sinister presence of alcohol and vice." Most people in Lawrence disapproved of the wartime excesses but also saw them as just that: wartime excesses. Once the war was over, Lawrence would try to turn back the clock, banning dancing in any place that held a beer license in an attempt to prevent the explosive combination of liquor and sex. In the meantime, the dirty windows downtown served as symbols of lower-class immorality to many of Lawrence's citizens, and town leaders concentrated their efforts on containing trouble and managing the new residents.[16]

In practical terms, concern about the illicit sex and drinking that commonly flourished around military training camps and war-worker encampments quickly led to the expansion and reorganization of the county health unit.[17] What had been a small, part-time unit, concerned largely with sanitary inspections (particularly of milk production), was reconstituted as a full-time, federally funded agency, meant to play a key role in Lawrence's war. Sanitary issues became ever more important with the influx of ordnance-plant workers who overtaxed Lawrence's supply of adequate housing, already depleted by years of economic depression. The true justification for the health department's expansion, however, lay in wartime fears of unchecked venereal disease.

Statistics about venereal disease in the Great War were employed with great success as Americans began to mobilize for another war. Over and over, the American public heard that venereal disease had cost seven million man-days of service during World War I, and in the first months of war an anti-VD short film played in movie theaters throughout the country. *In Defense of the Nation* showed a "snarling Edward G. Robinson type" with a defense map of the United States. "Women and girls are sent out, according to carefully laid plans, to brothels, to low cafes and bars, and to the streets, where they spread venereal disease and disorder among those upon whom the defense of the nation depends," the narrator proclaimed.[18]

Much of this sounds like moral hysteria masquerading as national defense, and as hundreds of communities scrambled to shut down their red-light districts in the wake of the May Act, passed by Congress in the summer of 1941, it may have been. Yet it is important to remember the possible physical consequences of venereal disease in the days before penicillin offered a quick and painless cure. The task of preserving public health and military readiness among a highly mobile population—where an infection contracted in one state was quite likely to be passed along in another—was a major bureaucratic challenge for a nation at war. In 1938 Congress, accepting the logic that "these germs do not know state lines," had passed the National Venereal Disease Control Act, which provided funds for local VD clinics and diagnostic equipment to private practitioners. Thus, as the Roosevelt administration intensified war preparations in the final year of a bad decade, venereal disease occupied the time of a considerable number of officials, both civilian and military.[19]

In Lawrence, the Board of Health viewed federal funds for controlling venereal disease with suspicion, even as the town was flooded with servicemen and war workers. Despite board members' reluctance, during the first year of war the Douglas County Health Department accepted more state and federal funds than ever before, and many who had been wary of the New Deal worried anew that this flow of money could lead to "unwarranted" interference from the federal government.[20] The magnitude of the problem they confronted, however, made it difficult to stand on principle.

The new full-time head of the health unit was a Lawrence man with no particular agenda about local autonomy or federal power. Dr. H. L. Chambers, known as Harry, was 73 years old at the beginning of the war. A native Kansan, he had received his medical degree in the previous century; had served as a doctor in France during the Great War; had founded KU's student health services; had even served a stint as county director of public health in the 1920s. However, when called upon to replace the county public health director, Dr. Mott (a younger veteran of World War I who spent World War II commanding a hospital in Anchorage), the septuagenarian Harry Chambers was not coming out of retirement but instead giving up his private practice.[21]

Harry Chambers found himself in a difficult position in regard to his VD clinic. He wanted—and needed—to acknowledge the full scale of the medical problem. During the war the clinic carried a far heavier caseload than in the prewar years. Clinic visits for treatment in 1941 totaled 1,107; the 1943 total was five times that number.[22] At the same time, he did not want to raise public alarm with these statistics, fearing that they would provoke a moral backlash against sexuality in general. Thus he attempted to manage public fears about sexual immorality by putting a careful spin on the information he released.

By the spring of 1942 public concern about the town's "moral health" ran high. In the wake of a rumor, circulating among Lawrence parents, that schoolgirls were taking up with soldiers and war workers, the health department board invited the public school nurse to speak at its monthly meeting. She stamped the rumor false, but even her insistence that Lawrence schoolgirls had not succumbed *en masse* to the lure of wartime promiscuity did not put it to rest.[23]

Local rumors certainly stemmed from observable events, magnified by small-town gossip. Many a girl, sending a boyfriend off to war, behaved in ways she might never have considered under ordinary circumstances. And others were drawn to the good times that wartime money offered after a decade of deprivation. Sexual behavior did change in Lawrence during the war. But the rumors that flew from house to house in 1942 were also given shape by alarmist portrayals of sexually active girls in the national media.

In November 1942 a *Newsweek* story on "teen-age crime" cited the example of Kansas City, which was just over the border in Missouri, not far from Lawrence. The article explained the rising danger of "prostitution, both professional and casual, by girls anywhere from 12 on up—feminine camp followers, popularly dubbed 'Victory girls' and 'cuddle bunnies' . . . who defended their relations with men in the armed forces on the grounds of patriotic duty." Posters expanded portrayals of dangerous women from the obvious prostitutes to include wholesome young girls; one caption read: "SHE MAY LOOK CLEAN—BUT . . ." The March of Time newsreel

"Youth in Crisis," which appeared on movie screens throughout America in 1943, showed an "adolescent girl with experience far beyond her age"—a "Victory Girl"—necking with a sailor on a public street. And just days before the outbreak of rumors in Lawrence, *Time* had informed its national readership that the "khaki-mad 'Victory girl' was a worse menace than the prostitute," perhaps accounting for as many as three out of four venereal infections. These Victory girls and prostitutes "who do not charge for their services" were presented as threats to the nation, undermining national security through sexual delinquency.[24] The wartime behavior of Lawrence's girls and young women took on added significance because it was part of a national phenomenon—and was scrutinized in the light of a national emergency.

While rumors raged, Lawrence public health officials tried to shift public suspicion away from girls and women, even in the face of coordinated national campaigns that personified VD as a woman—whether prostitute, diseased hag, or innocent young thing. At the same time, these officials followed national procedures for managing venereal disease that enacted a sexual double standard and heavily penalized sexually active young women.

Attempting to quash what he saw as counterproductive fears about sex and rumors of female promiscuity, Dr. Chambers entered the public arena with his own diagnosis of wartime morality in Lawrence. In his letter to the president of the Chamber of Commerce (published almost in full in the *Journal World*), Chambers began with reassurance. "Moral conditions in Lawrence are not noticeably out of line with those in other parts of Kansas and of the world," he insisted.[25] The dislocations of war had loosened the "old puritanism," but "the rules of good sex morals" had not changed "so much nor so fast" in Lawrence as in other places.

This claim may have helped calm fears about promiscuity, but it left Dr. Chambers with another problem. How, if "good sex morals" were holding strong in Lawrence, could he account for the much enlarged VD clinic, which had been the prime reason for the controversial increases in federal funding for the health department?

To manage this seeming paradox, Chambers employed the class-based analysis that pervaded virtually all of Lawrence's wartime efforts to manage sexual conduct. "Our unusually large and successful venereal disease clinic," he wrote, had little to do with changes in Lawrence due to the war or to "any other phase of the newer thought." In fact, he claimed, Lawrence had seen no increase in the venereal disease rate. This statement is completely at odds with his own statistics, which recorded 256 clinic calls in January 1943, up from 39 a year earlier. But Chambers made a significant distinction between populations. Much of the surge in the VD rate, he claimed, was due to the selective service's screening out of many cases of "late latent lues" (luetics), those with advanced venereal disease whose symptoms had receded but who were nonetheless infected. These men, he explained, had lived in the county for many years, and their long-standing infections had nothing to do with wartime moral lapses. If not for physical examinations for the draft, their infections might never have been discovered. Presented here, implicitly, as marginal men who were drawn into the town's purview only because of the national emergency, these men did not appear as threats. They were already contained in the social geography of Lawrence and Douglas County.

In addition to the newly diagnosed luetics there were, Chambers admitted, many new cases. Those, however, could be explained by "the influx of several thousand unattached and more or less irresponsible men" to the Sunflower Ordnance Works. In his explanations Chambers carefully preserved existing presumptions about morality and middle-class respectability. The problem of venereal disease, which demanded increased spending and an expanded clinic, was not a sign of fundamental change in Lawrence and did not require a new approach. It was still a matter of managing the sexuality of lower-class "others," marginal and transitory men who did not really count as part of the community.[26]

Just as Dr. Chambers emphasized class distinctions to reassure Lawrence's middle-class citizens, he reoriented assumptions about gender. Both groups to which he attributed responsibility—the "late latent lues" (diagnosed because of the draft) and the "irresponsible" newcomers—were exclusively male. Almost all new cases of VD, however, came from heterosexual intercourse. Women were involved. In his attempts to shift public concern from (local) women and girls to (outsider) men, however, Dr. Chambers was disingenuous. Despite his rhetoric, in practice women bore the greater burden of blame for the spread of VD. Lawrence, like cities across the United States during World War II, addressed the problem of venereal disease by incarcerating infected women.[27]

Throughout the war, women who were identified by male VD patients as possible sources of their infections were picked up by police for testing and held in custody while awaiting test results. Those deemed "incorrigible" or "delinquent" were then detained through the course of treatment for their infection. Not all women were subject to detention. Dr. Chambers had complained to his health board in 1942: "It always shocks me to have a man in the army report that he got his gonorrhea from his wife on a recent visit to his home"; that wife would probably have been exempt from incarceration, and daughters in middle-class families may well have escaped detention as well. But women who fell outside the bounds of "respectability" and who transmitted venereal disease were defined as public health hazards and quarantined until cured. Some were prostitutes, others simply "promiscuous" or underage. These women were not convicted of the crime of prostitution. Rather, they were picked up on the strength of a "contact report" and confined as potential threats to public health.[28]

Only women were subject to such action. Civilian men faced no such penalties, and the military had, early in the war, emphasized prophylaxis over punishment. Condoms and prophylactic kits were standard government issue, and most servicemen who were diagnosed with VD faced few penalties and no punishments. It is true that men who got VD while in the service were likely to have caught it from civilians, for no one with untreated syphilis or gonorrhea was inducted into any branch of the armed forces.[29] However, this policy held men harmless for an act that emphatically took two. And it was quite possible for a civilian woman to be infected by a serviceman who had acquired VD after his induction. On the basis of contact reports, a woman with no prior sexual experience could be held responsible for a less abstemious serviceman's syphilis. Contact reports left women vulnerable—without legal recourse—to rumor, retribution, and just plain ignorance. While Dr. Chambers's public presentations on venereal disease in Lawrence tended to obscure women's role, punishment did the reverse by falling heaviest on women, especially those who lacked the protections of class, race, and marriage.

Dr. Chambers consistently downplayed any sense of emergency over Lawrence's "moral health." But while his public statements tended to displace responsibility from Lawrence's citizens to outsiders and to focus solely on men, his reports to the Board of Health did the opposite. In April 1944 he emphatically rejected the idea that VD was spread in Lawrence through "traffic in white slaves." The term "white slaves," which had been current during the Great War, in Chambers's youth, metaphorically defined prostitutes as women captured, virtually enslaved, for "immoral purposes." Chambers made it clear that women in Lawrence were acting of their own volition. He told his board:

> The traffic in white slaves is a problem anywhere but not especially so in Douglas County. Most of our girls [under care and confinement for VD] are local citizens and have been swept off their moral moorings by three or four considerations:
>
> 1. The general liberalizing of moral standards, prevalent everywhere.
>
> 2. The pseudopatriotic desire to make the man in the armed forces happy.
>
> 3. The inclination to grab off a little easy money.
>
> 4. The personal pleasure for themselves.

Chambers reported that he had consulted with the parents of girls "under care and confinement," who almost unanimously believed "they could do better with them if allowed to try again." He was dubious, after making "tentative experiments."[30]

Despite such doubts, Chambers made it a policy to "lean to the side of mercy and kindness," which meant exercising his right to "parole" patients rather more frequently than the police or the city commissioners deemed prudent. (At his eightieth birthday party a few years later, he explained that, at his age, "the idea of salvage makes more of an appeal than it formerly did.") Many among Lawrence's governing structure disapproved of his actions, and more than one called him "soft" to his face. He took the question to the health board, which backed him up. At this point the police stopped cooperating with the health department, refusing to bring in suspects or to pick up people who missed their treatments. They saw no point in bringing in suspects only to have them released. The 77-year-old doctor fumed to his board: "As you were told before, I am always ready to hear advice and requests, but am totally deaf to dictation by irresponsible people. Our delinquent list [people who missed treatments] is large and growing."[31]

The problem of VD in Lawrence would succumb to national, rather than local, action. The discovery of penicillin would change not only treatment protocols but the significance of venereal disease. Five intramuscular shots of 40,000 penicillin units each in eight hours "is said to succeed like magic," Chambers reported in September 1945, soon before the drug became available for civilian treatments. No longer would long-term detention for treatment be medically justifiable. But the most significant change affecting VD rates was the end of the war. Employment at Sunflower Ordnance Works dropped from 12,000 to fewer than 2,500 in four months. VD rates made parallel declines.[32]

—

Rates of venereal disease are one of the few ways to measure changes in sexual behavior in Lawrence during the war. The rates went up significantly, strongly suggesting that non-monogamous sex was more common during the war years.[33] But VD rates are not particularly revealing about the meaning or character of sex.

The traces of wartime sex that remain are primarily the attempts of various elites to manage or control it. The people who were having illicit sex did not publicly proclaim their right to do so; did not write letters to the editors of the newspaper or stage demonstrations. This leaves us uncomfortably dependent on the pictures drawn by town elites, but it does tell us something. As much as "the old puritanism" loosened during the war, those who stepped outside the bounds of "good sex morals"—unlike later participants in the sexual revolution—did not directly contest the meaning society assigned to their actions.

That doesn't mean people did not defy attempts to control sex. Dancing and drinking beer in an outlying tavern were public rejections of elite control, as were many sexual acts and relations that fell outside the bounds of propriety or conventional morality. But these sorts of evasions and rejections were not antithetical to the larger system. They had been going on, in more limited forms, for a long time. At the time no one knew if the changes were simply short-term reactions to war or the shape of things to come. In Lawrence, those who piloted the town's public life worried about defiance and disruption, but were able to situate the sexual misconduct they witnessed within existing paradigms of class, gender, and sexuality.[34]

This was possible partly because no persons or groups in Lawrence directly challenged the definition of their sexual behavior as illegitimate. Some lacked the cultural authority to do so; others had no interest in changing the status quo; still others were much too vulnerable. Many who had nonmarital sex during the war years were members of groups who had never been part of the "respectable" middle-class order. The war brought many lower-class urban and poor rural people into intense contact with the middle-class mechanisms of national culture for the first time. They had little power to challenge the sexual order of America's middle classes.

Many who violated the rules did come from America's "respectable" classes. Historians and contemporary observers alike document the "virtue under fire" of the war years, when many of the tenets of sexual morality were strained or broken.[35] And yet the most obvious change during the war was a skyrocketing marriage rate. Most middle-class Americans believed the looser sexual mores of the war years were simply "for the duration," brought about by the emotional intensity and the temporary dislocations of war. Few saw them as a permanent shift in patterns of sexual behavior. Certainly no one claimed them as conscious revolutionary practice.

—

In Lawrence, those who had public voices and public power located sexual threat in the "irresponsible and unattached" working-class men at SOW, thus, to some extent, neutralizing any challenges to the established order. As the chief of police explained to a meeting of the Lawrence Council of Social Agencies in 1944, it was "these 'new' people" who had accounted for 75 percent of the preceding year's arrests.[36] These men were outsiders, by virtue of both their temporary-worker status and their class status. They had to be controlled, but their redemption was not, strictly speaking, Lawrence's responsibility.

There was another large group of men temporarily located in Lawrence: several thousand military trainees. These, however, were not the diverse group one would find at an army basic training camp. They did come from all over the United States, so one could not call them a homogeneous group. But they were all deemed capable of advanced study and high achievement. The majority were officers-in-training, most of them (with the exception of the naval air cadets) students in regular degree programs at the university. Many navy men were studying engineering; the army men concentrated in the liberal arts and the school of medicine. These men were judged to have the ability to succeed in college at a time when college education was not common. Moreover, war planners had decided that training them was important enough to justify holding them back from the war itself, at least temporarily, despite the pressing need for combat soldiers.[37]

Lawrence's leaders did not see this group as equivalent to the war workers. When planning for venereal disease prevention, officials almost never mentioned the military men in their midst. That is odd, for the federal actions that provided funding and legal authority for their local VD program were meant to maintain military preparedness. Lawrence's focus on war workers does make sense, because military doctors managed military VD while the public health department was responsible for civilian cases, including those contracted by transient war workers. However, class bias certainly played a role: the men in college classrooms seemed less of a threat to the public order of the town than their counterparts in the defense plant.

Though some townspeople did question why thousands of able-bodied young men were sitting in college classrooms while their own sons and husbands were on the front lines, the men's college status mainly worked to their advantage. Lawrence was accustomed to college students, and in some ways these young men seemed quite similar to the students they replaced.

While Lawrence citizens were less concerned about protecting their town's "wholesomeness" from the men in uniform than from those in overalls, they did believe the military presence required planning and careful management. At first the rationale was patriotic: it was Lawrence's "responsibility" to provide "hospitality" to the young men who would fight for their country. A year into the war, however, as military men overwhelmed the still-small town, those involved understood their service in different terms. Writing to the mayor, the head of the Community Service League insisted: "We must provide wholesome entertainment for those servicemen during their week-ends at liberty; this is no longer merely a need, but an urgent necessity."[38]

Marge Stockton, the woman who made this claim, was a middle-aged, upper-middle-class married white woman with almost-grown children. She was a member of the local elite, a civic-minded woman in the old progressive mode, who hoped to control, through a program of wholesome recreation, the dangerous desires of all the respectable young men and women caught in the dislocations of war. Paradoxically, it was in her experience, not in the experiences of the youth she tried to manage, that the changes most significant for the sexual revolution were manifest.

The war had greatly accelerated the pace of change in Lawrence. The Sunflower Plant and the military training programs created social problems that stretched local resources beyond capacity, and that were, ultimately, beyond the ability of local leaders like Marge Stockton to manage. Both

Sunflower and the training programs were subject to federal oversight. Both also brought many "outlanders," as the KU registrar called them, to Lawrence. As a byproduct of war, new voices emerged in policy decisions.[39] "Outside" institutions, authorities, and funding were increasingly necessary to handle large-scale dislocations that were due to the war, but that were to a great extent experienced, in Lawrence, as results of rapid economic-industrial growth.

As a result, local hierarchies of power and mechanisms of social and sexual control weakened during the war years. The "sexual revolution" was possible, to a great extent, because these local forms of authority lost ground while national forces—from the media to government agencies to the postwar market economy—increasingly offered alternate sources of cultural authority to people who contested the traditional social controls. Stockton and those like her fought hard to maintain the social—and sexual—order of their town. Her struggle against forces she saw as disrupting the civic order and undermining coherent community must be understood as an early battle in the "revolution."

Marge Stockton came from a distinguished Lawrence family. Her husband was Frank Stockton, the dean of KU's business school. During the war he chaired Lawrence's Defense Planning Committee, and he almost singlehandedly lured the Sunflower Ordnance Plant to Douglas County. In the gendered tradition of American industrial capitalism, Marge Stockton devoted herself to creating moral and social order in a world destabilized by the efforts of her husband, and of men like him, to promote economic growth. As an earlier generation of American progressives had understood, industrialism and market capitalism were disruptive forces. Though they benefited elites both socially and economically, they held the potential for human suffering and for social upheaval. Women like Stockton applied their considerable talents to maintaining stability in this system. They worked to alleviate the effects of poverty and also, quite explicitly, to develop mechanisms of social control. As Stockton wrote to a friend in 1943, "Lawrence is just learning to be an industrial city instead of a liesurely town, and we must develop social controls that have been found helpful elsewhere."[40]

Marge Stockton's wartime work with the Community Service League was not born of a sudden flush of patriotism. She had been active in various forms of community work throughout her life. Reared in an atmosphere of upper-middle-class noblesse oblige, with a mother whose life was "gracious" and a father who came from "a long line of lawyers," she acted in accord with a relatively old-fashioned ideology that conjoined privilege and responsibility, espoused democratic values, and unquestioningly situated social power and cultural authority in the hands of a benign local elite. The war gave some temporary credence to this world view. Lawrence did need the efforts of these capable (and mostly female) volunteers during the war. These citizens, in turn, enhanced their importance by refusing outside help (specifically in the form of the USO) even as they acknowledged that the problems they faced were not purely local. This approach to social problems, even as it was briefly confirmed by wartime exigencies, was doomed by the changes the war brought about.

In early 1943 Stockton found herself virtually confined to her home as she cared for her mother, who was in the late stages of a debilitating illness. During this period, exhausted, worn out from caring for her mother and cut off from all her "world saving" projects, she took stock of her life in a series of letters to friends in Lawrence, explaining to one that she'd always loathed "telephonic communication," probably "due to some overdose of peasant blood they've kept from the family records." Though she lamented that the "world is so troubled, so torn with the disappearance of all the old norms and the non-appearance of substantial new ones to replace them," she clung to her vision of social order and community service.

"I have a disease: civic mindedness," Stockton wrote to a friend.[41] The child and grandchild of lawyers, she had intended to practice law herself, in either juvenile or domestic relations court. Against her father's wishes, she left law school to marry. He, though, exacted his daughter's promise that she would use "what she had" to "effect a better social system." "I've kept the faith," she told her friend. "Perhaps that will explain to you, at least in part, why all these years I've collected old clothes, washed and mended them for poor children; why I've slaved for PTA; why I've been so interested in the juvenile court's borderline cases; why I've slaved for community recreation. If I weren't such a dyed-in-the-wool Republican, I might have been an ardent New Dealer." Stockton's social vision was sorely shaken during the war, even though in practical terms her efforts were quite successful. Her correspondence reveals both her attempts to perpetuate her ideal of social order and her growing awareness of its insufficiency.

Stockton's Community Service League operated a servicemen's center in the Lawrence community building from July 1942 through January 1945 (with the exception of five weeks in the winter of 1943 when the league ran short of funds, not coincidentally the same time that Stockton wrote the above letter).[42] The center offered USO-type amenities—playing cards and writing paper, cookies and Cokes and ping-pong tables—but its major function was to stage a dance every Saturday night. This "non-commercial recreation" was meant to keep the young men out of the beer halls and taverns—and out of the arms of the wrong sort of women. While the dances were open to all men in uniform, they were not open to all women. Instead, they were staffed by members of a "Junior Hostess League." These young women had been approved by the Service League committee on the basis of an application, two letters of reference from adults in the community, and evidence of parental permission for those who were not self-supporting.

The women who supervised the dances intended to guarantee the respectability of the young hostesses. Though any woman 18 or older might apply for membership, the executive committee actively recruited their "young friends" and members of KU sororities. (Jeanette Woodruff, the wife of the university registrar, chaired the Junior Hostess committee.) Junior hostesses had to pledge not to arrive or leave with a serviceman as escort, and they were prohibited from leaving the building at any time with one or more of the men. Unlike some USO programs, where chaperone rules were largely on paper and directors were grateful for almost any volunteers they could find, these sponsors took the job of screening women seriously. At each dance a senior hostess greeted attendees, making sure that no woman or girl who was not a junior hostess entered without her approval. It was a sensitive task, for she was charged with distinguishing between the legitimate fiancée from out of town, who merited a "guest badge," and the unsuitable local date. The latter was to be turned away, without "causing offense" or provoking a scene—if possible.

These were not dances for young men on the verge of battle or recovering from it, and the league faced few of the problems of control that many USOs confronted. In Hawaii, where men rotated away from the front for R&R before being sent back into the horror of the Pacific war, USOs had to contend with huge crowds of men jostling for the attention of a small number of women. Drunken brawls were common, and some men were lewd or sexually aggressive toward the women who had volunteered to dance with them. In Lawrence, the dances were not very different from college mixers, and Stockton's servicemen's center operated without public incident for almost three years. At the end of the war she received a letter of commendation from the commandant of the 9th Naval District.[43] It seems that her strategy of control had worked. Why, then, was her wartime experience one of *losing* control?

For most of her life Marge Stockton actively worked for a certain vision of social justice, and as she herself said, she might have been an ardent New Dealer—but for one thing. She believed wholeheartedly in local authority. That's why she was such a "dyed-in-the-wool" Republican. She feared the intervention of national organizations, particularly the programmatic efforts of the federal government, which might overwhelm or simply ignore her faith in a morally grounded society steadied by the sure hand of local elites. She saw in the New Deal and the expansion of federal power and national culture during the war a fragmentation of cultural authority. She feared the rapid multiplication of institutions and of authorities who claimed to manage a rapidly fragmenting citizenry.

In a confidential letter to a friend, Stockton's concerns about control became uncomfortably clear. She wrote: "The six organizations which make up the USO—Salvation Army, Travelers Aid, Jewish Welfare, National Catholic Community Service, YM and YW—find it hard to 'get along.' For example, a unit went in at Junction City under Jewish Welfare; the Catholics couldn't get along with them, so another one was put in; there are now two small USO units there . . . That is only one example, many places there is dissension . . . In some places the service men felt that the Jewish element is so predominant that the 'gimme' attitude sours the hospitality." Stockton rejected USO involvement because she believed in local control; however, one must reckon with the anti-Semitism and suspicion of "outsiders" that animate her concept of local control. But even she admitted, finally, thinking of the bars and taverns that had sprung up in Lawrence, "our problems aren't local here anymore."[44]

The Stocktons, along with many of Lawrence's leading citizens, had sought defense industry for their town. But they had not foreseen just how hard it would be to control such rapid growth, or how unsettling the influx of people and dollars would be. New people were making new public claims—through actions, if not words. And as national institutions became increasingly involved in managing these large-scale changes, local leaders like the Stocktons increasingly found their form of "moral" authority inadequate or, worse, beside the point.

Hundreds of towns and cities throughout America underwent similar changes. War had changed the nation in fundamental ways, and the recasting of American society did not end with the coming of peace.

Even as the nation demobilized, towns and cities across the country continued to feel the impact of wartime dislocations. The yearly marriage rate, which had held fairly stable in Kansas since recordkeeping began in 1913, increased almost 600 percent over prewar figures at its 1946 height. Marriages could well mark a settling down, but they were accompanied by an alarming rise in the divorce rate. Measured as divorces per thousand population per year, Kansas's divorce rate jumped from a prewar average of between 2.3 and 2.5 to 5. In Douglas County the number of divorces almost tripled from 1940 to 1946.[45] Some of these divorces dissolved fragile unions contracted by teenagers who had never known each other very well, but others marked the heartbreaking toll of extended separation amid the harsh realities of war. Men who had gone off to fight had lived in very different worlds than the women they'd left behind, and reunion was not easy even for the most committed couples. National magazines were full of advice for women about how to treat their returning veterans, but other sorts of information also circulated—such as the government estimate that three-quarters of the men returned from the military more sexually experienced than when they entered.

Lawrence's county commissioners were alarmed by the potential problems of reassimilation. At a Council of Social Agencies meeting in May 1945, they raised some of their concerns. Noting that none of the veterans showing up in Lawrence wanted farm work, or were even "farm-trained," one speaker reported a "consensus of opinion" that the veterans were going to be "'dead-beats' and expect too much." Though the World War I veteran Dr. Chambers tried to moderate that sentiment, arguing that it "takes some time for a man to readjust himself," one of the commissioners countered with government statistics: "Recent figures show that of these discharged vets 20% are morally sound, 20% debauched and wild, 60% in between." The in-between group could probably be managed by local churches and chaplains, this commissioner felt, but what of the debauched twenty percent? Churches "can't be expected to carry [the] entire responsibility for moral readjustment."[46] But who could? And what impact would these men have on the moral well-being of the town?

World War II ended on a note of uncertainty in Lawrence. Though town leaders had entered the war with great assurance that local planning and supervision could ensure a "wholesome" atmosphere in the face of rapid social change, the experience of war had undermined both that faith and their ability to manage Lawrence's population. If the changes in

Lawrence had been only "for the duration," old patterns of social hierarchy might have reemerged as "outsiders" left and those who fell outside the boundaries of respectability vanished from the social landscape of the elite and the middle class. But Lawrence was not going to settle back to "normal," whatever that meant in 1945. By 1945 Lawrence was, as Marge Stockton understood, no longer the "liesurely town," no longer the "cultural little city on the Kaw" against which the *Journal World* had played out its apocalyptic fantasy in 1942.

—

In the years following World War II, economic growth, combined with federal actions, further undermined the authority of local social and business elites. In Lawrence, changes in the social structure were especially significant. When the war began, almost half of the town's adult men had eight years or less of formal education. After the war federal authorities, supported by the managers of America's leading corporations, sought universal high school education. By 1950, 86 percent of Lawrence's 14–17-year-olds were still in school; by 1960 it was 91 percent. Because of the G.I. Bill, many veterans from economically lower-class backgrounds got college educations; for several years veterans made up well over half of KU's burgeoning enrollment.[47] These changes would broaden the pool of those who had the skills and the social positions to engage in public decisions about social policy and social order.

Nonetheless, the greatest challenge to elite control—particularly of sexuality—did not come through reconfigurations of class. This class reconfiguration was a broadly assimilative process that centered around the ideological construction of an American middle class. These new high school and college students were being taught middle-class behavior and values. These values most emphatically included the importance of sexual respectability. Instead, the power of Lawrence's elite to draw sexual boundaries for the community would be further weakened by a national consumer culture and the growing influence of the market in postwar society.

The problem with market forces in a rapidly expanding national economy was that they were not amenable to local control. The market forces that had brought thousands of war workers to a small Kansas town during the early 1940s continued to alter Lawrence's demographics in the next decade, as the town successfully competed for industrial development and economic growth. Many of Lawrence's citizens, boosters that they were, meant to take advantage of new economic opportunities as America emerged from the war. They actively sought change even as they bemoaned its effects. The town's population surged in the postwar years, partly because of the baby boom but also as the town grew physically by annexing surrounding land and by attracting industrial development. Between 1949 and 1956, $40 million in industrial growth took place in the Lawrence area, including the reactivation of the Sunflower Ordnance Works for the Korean War. The university also grew dramatically as enrollments boomed under the G.I. Bill. This huge crop of students was good for the local economy. In 1950 retail sales in Lawrence were 38 percent above the national average.[48]

But the economic and physical growth of the town undermined the ability of a small group of men and women to create their own version of social order. Before the war Lawrence's elites had been able to dictate the terms of respectability for their part of town, partly because class boundaries rendered so many who did not observe these tenets of social/sexual respectability irrelevant and, more fundamentally, powerless. The war had altered Lawrence's social geography, and it would never return to prewar patterns.

Lawrence, like cities and towns throughout the nation, became much less isolated in the years after World War II. Part of it was physical: by the mid-1950s the National Highway Defense Act was traversing the nation with a system of high-speed interstate highways. The Kansas Turnpike was supposed to go several miles north of Lawrence, but the Chamber of Commerce lobbied hard and succeeded in changing the proposed route. Suddenly both Kansas City and Topeka were much, much closer. Affluence also made a difference: in 1947 alone 9,170 licenses for "pleasure cars" were issued in Lawrence. By late 1955 Lawrence had direct long-distance dialing—one of the first cities in the country. Different kinds of people came to Lawrence. Industrial growth attracted new workers. As KU expanded, it drew a more diverse student body. Perhaps more important, it began to attract a more diverse faculty, hired from a national pool of newly minted PhD's.[49]

And popular culture increasingly tied Americans together. Lawrence's shops and airwaves were filled with the products of the national consumer culture. The *Ed Sullivan Show* presented Elvis, minus pelvis, on national TV in September 1956. The largest audience in television history—60 million

Americans—saw the stand-in host Charles Laughton introduce him as "Elvin Presley." Along with the rest of America, Lawrence watched. Nobody made a public complaint. In fact, Elvis had played in Kansas City a few months earlier, and Lawrence had sent its share of fans. That concert had ended in a full-scale riot, with fans storming the stage, destroying instruments, and even tossing one band member into the orchestra pit.[50]

At that point, never specifically mentioning the Kansas City incident, the *Journal World* had gently scoffed at those who saw "the whining, shouting, sobbing Elvis Presley" as a source of "grave concern." The editor asked: Remember "Rudy Vallee, the so-called Vagabond Lover"? Remember "Frank Sinatra, the frail, tone-bending star psychologists said brought out the 'mother instinct'"? Remember Johnny Ray? Dean Martin? This editor was much more concerned about the "leg-art" and "off-color activity" in a Judy Garland television special earlier that spring. It was less the bare flesh and suggestive posturing that offended him than the fact that in the show Judy Garland, she of "Somewhere Over the Rainbow," failed miserably. Maybe someone else could have pulled it off, he concluded, but "the fact of the matter is that she doesn't have the equipment for such a display."[51]

During the 1940s and 1950s the *Journal World* would occasionally editorialize about "off-color" material, and once in a while the bodice-ripper version of a movie ad would disappear from the pages of the paper after a day, replaced by a less sexy version. But what is significant is not whether some cultural arbiter in Kansas worried or didn't worry about Elvis, but rather that the products of a more and more sexualized national culture were beyond local control. They were there for the taking, on national radio and television networks, on movie screens, in bookstores and record stores and drugstores—if not in Lawrence, somewhere close, or at least through the mail. And ever greater numbers of Lawrence's people had the means—financial, cultural, educational—to participate in this larger world.

Some of Lawrence's citizens tried to control sex and to circumscribe this sexualized culture—and discovered that they couldn't control the marketplace. In February 1946 the Douglas County commissioners passed a regulation banning dancing at any establishment that sold beer. Their action was based on a report from the county health department, which in turn was based on information received from military authorities, that most of the new VD cases in Lawrence during the war had resulted from contacts made in such establishments. The new regulation was actively backed by a wide range of religious groups: the Lawrence Friends Church, the men's class of the First Christian Church of Lawrence, and the nonde-nominational Men's Christian Alliance.[52]

The regulation had some unintended consequences, as when the Lawrence Country Club had to cancel a dance scheduled for high school students—even though no beer was to be served—because the club held a beer license. The county commissioners had meant to target the beer joints and taverns, not the country club. But worse, the regulation didn't seem to reduce drinking. People just got in their cars and went somewhere else. The businessmen who ran the taverns and clubs refused to stand by and watch their own economic ruin. They flouted the law. Defending his position, the owner of the Skyline club, out on 23rd Street at the margins of town, told a reporter: "Young people come out to my place and order a glass of beer and then they want to dance . . . when I tell them they can't dance in my café, they finish their beer and go off to Topeka or Leavenworth or Kansas City where they can drink and dance in the same place." If controlling sexual contact was the issue, these boundaries were too permeable for local control. After a seven-month struggle the commissioners rescinded the rule, warning club proprietors that they would be held responsible for the conduct of their patrons, and that they must "operate along decent respect-able lines if they want to remain open." The rhetoric was face-saving at best, for this effort at control had been decisively defeated.[53]

The larger consumer marketplace encroached more and more in the years after World War II, prompting various efforts to reinforce bounda-ries. The American landscape had become progressively more sexualized in the twentieth century: the first moving pictures had titillated audiences with close-up shots of couples kissing. Advertisers had adopted the sexually suggestive style of tabloids in the 1920s, and the pin-up girls of World War II served as patriotic symbols and decorated the exteriors of the nation's fighter planes.[54] But in the affluent consumer culture of the postwar United States, sex—or, more accurately, representations of scantily clad women in suggestive poses—claimed new territory.

By the late 1940s a young and flourishing paperback industry was using more and more sensationalist covers to sell books. Probably the most famous was Popular Library's 1948 cover for the 1925 bestseller *The Private Life of Helen of Troy*. "Her lust caused the Trojan War," a banner headline proclaimed, and Helen appeared in a tight, gauzy drapery that concealed nothing, including her lack of pubic hair. Popularly known as the "nipple cover," it came to represent the commodification of sex in pulp paperbacks.

But Helen had a great deal of company: classics were frequently recast as steamy tales of lust, and science fiction and detective novels regularly featured half-naked women on their covers. These cheap paperbacks, available in drugstores and newsstands, told stories of sexual passion; prominently displayed were tales of lesbian love, targeted to voyeuristic male readers but equally available to those with other interests.[55]

Playboy magazine, introduced in December 1953 with photos of Marilyn Monroe that went well beyond World War II cheesecake, sold an astounding 53,991 copies of its first issue. In terms of pictorials, *Playboy* had replaced *Esquire*'s airbrushed drawings with airbrushed photographs; the fantasy women drawn by Petty and Vargas became, in time, "real girls next door." As *Playboy* became a commercial success, sold on newsstands across the country and even marketed by special college distributors (including one at KU), it spawned scores of imitators and created space for raunchier publications in the less respectable venues.[56] Meanwhile, magazines like *True Confessions* and *Confidential* targeted women with tales of sexual seduction; bodybuilding and physique magazines provided grist for homosexual fantasies; and comic books had become, in the words of a Senate committee report on juvenile delinquency, "short courses in . . . rape, cannibalism, carnage, necrophilia, sex, sadism, masochism, and virtually every other form of crime, degeneracy, bestiality, and horror," selling at the rate of about 60 million a year. This sexualization of mass culture was largely a matter of renegotiating the boundaries of respectability, for much more sexually explicit material had been available before this postwar turn, but it had been under-the-counter stuff, "circulated in barbershops, saloons, and Army posts," not set out side by side with the *Ladies' Home Journal* and *Life* on drugstore and newsstand shelves.[57]

This shifting of boundaries proceeded quite rapidly in the realm of commerce, but was not so readily accepted in the realm of culture, however middlebrow. In October 1952 *Reader's Digest* (circulation 10 million) ran an exposé entitled "Filth on the Newsstands." By December the House of Representatives was holding hearings on what its chairman called "the kind of filthy sex books sold at the corner store which are affecting the youth of our country." This would not be the last such mobilization. A young lawyer in Cincinnati began "Operation Newsstand," which developed into Citizens for Decent Literature, with chapters throughout the nation. The General Federation of Women's Clubs, the National Association of Parents and Teachers, and the Roman Catholic National Organization for Decent Literature all tried grassroots organizing, and congressional hearings on sex, mass culture, and youth raged for most of the decade.[58] In the case of popular culture, issues of community standards and parents' control over their children did not fit comfortably with national systems of production and distribution.

In the midst of these national campaigns, the Lawrence PTA's Juvenile Protective Committee launched its own drive against "inappropriate" magazines, comics, and paperback books.[59] Volunteers visited all the groceries, drugstores, and newsstands in Lawrence, compiling detailed records on the "objectionable material" they found on the shelves. Detective, romance, confidential, and "male" magazines were targeted, along with paperback books and comics. The information about individual stores is difficult to compare, for it may well tell us more about the sensibility of the surveyor than about the store's stock; one woman found a great deal to object to at every store she visited, while another seemed offended by little. But of the twenty establishments surveyed, only three displayed nothing deemed objectionable. In general, drugstores were worse than grocery stores, and the worst case of all was Green's Newsstand, where approximately one-third of its 380 items were deemed unacceptable. Lawrence's citizens certainly had a wide variety of material to choose from, with the newsstand alone boasting 64 different "male" magazines, 35 in the "Romance/Confidential" category, and more than 150 comics, which were not even included in the newsstand's total of "objectionable" items. Clearly, sexual material was proliferating in public places frequented by "respectable" people.

A local radio news station ran an editorial praising the committee's efforts. Let the drugstore and newsstand owners know "how you stand," the station manager exhorted. And let the PTA know that you "approve of this effort to make the sale of defamatory, sadistic, sensational, violent, vulgar, pornographic, sexy material, a *local* issue."[60] This campaign, too, failed. More of Lawrence's citizens were interested in buying such materials than were interested in boycotting the many stores that sold them. Equally important, this was *not* a local issue. The "objectionable literature" was produced for a national market that either demanded or accepted the increasing sexualization of public culture. Several of the stores in question were not local stores but national chains. And local stores tended to have even more of the objectionable material than did the national chains, perhaps as a means of competing with the chain stores, which held other economic advantages. Ultimately, the boycott failed because standards of middle-class respectability were less uniform, and Lawrence's population more diverse, in the postwar decade than before. The borders were, once again, too permeable.

—

In the 1950s the sites and subjects of struggle would continue to change. It was not that Lawrence's hierarchies of power dissolved, or that local elites were displaced, but that they had lost their power to dictate the terms of social order. As the nationalizing forces of war and its aftermath drew Lawrence into a larger and more complex world, new issues emerged concerning sex and its control.

One of the most significant changes was the increasing centrality of youth in American society. With the rise of a national youth culture—however mediated by race, class, gender, region, religion, and other significant categories of identity—a new group of potentially revolutionary actors began to emerge. In the prehistory of Lawrence's sexual revolution, the scene of conflict shifted from town to university, from local matrons like Stockton and professionals like Chambers to university students seeking new social, intellectual, and sexual frontiers.

Struggles to control sex were still at the heart of the story, with university administrators seeking new forms of cultural authority to deploy in their efforts to stem the sexual transgressions of youth. The university students, for their part, continued to transgress, their actions an odd blend of confrontation and evasion. From the student newspaper accounts of serenades and pinnings and engagements, it is clear they were still a long way from revolution. But there was a great roiling tension beneath the surface, and it was becoming ever more difficult for all concerned to manage the dissonance between the public norms and the private acts of American sexual culture.

2

Sex and the Therapeutic Culture

In the spring of 1952, as the police action in Korea dragged on and as support for Eisenhower's presidential candidacy grew, college campuses throughout the nation erupted into violence. Windows were smashed, buildings briefly occupied. Students fought police—and one another—while the media breathlessly reported each new riot.

The panty raids—for that is what they were—broke out like brushfires that May. At the University of Wisconsin 5,000 students charged the women's dorms, urged on by bugle calls. At the University of Alabama women's lingerie was locked in trunks to prevent a raid, and the girls were reduced to throwing socks to the boys massed below their windows. At the Indiana University the director of women's residence halls sent out a "barrelful of female undergarments in the hope that the males would help themselves and go home quietly." At the University of Oklahoma 2,000 students "battled" state police in what local authorities politely called a "lingerie raid." In Missouri Governor Forrest Smith called out the National Guard when local police were unable to contain a mob of more than 2,000 men who were battering down doors and smashing windows at the women's dorms. The Lawrence police, who were called by dormitory officials and sorority housemothers when a large crowd of men began to surround women's residence halls at KU, told the women "to leave the doors open and not to resist." They refused to come to the scene, arguing that the students were looking for resistance, and that police presence would just "incite" them. Close to a thousand men stormed three dormitories and five sorority houses that night, but only a "single pink brassiere" was reported taken.[1]

Alfred Kinsey, when asked his opinion of the panty raids, said simply: "All animals play around."[2] The dean of men at KU was willing to go along with that analysis: youthful high spirits, springtime, the end of the semester. He thought the Lawrence *Journal World,* with all its talk about "mobs" and scornful references to "'educated' students," had paid the raids far too much attention. But he, and every other college administrator who saw his or her job as controlling these youthful energies, recognized the danger of the riots. They were a contest for power between the young and their elders. They challenged authority. When the University of Alabama's president, John Gallalee, appeared at a women's dorm that was under siege and gallantly shouted to the girls hanging out the windows, "Don't worry, everything will be all right," they threw eggs at him.

More alarmingly, the panty raids linked this challenge to authority to the potentially explosive power of sexuality. When Princeton students rioted through town in the spring of 1953 and then marched on Westminster Choir College screaming, "We want girls! We want sex! We want panties!" most adults certainly understood how potentially dangerous this rite of spring was.[3]

Magazines were full of titillating accounts, complete with much verbal hand-wringing about the state of the younger generation. None of this was really new. Stories about the (often sexual) misconduct of college youth had been a staple of journalism in the 1920s, and the panty raids of the 1950s were just the latest elaboration of a long tradition of college riots that reached back at least to the eighteenth century.[4] But as the panty raids became a national phenomenon in the spring of 1952, their volatile mix of youth, sex, and failed authority shone a spotlight on the anxieties of postwar America.

The fifties were not a decade out of time, and the shadows of depression and war lingered on well past the return of prosperity and relative peace. The panty raids were taking place against the backdrop of combat in Korea and the intensifying Cold War. They were vicariously experienced by a nation on the move: from family farms to new suburbs; from urban ethnic neighborhoods to new suburbs; from working class to middle class; and from parental home to college dorm. In the midst of such change, Americans worried about issues like economic stability, international communism, and its "threat to democracy," and whether "American" or "traditional" values were being lost. Could members of the rising generation protect their country against new and greater challenges, or were they being spoiled by affluence and indulgence?

Attempts to prepare youth to maintain America's democratic system, economic growth, and (variously defined) values led to well-funded and carefully crafted programs, including those aimed at instituting universal high school education and expanding the college population. But this focus on youth was not bred of optimism. Instead, most adults acted out of a widespread concern that young people would be incapable of preserving essential American ways and values in the sharpening bipolarity of the Cold War world. As educational policies and curricular reforms were crafted in attempts to fortify the nation's younger citizens, inchoate fears about youth led to panic about juvenile delinquency and to widespread condemnation of the immaturity and herd instincts of young adults.[5] The spectacle of mindless "mobs" of college men—the privileged ones, the "educated" ones, the ones who were being prepared to lead in America's future—roaming their campuses in search of *panties* touched off alarms.

The college and university officials who were engaged in a highly self-conscious effort to manage, control, and shape these crucially important college youth had a more complex view of the phenomenon, for they—unlike most readers of sensationalist accounts in magazines and newspapers—could see the panty raids in context, as infrequent eruptions in a generally manageable student body. But even they worried that the epidemic of panty raids was merely the tip of a very troublesome iceberg. To the college deans and their staffs, trying to defuse the momentum of a thousand or more young men who were on the verge of mob action, aware that property damage was almost inevitable and that sexual assaults were more than possible, the panty raids did not look like harmless springtime frolics. No matter how they were resolved, no matter what the students' intentions, both university officials and the American public saw the panty raids as very public challenges to authority.

By the early 1950s the professional organizations for what were called "student personnel workers" frequently discussed the problem of lost authority. In the new "democratic" university, the "authoritarian dean is becoming more and more of an anachronism," wrote the dean of Swarthmore College in 1953, and his tone was not exactly celebratory. At the same time, college administrators felt their roles in shaping youth were more

47

important than ever. "[Our profession] is pushed to the very forefront," wrote the editor of the *Journal of the National Association of Women Deans and Counselors* a few years later. "It is the counselor, not the clergyman, who must develop youth's conscience; it is the educator who is called upon to take the leading ethical role."[6]

These statements and much of the concern that gave birth to them focused on the sexual conduct and misconduct of youth. Sex was the nexus that brought together concerns about youth and authority. The college rite of spring that quickly standardized across the nation as the "panty raid" was sexual, as Kinsey had noted: young men intent on what was variously understood as a form of flirtation or of sexual violence. Panty raids gradually disappeared in the 1960s, but they were only the most public of college sex problems. What lay behind them was infinitely more complex. Young people often did violate both the spirit and the letter of the law in sexual matters, and though these challenges to the mores of polite society were rarely so confrontational as the panty raids, they demanded much in the way of time and attention from deans of students.

The deans did not find it easy to control the sexual energies and behavior of youth, especially as justifications for restraining sexual conduct became increasingly tenuous. While many Americans continued to believe in absolute moral sanctions grounded in religious teachings, religion could not serve as the ultimate justification for public rules and laws governing sex in a society that proclaimed individual freedom of religion. From early in the twentieth century, scholars—many of whom fully accepted contemporary interpretations of Judeo-Christian sexual morality—had sought scientific bases for societies' sexual mores. Whether based in physical studies of the human body, psychological analysis of human nature, or sociological investigations of human communities, these "scientific" sexual systems were less absolute than the religious beliefs they often overlay, as all had to deal with variations or differences—physical, psychological, or cultural—among humans, and as all were open to questions about samples, interpretations, and methodologies.

Perhaps scholarship on human sexuality would have remained a purely academic endeavor had not American sexual mores seemed so much in flux, even in the early part of the century. And by the century's midpoint, as scientific and medical advances made fear of disease and even pregnancy less powerful disincentives to nonmarital sex, and as more Americans from different backgrounds were incorporated into the nation's civil society, it became more necessary to articulate and justify the rules governing sexual behavior.

Colleges and universities were often at the forefront of the struggles over the control of sex. Most scholars of sex or of "family life" held teaching appointments at universities, so the new discourses of sexual science were in and of the American university. Perhaps most crucially, higher education concentrated large numbers of sexually mature but unmarried young adults in an intense peer culture. Most young people, especially in the 1950s and early 1960s, never directly challenged the system of sexual controls, whether because of religious beliefs, "scientific" knowledge, or social sanctions. But many did evade the controls and violate the rules without ever openly rejecting them. The widespread covert violation demanded attention, which it received both in the multiplication and elaboration of rules governing behavior and in the creation of systems of discipline and punishment for those whose misconduct crossed newly negotiated lines.

In the three decades following World War II, deans of students found themselves more and more enmeshed in questions of sexual discipline. Larger and more diverse student populations required more explicit statements of rules governing sexual conduct. Even though the mass of World War II veterans had passed through America's colleges and universities by the early 1950s, enrollments stayed high, and then rose higher. The G.I. Bill had propelled hundreds of thousands of young men into a new socioeconomic class through higher education, and those who came after them increasingly saw a college degree as a prerequisite for a "good" job and a middle-class life. The economy was strong, so college was within reach of more of America's youth than ever before. A great many of these young men and women were the first in their families to attend college. Though universities had survived the first shock of growth, they were in the process of transformation that would yield the modern research university. Struggling to clarify their mission and identity, they also had to cope with the growing size and heterogeneity of their student bodies.

Faced with the daunting task of managing student behavior, university officials sought new forms of authority and new methods of control over student conduct. Two distinct approaches emerged. The first developed directly from the military use of psychiatry during the war. With a sizable cohort of military-trained psychiatrists and psychologists to draw on, universities attempted to take advantage of their expertise in evaluating and managing large and diverse groups of young people. In shifting some of the authority over student sexual misconduct from dean to psychiatrist, universities redefined certain sexual behavior from misconduct (or sin), meriting punishment, to mental illness, deserving treatment, and so fundamentally changed the way universities handled whole categories of sexual transgression.

The other new approach was closely related to the Cold War–era curricular reforms intended to develop "mature," responsible citizens through university education. Advocates of this approach insisted that students must learn to make responsible choices in their lives, and attempted to reframe the regulations concerning students' nonacademic lives as a crucial part of their training for democratic citizenship.

Both these approaches to managing student sexual behavior were implemented through the deans' offices, but the two were located in different constituent bodies and were not always comfortable allies. What they had in common, however, overrode their significant differences in orientation. Both called attention to the constructed nature of human sexual behavior, for the turn to psychiatry drew attention to the gray area between normal and "deviant," and the emphasis on "responsible choice," even if the proper choice was clearly indicated to students, made the range of possible choices more visible to all.

Both psychiatric authority and this peculiarly American brand of existentialism contained the seeds of their own destruction as mechanisms of control. Students would challenge the system of rules about sexual behavior with the very same arguments about responsibility and democratic citizenship that university officials had used to buttress that system. The shift to psychiatric authority, in contrast, did not offer students powerful tools with which to challenge that authority. Instead, it created problems for the administrators and officials themselves by introducing criteria for judgment about sexual behavior that made it difficult to draw clear distinctions between "right" and "wrong." Both the psychotherapeutic system of control (discussed in this chapter) and the democratic-existentialist system of control (discussed in Chapter 3) would ultimately undermine the ability of university officials to control sex and sexual transgression.

—

In the spring of 1947 a KU undergraduate whose first name was Oral, though he preferred to use his middle name, was discovered to be in homosexual "difficulties" and was asked to leave school, pending psychiatric evaluation and treatment.[7] In September the young man appealed to the chancellor to reconsider his case, and he was referred to the new student "mental hygiene" clinic for evaluation. Oral's own psychiatrist, a professor at the KU medical school, submitted a statement to the dean. "In my opinion," he wrote, "it is not likely that Mr. Hill will repeat the undesireable conduct that caused so much concern and embarrassment for all concerned, this past spring. I am not convinced that he is a homosexual, in the sense that term is generally used." Oral did come from an "unusual home environment" and had been going through a "period of nervous tension," but was not "psychotic" or "mentally ill to the point he should be rejected automatically on that basis." He did suggest that, if readmitted, Oral should "take advantage" of KU's mental hygiene service.

The psychiatrist in residence at KU's mental health center, Dr. Sigmund Gundle, disagreed: "The patient . . . still is unable to control his aggressive tendencies . . . [and] he has neither made any progress in solving his homosexual difficulties. In view of this I feel that there is very little or practically no assurance that the patient will not get into any difficulties should he be reinstated. There is even less assurance that he will not get other people into difficulties and disturb other students with whom he is bound to have close contact." His conclusion: "As a psychiatrist I would hesitate very much to assume the responsibility to let this student return to school as I can only see how unable this patient is to overcome his difficulties." As a virtual postscript, he added: "During the interview I noticed distinctly that this patient has strong paranoid elements and seems to move in the direction of schizophrenia."

The "patient," however, appeared once again at the beginning of winter term, with yet another psychiatric evaluation from a private clinic. "I can neither substantiate nor deny the evidence of homosexuality in this case, although he can be described as being aesthetic in temperament and somewhat effeminate in speech and manner. Certainly I was unable to bring out any active homosexual tendencies which could be considered dangerous to others," wrote this third psychiatrist. "In short, from a psychiatric standpoint, I see no mental abnormalcies which would prevent him making high scholastic marks in a University, nor can I definitely say that his enrollment in any University would be detrimental to the faculty, student body, or reputation of such school." Emphasizing that Oral was of superior "native intelligence," he argued that such "assets of the personality structure" should be "weighed against behavior trends, possibly sexual abnormality," in determining eligibility for enrollment. At the very least, he requested, the hold on Mr. Hill's official transcript should be lifted so he could enroll at another "'Grade A'" university.

The dean, caught between conflicting psychiatric judgments, played it safe. He wanted a unanimous decision, and would allow readmittance only if Dr. Gundle at KU's mental health clinic believed the young man was no longer "dangerous." Moreover, the dean was concerned about the possible consequences of releasing Oral's records, noting in the file, "We should not pass his record on to another school without letting them know of the boy's past, then if they wish to take him we are in the clear if anything happens there." As of the following summer, the "boy's" record still read: "Not eligible to re-enroll on recommendation of Student Health Service."

The point here is not that homosexuality was treated as a basis for expulsion. In fact few of the KU students brought before the dean or even before the criminal courts for homosexual acts were expelled. More significant is the shift of authority from dean to psychiatrist, and the basis on which the psychiatrists made their recommendations. It is not homosexuality that is primarily at issue here, but instead the level of "danger" that an individual's homosexuality may present to the university community.

Two other cases from this era are useful here. The first, in which a respected faculty member left KU under a cloud of allegations about homosexuality, was treated quite differently by the same dean. The former faculty member, who insisted that the "intent and drive of [his] behavior were misjudged," wrote to inform the dean that after working with a psychiatrist he was confident there was no "ghost of a chance of a recurrence." He was, however, concerned about what the dean would say when asked for references, as he needed good letters of reference to obtain another position. This same dean, with many kind words, assured him that he would merely refer to "an illness which for a time incapacitated you," and closed with, "I feel so happy over your recovery."[8]

The other case involved a graduate student in the School of Fine Arts who confided to one of his professors that he was homosexual.[9] The professor reported the conversation to the school's dean. The dean notified Dr. Gundle, who then attempted to bring the student in for a conference, though he did not succeed until the young man discovered that his enrollment had been blocked. Dr. Gundle evaluated him as "unlikely to cause us any trouble through overt or aggressive acts" and recommended he be allowed to reenroll. When the Fine Arts dean resisted, the chancellor intervened on the student's behalf. However great his sense of betrayal, this young man was allowed to complete his degree, but only on condition that he stay in "continuous contact" with the health services psychiatrist.

Each of these men had his life turned upside down, and all surely suffered. But only one of the three was forced out of higher education entirely. The academic pecking order must be taken into account: the one whose records were so fully blocked was an undergraduate; the faculty member and the graduate student were somewhat better treated. However, plenty of other undergraduates found themselves in homosexual "difficulties" in the next few years, and very, very few were expelled. It becomes clear that it was not "homosexuality," as such, nor even a discovered act of sodomy, that merited expulsion. Instead, the decision was based upon psychiatric evaluation: is the patient a danger to himself or to others?

A case from the 1920s demonstrates how much had changed.[10] In the summer of 1921 an instructor who had been teaching at KU since before the Great War discovered that his contract would not be renewed and that, moreover, the chancellor had personally blocked his appointment at another Kansas university. The charges against him were vague initially, the dean's letter mentioning only "rumors . . . about your conduct here in the years just preceding the war." The instructor responded with a barrage of letters, mounting a scattershot defense that ranged from his "attempt to get to the bottom of rumors slandering the character of Walt Whitman" to his claim that "practically every act and almost thought of my life has been determined by my understanding of the answer to the question, 'What would Jesus do?'" to a genealogy that reached back to James Otis and the origins of the American nation.

Eventually the specifics emerged. The dean explained that "the men who have said that they were willing to state their personal relations with you charge you with the specific act of having kissed them . . . There has been some presumption and there have been rumors of conduct which would be considered in any court of grave immoral nature." The instructor readily admitted that he had kissed friends and students, both men and women, but insisted that his kisses were "manly" and "pure." He vehemently denied any "definite act of immoral nature" (with the sole exception of one "unfortunate experience during the night" that occurred while he was asleep, and for which he apologized when he learned of it) and demanded to face his accusers. Several men wrote on his behalf, one of whom insisted, in a long and impassioned letter to the dean, that though this man had certainly kissed some of his male students, including himself, the kisses were given "in a manly way without a trace of impurity or immorality." He declared that there was no "proof that he has gone further and had immoral relations with them," noting in his former instructor's defense: "Certainly there was opportunity for advances of an impure nature, yet [he] was always clean and straight with me."

In the end, the instructor's contract was not renewed. The university, the dean wrote to him in the summer of 1921, "brings no charge of immorality against you," but nonetheless deemed his "unwholesome habit of kissing" sufficient grounds for dismissal. Wholly ignoring what the loss of livelihood and profession might mean, the dean advised the increasingly desperate man: "As to 'carrying on' in spite of rumors i.e. individual interpretations of what you must feel were 'injudicious acts' making for what are considered by most people 'unwholesome relations as obtaining between men,' my feeling would be that no misinterpretation should unbalance one, if his conscience is clear."

Everyone in this case—the accused, his defenders, his accusers, his judges, even the gossips who circulated the unproven rumor—spoke a language of morality. The dean's investigation centered on whether or not any act of an "immoral nature" had occurred, with the accused denying it to the end. The postwar cases, in contrast, were conducted in a therapeutic framework. The deans and psychiatrists never used the word "immoral" or any of its cognates, and they did not seem particularly interested in ascertaining information about specific acts. Instead, they discussed diagnosis, illness, and recovery.[11] Homosexuality, in the postwar cases, was defined as a condition which might or might not stem from "serious" mental illness ("serious" because homosexuality itself was considered a mental illness). The university's course of action was not determined by the discovered fact of homosexual identity or homosexual acts, but rather was based on a fairly complex judgment about whether the individual posed any "danger" to the community.

The shift from a moral to a therapeutic framework is significant, though perhaps more for those who handed out the judgments and penalties than for those who were judged. Even though it appeared that a system of moral absolutes had been replaced by a much more flexible system of evaluation, the two systems remained enmeshed, with new "scientific" analyses often used to support the old "moral" claims. Within the system of moral absolutes that condemned homosexuality as sin, there had been some flexibility: were the instructor's kisses evidence of "immoral relations as obtaining between men," or were they "manly" and "pure" acts of friendship and Christian brotherhood? Conversely, within the therapeutic system, "mental illness" was often treated as the moral equivalent of sin. Thousands of men rejected by or discharged from the armed forces on psychiatric grounds during World War II returned home with official documents (requested by all prospective employers) labeling them "sexual deviants." Many of these men would never have come to the notice of authorities at all had not psychiatric screening and the detection of psychological abnormality become a priority in large and powerful institutions like the U.S. military.

At the same time, the turn to psychiatric expertise created a gray area, a much less absolute approach to the problem of sexual misconduct. The criterion of danger to the community complicated judgment, for while moral judgments are based on how an individual's actions are evaluated ("manly" and "pure"? or "immoral relations"?), the same act may seem very dangerous in one community and relatively harmless in another. That relativity was difficult to reconcile with moral absolutes. And psychiatrists disagreed, as did those who judged poor Oral so differently within five days in 1947. How were deans supposed to act on psychiatric evaluations when psychiatrists could find no consensus? And then there was the problem of distinguishing between categories of sexual transgression. Some transgressors, like the young men and women occasionally found drunk and disheveled in an off-campus apartment, were still treated according to the older system of moral absolutes. Others, such as two men caught having oral sex in the men's room of the student union, fell under the new therapeutic system. The distinction between the two was usually quite clear: "normal" behavior was punished while "abnormal" behavior was treated. Still, drawing such distinctions complicated, and eventually weakened, the authority of absolute standards. Even though it may be scant comfort for those who found their lives just as shattered by psychiatric judgments as by moral ones, the new therapeutic language helped to dissolve the power of absolute categories and unanimous verdicts.

The turn from moral authority to psychiatric expertise at KU, as across the nation, had not been sudden. The "medicalization" of homosexuality (and of human sexuality in general) can be traced to the previous century. A simplified and sexualized Freudianism had swept through American culture in the 1920s, and psychological explanations for various actions had gradually gained currency, frequently coexisting with moral judgments when it came to sex. Before World War II, psychiatric concepts were widely available, if not widely understood. For example, in 1938, asked by the chancellor if he could shed any light on the actions of Don Henry, a KU student who had embraced communism and left Kansas to fight and die in the Spanish Civil War, the Men Students' Advisor speculated that Henry had "a prepsychotic make-up."[12]

The specific experience of World War II, however, decisively shaped the role psychiatry would play in institutions of higher learning in the postwar years. During the war military psychiatrists and volunteer physicians, many of the latter general practitioners given a crash course that was sometimes referred to as "a child's guide to psychiatric diagnosis," attempted to act as gatekeepers for the armed forces by determining fitness for service. Their assignment was not to offer treatment to individuals with psychiatric disorders but rather to screen out individuals who might pose a danger to the integrity and power of the military unit.[13]

In 1940, when Congress authorized a military draft to bolster the nation's defenses, prominent psychiatrists lobbied for psychiatric, as well as physical, screening of inductees. Their arguments were immensely practical. Neuropsychiatric casualties from World War I had thus far cost more than a billion dollars in compensation and care. Adequate psychiatric screening, its advocates argued, could not only save taxpayers "the enormous cost of taking care of those who develop psychiatric disorders after being inducted" but also spare the wartime military the "futile attempt to make fighting men out of ill-adapted material." Furthermore, by excluding men who, for whatever reason, would not "integrate smoothly into military service," the military could prevent a negative impact on the morale of the fighting unit. Military psychiatrists acknowledged that their approach, which allowed chronic malingerers and "reckless, wayward, spineless, unadjusted male adults" to evade service, might seem unfair. But the larger goal of creating a strong military had to override such concerns. Military service, with war on the horizon, could not serve as a "course of discipline and treatment" for the maladjusted. The first priority had to be "build[ing] an intelligent and dependable soldier as a unit in the defense of our homes."[14]

At the center of the effort was the Menninger Clinic, one of the most prominent psychiatric training and treatment centers in the nation, which was located in Topeka, Kansas, not quite thirty miles from Lawrence. Menninger staff members led "seminars for practical psychiatric diagnosis" in cities throughout the nation in 1941, and William C. Menninger served as a psychiatric consultant for the army, eventually attaining the rank of brigadier general. Throughout the war the Menninger staff worked hard to influence the development of military psychiatry through its publications, which were provided without charge to all psychiatrists in military service.

Despite the best efforts of America's psychiatric profession, the process of psychological screening never became fully coherent or standardized in implementation. Psychiatrists disagreed on the classification and etiology of mental illness, and their diverse criteria were filtered through layers of Washington bureaucracy and military hierarchy before being communicated to the volunteer local physicians attached to draft boards, most of whom were completely unfamiliar with psychiatric diagnosis. Nonetheless, it is clear from discussions of screening procedures that most psychiatrists were not *especially* preoccupied with sexual "abnormality." The *Bulletin of the Menninger Clinic* published a special issue on military psychiatry, which devoted much less space to such "abnormality" than to advice on screening out psychopathic personalities, the feeble-minded, and those suffering from psychoneuroses, including "paranoid personalities," who were deemed "likely to stir up dissension in the ranks . . . and cause all kinds of trouble," and "dependent" personalities, who might try to enlist in order "to get 'on the government' for life by sustaining an injury or breaking down in the armed forces." "Overt sexual perversions" appeared as a category of concern, "especially homosexuality, exhibitionism, or fetishism," which might endanger the unit's morale, but readers were advised that "otherwise well adjusted cases of perversion" might be "useful members" of the army. One writer noted that while a man "with strong unconscious homosexual conflicts" might be "threatened" by the constant association with large groups of men, a "normal" man might find segregation from women psychologically stressful and become hostile or anxious. Each man was equally likely to disrupt discipline or morale.[15]

While some psychiatrists attempted to maintain such diagnostic distinctions, in the hands of barely trained laypeople or of psychiatrists who were allotted three minutes to evaluate each inductee, the screening procedure was a blunt instrument. Questions such as "How often do you 'date' girls" were used to detect sexual abnormality, and either overt homosexuality or effeminacy of manner might lead to disqualification or dishonorable discharge on grounds of mental disorder.

William Menninger was very aware of the compromises psychiatry was making in the military. He attempted to justify those compromises—the standardization and bureaucracy, the simplified classification system for psychoneurotic conditions—by reminding his colleagues of the larger picture. Their civilian practices had focused on the individual patient and his treatment. Their military service, however, focused on winning the war. Their first responsibility was to "maintain" the organization—Army, Navy, Marines—by filtering out those who posed a danger to the unit's efficacy, "quickly salvag[ing]" those who could be salvaged, and getting the unfit out of uniform before they caused further damage.[16]

Psychiatric screening shifted the military's focus from the outlawed act of sodomy to the homosexual individual. Instead of punishing an illegal act, these policies declared certain persons unfit for military service because of their sexual orientation. It was not necessarily anything they did that created a problem; it was who they were, and how their sexual identity was assumed to threaten the military institution. In the case of gay men and women during World War II, this shift in policy and practice undoubtedly injured individuals and further undermined the already precarious status of homosexuals in American society. However, these new policies were aimed at all forms of "sexual abnormality" that were believed to threaten the war effort, not just at homosexuality. Psychiatric screening based on the concept of danger, forged in war, would have different results when applied to sexual "deviants" in civilian life.

The psychiatric profession expanded rapidly during the war years. By 1945, 2,400 physicians were serving as military psychiatrists—a number that equaled the total prewar membership of the American Psychiatric Association. Most of them had been trained in the military. Many now believed that the benefits of psychiatry could—and should—be extended across a greater territory, fostering mental health among the American people in peace as well as in war. William Menninger argued that psychiatry's wartime experience made it "vividly apparent that psychiatry can and must play a much more important role in the solution of health problems of the civilian."[17] Congress passed the first federal mental health act in 1946, establishing the National Institute of Mental Health. The Cold War defense budget included lavish funding for psychological research. And American institutions—from businesses to public health centers to universities—sought psychiatric and psychological expertise.

The University of Kansas, probably because of its proximity to the Menninger Clinic, was well ahead of the curve in developing mental health facilities. Its mental hygiene clinic opened in 1947, and by 1950 it was accepting psychiatric residents from the Menninger Clinic for six- to twelve-month rotations. KU's Dr. Gundle promoted the development of similar clinics across the nation. He surveyed 1,141 colleges and universities in the United States and Canada in 1953 and reported that only 99 of them had full-scale mental health clinics. However, that was up from 43 schools offering students psychiatric consultation in 1936, and much higher percentages of large universities had clinics: 52 percent of those enrolling 5,000 to 10,000 students, and 81 percent of those with student bodies of more than 10,000.[18]

The World War II military experience profoundly shaped the development of university mental health programs. The vast majority of psychiatrists in the nation at that time had served in the military. In Kansas, Menninger's wartime role certainly had an impact on the university's mental hygiene clinic. And many physicians with other specialties had obtained some familiarity with psychiatry in their wartime service. The man who ran KU's student health program from the 1950s through the 1970s, an obstetrician, had been given the brief course in psychiatric diagnosis at the beginning of the war, and had asked thousands of Kansas inductees questions like "How often do you 'date' girls?"[19]

As universities established or expanded mental health clinics, their psychiatrists often acted in the roles pioneered by military psychiatrists. Quite a few universities used psychiatrists and psychologists to screen applicants, hoping to weed out those who were somehow unfit for university life. Many set up clinics for their students, offering help with the common adjustment problems of young adults and emergency care for more serious cases. Like the military, most universities did not have the facilities or staff for long-term treatment of serious chronic mental disorders. As in the military, where psychiatrists tried to "salvage" those who could return to duty, university psychiatrists worked with those who were able, on some level, to meet their responsibilities as university students. Others were separated from the university, on the recommendation of the student health service. It wasn't a discharge, but these students usually found their registration blocked if they tried to reenroll or transfer. Also as in the military, the psychiatrist's obligation was to the institution as well as to the patient. The psychiatrist was "responsible," in the words of KU's Dr. Gundle, for evaluating individuals and advising the institution on a course of action. The question was essentially the same as it had been during World War II: Was the person, from a psychiatric standpoint, a danger to himself or to the university community?

Just as in the war, the focus shifted from unacceptable acts (sodomy, exhibitionism, voyeurism, even sexual assault) to the persons involved. The key issue, again, was their effect on the unit—in this case, the university community. Could they do their jobs? Did they pose a "danger"? But there was a big difference between the university and the wartime military. "Sexual perverts" were excluded from military service to prevent "disruptive" influences among groups of men who were going into combat with the fate of the nation at stake. This focus on disruption and danger had a very different impact in a different environment. The university student body was not the army, and education was not combat. "Danger" was not measured by the same criteria, or on the same scale.

The American Psychiatric Association classified homosexuality as a mental illness, and in the 1950s virtually all university psychiatrists and psychologists accepted that designation. But that did not mean that most believed homosexuals were, by nature, "dangerous" to the community or "unfit" for higher education. At a meeting of the National Association of Student Personnel Administrators in 1952 (with KU's dean of students, Laurence Woodruff, on the executive committee), a psychiatrist told the assembled deans:

> I do not think of the homo-sexual patient as one who goes around corrupting others—if the atmosphere on campus is a healthy one. I think of him as being quite a nuisance to others and of being an exciter of anxiety in other persons who are struggling with their own latent homo-sexual conflicts; but I do not subscribe to the idea that having such a person on the campus under treatment is going to do him any harm, or the campus any harm, as long as he knows that he has to maintain his own personal integrity in that field just the same as other students have to maintain their heterosexual integrity.[20]

The concept of danger governed the way many universities handled cases of sexual misconduct, and university psychiatrists promoted the use of that criterion. An article in the professional journal for administrators in the field of "student life" presented this model for handling student sexual misconduct and chronicled its results. At the University of Wisconsin, during the 1950s, 28 male students were referred to the psychiatric center because of homosexual difficulties. Of these, 25 were "cleared" to continue their studies. From today's viewpoint, these verdicts may appear to indicate a slight lessening of the era's homophobia, but it was not only homosexuality that was so treated. Of the 17 men referred to the psychiatric center for exhibiting their genitals to women, 15 were judged "very disturbed"—psychotic or on the borderline of psychosis. Yet 14 of the 17 were given psychiatric clearance to continue their studies. Overall, only 10 percent of the students evaluated by health service psychiatrists at the administration's request were considered a danger to themselves or to the community.[21] No matter how reprehensible the administrators found an act, the issue was not sexual morality but danger to the university community, and psychiatrists did not confuse the campus with combat.

—

By the 1950s various forms of sexual misconduct had been redefined. On the basis of clinical research, both experts and popular wisdom rejected the idea that homosexuality and certain other sexual "abnormalities" were the immoral or depraved acts of "normal" individuals. Instead, they were symptoms of mental illness. "Sexual deviates," thus, did not deserve punishment. They needed treatment. This approach was widely adopted, not only by mental health experts, but also by those charged with controlling the sexual behavior of the nation's youth.

In 1955 the dean of students at UCLA, along with his assistant dean, published an influential article on "the sexually deviate student" in the journal *School and Society*. The article, based on "years of painstaking committee study," proposed a procedure for dealing with these widespread and troublesome cases. "It is true that society does not understand nor tolerate sexually deviate behavior, nor should it," the authors wrote. "However, in our lack of toleration, we are much more likely to adopt punitive than remedial measures." Their goal was to develop a standardized procedure that focused on "proper medical diagnosis, prognosis, and therapy."[22] This procedure essentially mandated psychiatric evaluation, officially shifting the dean's authority to the psychiatrist, or at the least, shifting the basis of the dean's authority to psychiatric grounds.

At the University of Kansas, therapeutic models structured the dean's action in all postwar cases of sexual deviance. But the transformation from moral to therapeutic model, the marriage of dean's and psychiatrist's authority, often presented complications when applied to individual cases. Moral language was quite resilient, even though it was resolutely eschewed by university personnel. Deans often were personally ambivalent and also caught in the middle between the moral understandings of the general public, before whom the university's reputation had to be upheld, and the "permissive" tactics of university psychiatrists. How could they justify the continued enrollment of homosexuals and other sexual deviants at the taxpayer-supported state university, when most citizens of the state believed homosexuality was immoral and when sodomy was, in fact, illegal? This was not a case most deans looked forward to making publicly.

The triumph of therapeutic language and policies that emphasized treatment rather than punishment did not mean that deans and administrators began to *approve* of sexual misconduct. The personal distaste KU's dean of men felt for sexual deviance shows quite clearly in his notes, even as he wholeheartedly implemented the new policies. Most university officials understood the turn to psychiatric management as a way to keep the "red-flag" problems of sexual deviance from becoming public knowledge. Universities did not benefit from that sort of publicity.

Throughout the postwar era the deans of men at KU kept detailed files on student misconduct, much of it sexual. These files, such as the one compiled in 1947 when Oral appealed for readmission to KU, contain not only memos about the disposition of cases but also the deans' rough notes, students' handwritten statements, police reports, letters from and to the students' parents, newspaper clippings, even, occasionally, a notice of death or a query from another university or the FBI. The deans of women, in contrast, kept no such files. While the stereotypical dean of women—a prudish spinster obsessed with closing hours and sexual propriety—bears little resemblance to most of the women who acted as deans in large universities, the lack of records on women's misconduct is striking because women's sexual behavior normally was more closely monitored than men's.[23]

Emily Taylor, the dean of women at KU from 1956 through the early 1970s, purposely kept her records cryptic and then destroyed them in order to protect the students. When she noted an "inappropriate" level of physical affection between two women, she suggested greater propriety in public, not counseling. Obviously, the personality and beliefs of the individual who fills an administrative position can make a great deal of difference. But gender differences in the forms of sexual misconduct also explain the greater visibility of men. Women students' sexual misconduct was mostly "normal" and unlikely to disturb others or impose on them. Women were hardly ever exhibitionists or voyeurs; they didn't sexually attack men. Some were lesbians, but they didn't hang out in the student union restrooms looking for partners. Instead, women students tended to get pregnant. Most secretly found an illegal abortion or left school. They were rarely drawn into the therapeutic net.[24]

Even without women's records, the disciplinary files offer a much clearer picture of how sexual misconduct was handled than do all the policy statements and clinical research reports of the era. These are records of human tragedy, and there are no happy endings. But one sees, in these thick file folders, how the university's forfeiture of absolute moral authority in favor of therapeutic methods would eventually undermine the entire system of sexual controls.

—

In early November 1959 a university police officer appeared at the door of Bill Hawkin's dormitory room.[25] The officer, acting on information received by the department, was investigating a "sex offense." He told Bill that he did not have to go with him, but that the KU police would like to discuss his "activities" of the previous night. Bill agreed, and made a full statement to the police. In so doing he implicated his friend Fred, who may have been the one who called the police in the first place.

Bill, a junior, had been making the rounds of Lawrence bars that Friday night. He'd drunk beer at the Jayhawk, the Flamingo, and the Dine-a-mite, hitting the Rock Chalk around 11 P.M. There he met Fred, a freshman who came from the same town in western Kansas. Bill invited Fred along to visit a friend of his, a man who worked at the library and was known for being generous with his liquor. As Bill was knocking on the apartment door he told Fred to watch out, that people said this man was a "queer." There were a few young men gathered in the apartment, drinking, talking, and listening to music. The apartment's owner was lying on a davenport, dressed in pajamas and a dressing gown, but he welcomed them, giving Bill a Scotch and Fred a beer. About half an hour later another man arrived, and the atmosphere changed. Alex, who was "colored," put on

classical music and began what the report refers to as a "cultural dance."
The notes taken by KU's dean of men look like this:

> did a "cultural dance"—
> —smooth music
> Low light—(1 light) flashed against wall
> moved hands in hair air
> (1) shirt off
> (2) trousers "
> (3) shorts "
> —nude—

Fred had been confused about what was going on in the apartment
from the beginning. The hi-fi had created some sort of mechanical interference with the hearing aid he wore, and so he just sat back, drinking his beer,
while the other men talked. He sat quietly while Alex danced, but when the
nude man pulled him from his chair he tried to resist. Alex forced him into
the apartment's bedroom and undressed him, leaving only Fred's socks and
glasses. Fred was afraid to struggle too much because he didn't want to
break his hearing aid or his "special" glasses. He told the dean he thought
the quickest way to get out was to just go through it. Here the account
becomes Fred's:

> It started out with a kiss—having a man kissed one with a tongue
> stuck into my mouth didn't seemed right. I fought to leave the bed
> but Alex was on top of me and I quit . . . The green soft light was on
> and Alex did suck my privates. It was a very short one—because I
> didn't like it. Alex then got some vaseline to put on his private his
> private to stick it up into my hole. Alex stuck it up but it sure did
> hurt. I fought against him to leave—again he had a way to overpower
> me. He again stuck his prick up again—Again I didn't like it. I got
> mad. But it didn't help. Alex then said jack off—I had no idea what
> that meant. Finally he started playing with his so I played with mine
> . . . After my sperm was shot off I left the bedroom and went to the
> living room to pick up my shirt and coat and my friend to go back
> home.

Fred's account is poignant, as much from his ignorance as his victimi-
zation. "I never did anything to him because I had fear of doing something

with anyone else my own sex," he wrote in his statement to the dean. "I've heard about syphilis but I didn't know what it was like. So I *never* wanted to play or suck other's sex. My head was going crazy."

The police, after taking statements from Bill and Fred, turned both over to the dean. It seems that Bill had committed an "indecent act" of his own in the living room while Fred wasn't there, and he admitted to two other such acts in his time at KU. The dean interviewed both young men, making detailed notes about the layout of the apartment, the seating arrangements, the lighting and music. But he disposed of the case quickly. Both Bill and Fred were allowed to continue in school under disciplinary probation. Both were referred to the university psychiatrist, and each had to summon his parents for a conference with the dean about his "special problem." Fred's parents also accompanied him to the psychiatrist.

Bill and Fred were treated identically by the dean, even though he believed that Bill had engaged in sex voluntarily and Fred had been forced. (Nothing in the dean's notes suggests that he didn't believe Fred, and he never implied that Fred's account might stem from guilt or ambivalence about what took place in that apartment. The dean took Fred's account at face value, even though in cases of heterosexual misconduct he commonly speculated on ulterior motives and recorded unsubstantiated rumors about women's sexual promiscuity.) In this case, whether voluntarily or by force, both young men had engaged in "deviate" activity, and the dean was following a university policy developed in 1955—one month after the article about UCLA's procedures appeared in *School and Society*. This policy, developed by the mental health center and the dean of women's office, specified that unless the case had become irrevocably public—"charged by police and trial in court scheduled"—the dean was to work through the university psychiatry service, not the criminal justice system or the university's disciplinary organs. In fact, the memo detailing the policy strongly suggested the following procedure: warn the student that the matter was serious, tell him the dean's office would investigate, refer him to the mental health center, and take no further action.[26]

Alex's case was both more and less complicated. His actions suggested he might well be judged a danger to the community, and Fred said that he was telling the story because he wanted Alex expelled from the campus. But it turned out that Alex wasn't a student. He had come to Lawrence to attend KU, but when poor grades in chemistry thwarted his plans for a medical career, he had dropped out. Alex did not fall under the protective or punitive reach of the university. But no one in charge wanted publicity. Although copies of the KU police reports had been forwarded to the city attorney and to the Lawrence police department, the dean's notes suggest an off-the-record arrangement with city officials. Alex was "given 24 hours to 'clear out' of Lawrence" before the matter was turned over to the police.

That, however, was not the end of the story. The dean began an investigation of homosexuality on campus, making detailed charts and diagrams. He identified three discreet groups, listing names, addresses, even physical descriptions. He circled the names of those he believed to be "active and recruiting members of the group." He concluded that there were "H's 50—100" on campus, about half of whom "poss use dope." He found that a fairly active branch of the "young communist party" was somehow associated with homosexual activity, that the Acacia fraternity "may have problem w' h—uals," and that the "grapevine" had it that Alpha Chi Sigma was "noted for h—s." Most of those he identified were men, though a few women's names appear in random notes. The groups were multiracial, including white, "negro," and "Spanish" men. They were composed of students, instructors, university employees, and working-class men in town. One group was rumored to have some connection with a Kansas City nightclub, the Congo Club. The dean also listed "Recruiting Stations" for homosexuals, including the student union Trophy Room and a couple of local bars, noting, with some alarm, that "Lawrence is a 'congregation point' for the midwest."

The dean's investigation did not precipitate a witch-hunt. No action was taken against any of the persons identified, with the exception of Alex, whose behavior had crossed many lines. But in the questioning process, what seems to have been a fairly close-knit group of gay men on campus were given notice that their activities were being monitored, and that information about them was on file. This strategy of sexual containment had as its main goal preventing "danger" to the community, whether from homosexual "recruiting" or from unwanted publicity. While the dean worried a great deal about sexual deviance on his campus, he did not attempt to punish men for illicit sexual acts. Still, this policy may well have *contained* homosexuality by pushing it further underground. The next set of such cases recorded by the dean did not appear until a full student-generation later, in 1963.

Once again, the university did not follow this tolerate-and-contain procedure out of a belief that homosexuality was acceptable, or that it was simply the private choice of an individual. Similar approaches were taken with a wide variety of other forms of behavior that were considered sexually deviant. Danger to the community was the key criterion, and all these cases were managed through therapeutic, not disciplinary, channels. In 1955, when a 21-year-old married senior accosted three girls, two KU students and a 13-year-old, grabbing them and trying to force them to accompany him, he was charged with "assault and battery and molesting" the two students. However, he was turned over to university authorities, where the university psychiatrist determined that he was "not a menace to public safety—and furthermore, punishment is not in the best interest of the student or to the public." In 1961, when police picked up a KU student on charges that he had "grabbed a coed" and then let her go "for some unknown reason," they delivered him directly to the mental health clinic. Earlier, in 1956, a 26-year-old Lawrence man was picked up in the KU student union restrooms after propositioning two male students. The Lawrence police charged him with vagrancy and took a statement that revealed a history of "illegal sex relations by mouth," almost always in the union restrooms and usually with "colored" men (he was white). The police report, however, notes that the vagrancy charge was "pending in liew of investigation at the Bert Nash Clinic (Lawrence's community mental health clinic, established shortly after World War II) as to [his] mental condition."[27]

Psychiatric evaluation and therapeutic language were becoming increasingly widespread. The file of a young man the dean referred to the university psychiatrist because of exhibitionism in 1962 also contains a police report from the small town of Sunflower, Kansas. The deputy sheriff's report on a previous "incident of indecent exposure" concludes: "In our opinion, this subject has not reached the stage where there is a danger of an emotional upset to cause violence or improper sex attitudes . . . Again, in our opinion, [he] is ill; suffering a malady common to many of our citizens. We feel that he should have medical attention and treatment of some nature which should correct this illness."[28] When small-town police departments in Kansas also employ therapeutic language, it is clear that the new understandings of sexual deviance and therapeutic management are not restricted to cosmopolitan university communities.

While the shift from disciplinary to therapeutic procedure was widely accepted and implemented, many of the university administrators who were expected to manage and control youth's sexual behavior worried that this shift was undermining their authority and making their task impossible. The difference between the ways "deviate" behavior and "normal" sexual misconduct were handled violated the sensibilities of many. In practice, the therapeutic approach drew a line between forms of misconduct. Homosexuality, exhibitionism, voyeurism, even sometimes sexual assault, were understood to be—or to stem from—mental illness. Premarital heterosexual intercourse, in contrast, remained in the sphere of immorality. The first set of behavior required treatment, the second, punishment. Under the right conditions, and according to this logic, the boy who had sex with his girlfriend might be expelled, while the one who had sex with another man, or who exhibited his genitals to women he didn't know, might remain at the university with the offer of free or low-cost counseling. While the deviate might be "analyzed without suggestion of moral disapproval," those whose transgressions were based on socially acceptable urges might feel the full brunt of punishment. The logic didn't work for many of the people who were supposed to implement it.

Compare a case of "normal" misconduct to the previous cases: On June 11, 1960, at 2:45 A.M., the assistant director of a coed dorm flagged down Officer Hanna, a KU police officer who was making his rounds. She reported that a boy and a girl were missing from their rooms, and that she thought they might be walking around campus, as neither had a car. Officer Hanna immediately contacted the Lawrence city police and had them check with the cab companies to see if the couple might have taken a cab. They had indeed, to the Lawrence Motel.[29]

Detective Vernon Harrell of the Lawrence police met Officer Hanna at the motel. They awakened the proprietor, who told them that a young couple *had* checked in that evening, but had given the names Mr. and Mrs. John Keegus and said they were from San Francisco. They had arrived in a cab, without luggage, explaining that their car had broken down and they'd left it at Page's Garage to be repaired. The officers knew that Page's was not a garage but a filling station. Nonetheless, they woke up the owner of Page's to ask if a car had been left there ("so that we would not be getting the wrong people out of bed," the report said, an irony that may have been lost on the owners of the motel and the gas station). Having made sure that "Mr. and Mrs. Keegus" were not unfortunates whose car had broken down on a cross-country drive, the officers knocked loudly on the door of cabin #16. No one answered at first; probably the two were frantically trying to find some way out of their predicament. But after about fifteen minutes the missing young man came to the door and spoke briefly with the police; fifteen minutes after that the couple emerged. They were taken in the police car to the campus, where they were turned over to the dormitory director.

The police report, while detailed, is rather strained, for the form clearly was never intended to record such offenses. The blanks for "person(s) attacked" and "property attacked" are left blank; "how attacked" is specified as "failing to report at closing time" and "object of attack" is rather coyly rendered as "unknown." The offense was, however, treated with all seriousness. Later that morning Peter, the young man in question, was summoned by the dean of men and informed that, through "his actions with Miss Susan Holcombe" he had "forfeited his right to continue" as a student. Susan's case is lost to history, for she fell under the authority of the dean of women.

The young man's father, the dean noted, was "somewhat exercised by this disciplinary action," and apparently pushed matters, for Peter was allowed to reenroll for the fall semester, though he lost his summer school tuition payment and credit for the courses he'd begun. In a memo summing up the case, the dean noted that "discovered-behavior" of this sort could not be "tolerated among University of Kansas students."

Here again the criterion was harm to the community. The University of Kansas did not try to track down all sexual miscreants. The police did not patrol the back roads, apprehending disheveled students in parked cars. The dean had no illusions that he could or should expel all students who had premarital sex. That course, various people commented over the years, might well depopulate the university. This couple's behavior, however, had crossed the line from private to public. If they had been cleverer or more discreet, if they had had a car, if they had gotten back to their dorm rooms by closing time, their behavior would have been for all practical purposes irrelevant to the institution. But because of their passion or their clumsiness, they had brought themselves to the attention of the administration. "Discovered-behavior" of this sort could not be ignored. Public toleration would endanger the university community and possibly fray its moral fabric.

Significantly, there was no suggestion—much less requirement—that Peter undergo psychiatric evaluation or treatment. His misconduct was assumed to be voluntary, stemming from "normal" urges that he should have been capable of controlling. Because his misconduct was simply that—misconduct—and not "illness," it warranted summary expulsion.

The dean of men had no trouble labeling Peter's behavior as wrong. He likewise had no trouble believing that exhibitionists and homosexuals were sick and deserved help. In espousing those beliefs and implementing policies based on them, he never intended to foster sexual "permissiveness" or freedom. But the difference in procedures for handling "normal" and "deviate" misconduct made the rules seem ever more arbitrary and artificial.

Deans and other administrators who dealt with students were highly self-conscious about the complications and contradictions of their disciplinary role. Their professional association, the National Association of Student Personnel Administrators (NASPA), frequently addressed issues of authority and control in its journal and annual meetings. In 1952 NASPA framed its annual meeting around the question: "How can we effectively develop a sense of higher standards of personal integrity and individual responsibility in the university and college community?" While the keynote speech was given by a chaplain, the conference centered around a half-day session on the relationship between the dean and the psychiatrist. The deans were concerned about the implications of psychiatric authority, or, as one put it, the conflict between "the permissiveness of the psychiatrist and the moral standards of society." Though the psychiatrists attempted to explain that permissiveness was a technique, not a moral position (if we condemn a student's behavior at the outset, he'll stop talking and we'll have lost him), they were speaking a different language than most of the deans. Asked about how he would counsel a homosexual, the psychiatrist from Swarthmore replied: "I take the attitude to the patient that you have violated the customs of the community."[30]

Such relativism frustrated many of the deans. "[You] advise a student not to indulge in anti-social behavior, but to accept the standards of the society around him as a sort of common sense procedure which will make him happier, give him . . . more freedom from tensions, and more peace of mind," one dean began his critique. But by rendering "moral" standards as "conformity" to the standards of the community, by removing notions of right and wrong and replacing them with "freedom from tension," he argued, psychiatric authorities had left administrators in an indefensible position. Students, well aware that "standards" differed from one community to another and changed from generation to generation, too often saw administrators' insistence on certain proprieties as hypocritical. Thus punishment or penalties for violating what were, after all, *not* moral absolutes but simply the standards of a specific community seemed unjust within an institution that taught the social science concept of "relativity" in its class-rooms.[31]

The deans, who shared a conviction that they were expected to "up-hold the traditional mores of the communities which send their students to the college" and also "provide a certain cloak of respectability to the college," probably understood the implications of the shift to therapeutic procedures better than most of the psychiatrists. Though one dean suggested that the two groups might find common ground by recognizing that the shift was not in "morals and values, but in method," no one ever answered the dean's plea: "Are there any other standards than the standard of the community, which so many [students] reject?"[32]

As the line drawn between normal and deviate misconduct under-mined any notion of absolute moral authority, so too did the therapeutic process. This is not to say that psychiatrists condoned or accepted "socially offending" sexual behavior like exhibitionism or public masturbation or homosexuality. And there was no full agreement on the etiology of sexual disorders or on their treatment. But the sorts of therapy recommended for university students avoided all mention of absolute standards of morality. And some even emphasized the fluidity of sexual identity. In a paper presented to the Midwestern Association of College and University Psychiatrists and Clinical Psychologists in 1948 and later published in the *Journal of Nervous and Mental Disease,* Dr. Benjamin H. Glover, a psychiatrist from the University of Wisconsin, detailed his use of "direct psychotherapy" in working with homosexual students.[33]

Having made it very clear to the student that he is embarking on a "hard and lifelong project," Dr. Glover told his heartland colleagues, the therapist should begin with a description of "the early embryologic bisexuality in the human being." That information should open the way for a discussion about the "many possible intergrades between 'absolute masculinity and femininity.'" Then, using the patient's background (his firsthand knowledge of animal behavior, say, or for veterans perhaps the "conversion of an apparently stable heterosexual to overt homosexuality under stress of war"), the therapist should stress the "flexibility of sexual adaptation." Then comes the material on community standards:

> Explain [to the patient] the logical development of the restrictions of society on deviant sex practices. A practical, sociologic approach sprinkled generously with present-day tribal variations and religious

71

and superstitious influences serves to make more interesting a purely historical and ethnologic subject. Thus the early polygamy and mixed sexuality and practices of early man are brought down through history and conditions of living to the accepted monogamous and purely heterosexual practices of the present mores of civilized man.

72

This discussion is meant to demonstrate the "practical value of adherence to the basic taboos." In this stage of treatment, the therapist has to deal with the fact that some violations—"heterosexual familiarity or even promiscuity"—are tolerated by society, while homosexuality is not.

With the "academic preparation" finished, the therapy moves on to more "practical" aspects. The student works with his therapist to identify the outward signs of his homosexuality. Is it a question of appearance? Of manner? Over time the patient must try to develop a "manly first appearance" by practicing mannerisms that are "masculine in connotation or at least not doubtfully masculine." Dr. Glover described the changes in gestures, voice inflection, gait, and facial expressions as "conning in the dramatic arts." The point of this therapy was to "cure" homosexuality. But the whole content of the therapy emphasized the arbitrary, contingent, flexible, and nonabsolute nature of both sexual mores and sexual identity.

Dr. Glover's claims here were not far from mainstream thought. His explanations were true to the best research in the social, behavioral, and medical sciences at that time. Even the focus on "masculine" mannerisms meshed with what was appearing in popular magazines and advice books, with experts offering tips on how to *appear* more masculine or more feminine, and thus more desirable. Dr. Glover's therapy was grounded in common beliefs and common knowledge, especially as that knowledge was taught to the rapidly expanding population of college students. Scholarship that stressed the historical construction of social and cultural norms, including those governing sexual behavior and gender roles, reached far more Americans in anthropology and sociology classrooms than through this particular form of therapy. Many Americans at the time, including those within universities, accepted such "scientific" understandings without relinquishing any belief in "traditional" gender roles or *moral* codes of sexual behavior. But this social scientific knowledge could—and would—be used to critique the reigning system of sexual mores. In some arenas, such as universities, the rise of a therapeutic approach to sexual misconduct, with all its complexities and what many who were charged with implementing it saw as moral inconsistencies, made it more difficult for officials to defend that system of sexual mores when it was challenged.

It is difficult to know what the therapeutic approach meant to the young men who were sent to the psychiatrist instead of being expelled. It is even difficult to evaluate the process from the outside, for some of the acts treated that way, such as grabbing coeds or trying to make women look at one's penis, are still "socially offending" behavior. "Helping" these individuals rather than punishing them seems fairly progressive even by today's standards. In the case of homosexuality, however, the therapeutic approach appears in retrospect intrusive and oppressive, though perhaps better than expulsion because it did at least allow most of the men to continue their studies. Is a psychiatric "cure" worse than expulsion? Is it worse to be labeled mentally ill or sinful? All the men who turned up in the dean's disciplinary files suffered, and the men (and women) who sought gay liberation in the following decades would reject the therapeutic model just as surely as they refused a moral universe that declared homosexuality a sin.

While the shift from a moral to a therapeutic approach did not offer new freedom to individuals, it did undermine the ability of university officials to implement the existing system of sexual controls. That wasn't intentional, nor was it the work of sexual revolutionaries or of free love radicals. The deans and administrators who created and implemented the new approaches to student sexual misconduct were as conservative about sex as most Americans of their generation. Even the psychiatrists involved insisted that behavior be measured against the standards of the community—not against the standards of "enlightened" individuals or against what was acceptable in the nation's most cosmopolitan or bohemian enclaves. No one intended to foster sexual freedom, but by their actions they created a tear in the fabric of moral authority.

Despite these momentous behind-the-scenes changes, public codes of acceptable sexual behavior held firm through most of the postwar era. The claims to sexual freedom, the direct challenges to institutional authority, lay in the future. While the deans who were expected to manage students' sexual conduct agonized over their lost "authority," they still held power. New understandings may have chipped away at the edifice of absolute moral standards, but students who were discovered breaking the rules of sexual conduct still suffered consequences—as in the panty raid at KU in the spring of 1952.

In the disciplinary files of the dean of men is a handwritten letter from Cpl. William Cranston, United States Marine Corps. It is headed, simply, "May 26, 1952, Korea." Corporal Cranston was writing in protest and with great indignation, having read about the college panty raids in the *Stars and Stripes:* "College students are deferred from the draft to get a better education. And I don't think they are bettering there education by holding panty raids on girls dormitories. If it would be at all possible I'd like to see them all be drafted and sent over here. If its raids they like we have one raid a day but these raids are not on girls dormitories but on the Chinese Communist lines."[34]

The dean answered the letter immediately. He blamed the "scare-minded tactics" of the press for blowing the panty raids out of proportion, and he insisted that most college students were serious and responsible. But he also assured Cpl. Cranston that justice would be served: "The disciplinary action taken against the leaders . . . will undoubtedly result in the implementation of your suggestion that their urge for 'raids' be diverted toward the Chinese Communists' lines."[35]

In other words, the leaders would be expelled, and being expelled meant, quite likely, being drafted. Whether one believes today in the fairness of college deferments, whether one believes that panty raids were harmless diversions or hooliganism or violence against women, the leaders had stepped over the line of permissible behavior at the University of Kansas in 1952. The consequences to them would be all too real.

3

Responsible Sex

Most students at the University of Kansas never were drawn into the therapeutic system, never appeared in the dean's "Problems and Discipline" files. A great many of them, however, broke university rules and transgressed against the accepted standards of sexual propriety these rules were meant to uphold. Students broke—or stretched—the rules all the time, but few were ever caught. Neither university officials nor Lawrence police officers roamed lovers' lanes after dark, peering into parked cars. A woman who returned from dates rumpled and disheveled might get a talking-to from the housemother of her dormitory or sorority house, or even from her sorority sisters or friends if they were concerned about how her actions affected their own reputations, but she was not likely to get into trouble officially as long as she returned to her residence by the appointed curfew hour.

At KU most of those whose sexual misbehavior fell into the "normal" range (heterosexual and consensual) got into serious trouble with university officials only if they were blatant—or stupid—about it, like the couple who checked into a motel room for the night instead of returning to their dormitory rooms by curfew. (Pregnancy, because it was a visible sign of sexual misconduct, was a blatant violation of the unwritten but powerful* rules.) Even cases of sexual deviance at KU were not discovered through surveillance, but instead were almost always reported by someone involved, whether a woman who was attacked, a third party who witnessed a public sex act, or a man who received an unwelcome sexual advance from another man. For gay men and lesbians, any sexual overture that might not be fully and unambiguously welcome was risky, but heterosexuals had a fair degree of latitude in their sexual activity so long as their actions remained covert and did not force themselves to the notice of either their peer group or the adult world of authority.

The middle-class culture of respectability so widely endorsed in mid-twentieth-century America provided a clear set of rules about sexual behavior. At its heart was a simple stricture: no sex outside of marriage. At the same time, the sexual terrain that young people had to navigate was surprisingly complex. Various forms of authority, from parents to peer culture to popular culture to the legal system, interpreted and enforced that prohibition in different ways. Countless young men and women, along with many of their elders, worked around the strictures against premarital sexual intercourse, living up to the letter of the law much more often than to its intent. Thus young people had to negotiate the difference between the public rules and controls and a set of equally complex behaviors that were more or less acceptable so long as they remained private or covert.

The increasingly sexualized popular culture, widespread recognition that women were not the passionless and chaste creatures that populated Victorian-era advice books, and the rise of institutions, including the practice of dating, that allowed young men and women to spend more private time in each other's company, created new complications for those who attempted to control the sexual behavior of youth. Well before World War II, two systems of sexual control had emerged in America, one structural and one ideological. The ideological system of controls was more pervasive than the structural system and probably more effective. It centered on ideas of difference: men and women were fundamentally different creatures, with different roles and interests in sex. In sex, as in life, proponents of this ideological system insisted, women were the limit setters and men the aggressors.

Women did in fact have a different and more imperative interest in controlling sex than men did, for women could become pregnant. Few doctors would fit an unmarried woman with a diaphragm, though she might get one in the anonymity of a city with a cheap "gold" ring from a drugstore or by pretending to be preparing for an impending honeymoon. Relying on the ubiquitous condom in the wallet was risky and douching even more so. (Some young women in Lawrence used Coca-Cola as a douche, on the theory that carbonation prevented pregnancy: Coke bubbles were supposed to pop the heads of the sperm.) Abortions were illegal, and even though many took place, they were dangerous, expensive, and often frightening and degrading experiences.[1]

Dependable and available birth control would have made a difference, but sexual behavior and sexual mores were not based simply on the threat of illegitimate pregnancy. In his massive study *Sexual Behavior in the Human Female* (1952), Alfred Kinsey reported that only 44 percent of the women in his sample said that they "restricted their pre-marital coitus" because of fear of pregnancy, whereas 80 percent cited "moral reasons." Forty-four percent also noted their "fear of public opinion." As these women understood, a woman who was too "free" with her favors could lose value in the marketplace of courtship, and in this society a woman's future socioeconomic status depended primarily upon her husband. The consequences of a compromised "reputation" could be lifelong. While a girl was expected to "pet to be popular," girls and women who went "too far" risked their futures. Advice books and columns from the 1940s and 1950s linked girls' and women's "value" to their "virtue," arguing in explicitly economic terms that "free" kisses destroyed a woman's worth in the dating system: "The boys find her easy to afford. She doesn't put a high value on herself." The exchange was even clearer in the marriage market, which during the 1950s was in full force for women by the last two years of college. In chilling language, one advisor asked: "Who wants second hand goods?"[2]

It was not only the advisors and experts who equated virtue and value. Fifty percent of the male respondents in Kinsey's study of male sexual behavior wanted to marry a virgin. A young man who went to high school in the early 1960s recalled, "You slept with one kind of woman, and dated the other kind, and the women you slept with, you didn't have much respect for, generally." Even though a fair number of young women had sexual intercourse before marriage, and a greater number engaged in "petting," most of these women at least expected to marry the man, and many did so.[3]

Dating, for middle-class and "respectable" youth, was a process of sexual negotiation. A whole new set of "official" statuses emerged to designate the seriousness of relationships: going steady, lavaliered, pinned, engaged. Each of these was more serious than the last, and each step allowed greater sexual intimacy. Necking with a "steady" was one thing, necking with a casual date something else entirely. Among engaged couples petting was assumed and intercourse at least a possibility. But men and women

77

might go through the first two or three or four steps of that progression several times before actually marrying someone, and even "good girls" had to contend with their own sexual desires and with boys who expected at least some petting as a "return" on the cost of the date.

For these middle-class youth sex involved a series of skirmishes that centered around lines and boundaries: kissing, necking, petting above the waist, petting below the waist, petting through clothes, petting under clothes, mild petting, heavy petting. The progression of intimacy had emerged as a highly ordered system. Each act constituted a stage, ordered in a strict hierarchy (described by boys as "first base," "second base," and so on), with vaginal penetration as the ultimate step. A magazine article of 1959, "Sex and the College Girl," described the college ideal as having "done every possible kind of petting without actually having intercourse."[4] But as young women attempted to preserve technical virginity, many engaged in behavior that, in the sexual hierarchy of the larger culture, should have been more forbidden than vaginal intercourse. In the heterosexual youth culture of the postwar era, the missionary position was the final frontier.

Many young people acted in defiance of the rules, but in so doing most were still acting within the system of controls that distinguished between public and private, overt and covert. For America's large middle class and for all those who aspired to sexual respectability, nonmarital sex was overwhelmingly secret or furtive. Sex was a set of acts with high stakes and possibly serious consequences, acts that emphasized and reinforced the different interests and risks that sex held for men and for women.

This system of ideological controls was buttressed by a structural system, which worked by limiting opportunities for the unmarried to have intercourse. Parents of teenagers set curfews and promoted double dating, hoping that by limiting privacy they would limit sexual exploration. Colleges, acting *in loco parentis,* or, literally, in the place of parents, relied primarily on a system called "parietals," a word that disappeared from common usage in the early 1970s. Parietals were a set of rules governing when and under what circumstances women students could leave their residence halls in the evening and on weekends. These sign-out procedures and curfews applied only to women and, to some extent, were meant to guarantee women's safety by keeping track of their comings and goings. But the larger rationale had to do with sexual conduct. Men were not allowed in women's rooms (nor women in men's), and male visitors were received by women in downstairs lounges or "date rooms" where privacy was never ensured. By setting curfew hours and requiring women to sign out, indicating whom they were with and where they were going, college authorities meant to limit opportunities for privacy and for sex.

Because of a sexual double standard, "parietals" were not imposed on men. Young men traditionally had far fewer restrictions on their freedom, sexual and otherwise, and because colleges and universities were concerned primarily with controlling their own students, they did not find it necessary to restrict men's movements. If women students were supervised and chaperoned and in by 11 P.M., the men would not have partners—at least not partners drawn from the population that mattered. Other young women were not the university's responsibility. Physical safety was also an issue. Parents and university officials assumed that freedom to come and go as he pleased would not put a young man at risk, but feared that in similar circumstances a young woman would be a potential target for abduction or rape. Parents did not want their daughters running around unsupervised at all hours of the night. Most young women who went off to college had curfews at home, too.

Throughout the 1950s the system of structural controls became increasingly complex; by the early 1960s it was so elaborate as to be ludicrous. At the University of Michigan nine of the student handbook's fifteen pages were devoted to the details of women's hours and curfew regulations. Penalties for lateness at most colleges and universities (an institutional version of grounding) normally began after ten "late minutes," but late minutes could be acquired one at a time throughout the semester. At many universities, if a woman lost her "privileges" by returning late from a date, the man who had "taken her out" was expected to send flowers.

The myriad of rules, as anyone who lived through this period well knows, did not prevent sexual relations between students so much as structure the times and places and ways that students could have sexual contact. Students evaded controls and circumvented rules, climbing into dormitory rooms through open windows, signing out to the library and going to motels, spending hours making out in parked cars but signing in to the dormitory on time. Students said extended and passionate good-nights on the porches of sorority houses. They petted in dormitory lounges while struggling to keep three feet on the floor and clothing in some semblance of order. They had intercourse—or oral sex—in cars, keeping an eye out for police patrols. What could be done after eleven could be done before eleven, and sex need not occur behind a closed door and in a bed. But despite all the evasions, very few young people ever openly rejected the system of sexual controls.

The overelaboration of rules, in itself, is evidence that the controls were beleaguered. Rules do not have to be made explicit unless there is some doubt that people will otherwise observe them. The many exceptions and loopholes in the system demonstrate how strained it had become in coping with the changing realities of male-female relationships. Young people had developed systems for skirting the rules and evading penalties almost as overelaborated as the rules themselves. Nonetheless, this structural system of controls reinforced the distance between public and private, between what was "acceptable" behavior and what people actually did, between the rules and the evasions. No matter how often the evasions succeeded, the rules were not irrelevant, because they profoundly affected the ways young people experienced sex.

—

While we tend to think of "The Sixties" as the era of freedom and rebellion, the sexual-social landscape of most colleges in 1965 resembled that of 1955 more than that of 1970. Some students marched for Civil Rights or against the escalating war in Vietnam, but most lived in a world that still had room for serenades and fraternity mixers, in which "pinnings" were announced in the school newspaper and women had to sign out of and into their dormitories at night. This official world of rules and public rituals coexisted with and partially shaped a covert world of sexual experiences that did not fully correspond to the rules, but no matter how many young people pushed against the boundaries in their private acts, very, very few publicly rejected the fundamental premises of middle-class sexual morality.

By the mid-1960s, however, students on college campuses throughout the nation had begun to reject the rules that governed their nonacademic lives. Their challenges to the structural system of sexual control were not made in the name of sexual freedom, but the mass media made the connections between sex and protests against parietals quite explicit. In November 1966 *Time* magazine began its usual column entitled "Students: Moods and Mores" with the line: "At U.S. universities this fall, *in loco parentis* is suffering from *rigor mortis*." Like many of the articles on social and cultural change that appeared in *Time* during this era, this one offered the magazine's 10 million readers equal parts alarmism and reassurance.[5]

"On almost every campus," the article announced, "students are either attacking *in loco parentis*—the notion that a college can govern their drinking, sleeping, and partying—or happily celebrating its death." The *Daily Princetonian*, it reported (in alarmist mode), had proclaimed that "the university has absolutely no moral right to regulate the private morality of its students," but (in reassurance) Notre Dame "still insists that entertaining women in campus bedrooms is simply 'not socially acceptable'" and Smith women are honor-bound to report their "personal misconduct" to the student government.

To illustrate the consequences of the new system, the author turned to the University of Wisconsin, "where junior and senior coeds have no dormitory curfews even on study nights." There, "a favorite male pastime this fall has been to grab a girl and a bottle of Scotch and ride a slow boxcar 100 miles to Prairie du Chien." Sex and liquor and youthful rebellion, yes, but somehow an old-fashioned image. The "girl" was "grabbed," along with the bottle. She wasn't demanding the right to make her own decisions; she was along for the ride. In *Time*'s account, these couples certainly were stretching the limits of acceptable behavior, maybe pushing them too far. The slow boxcar was definitely presented as a challenge to the reigning system of sexual controls. Still, in 1966 *Time* did not really seem to recognize how significant and fundamental such challenges were becoming. Here the "attack" on *in loco parentis* and its consequences appeared as just another sexualized eruption among college youth, akin to the panty raids that had been documented and detailed in "Moods and Mores" columns in the recent past. Few of those involved in the negotiations over *in loco parentis*—students *or* administrators—saw it that way. Nonetheless, understanding that, at a university dependent on taxpayers for funding, public perceptions of the struggle mattered almost as much as the struggle itself, the dean of students at the University of Kansas had the *Time* article photocopied and filed under "Unrest."

The men and women at KU who, in 1965, began to protest the ways the university exercised control over their nonacademic lives acted in a sober and careful fashion. They held meetings and formulated questions about legal precedents and philosophical intent, which they posed in polite fashion to university officials. Their protests were a far cry from both the dangerous privacy of the slow boxcar to Prairie du Chien and the explosive danger of the panty raids that still threatened to erupt every spring, even though all three were, in different ways, struggles against sexual restraints imposed from above. The KU administration, having weathered too many panty raids, including a notorious one in 1956 during which KU students invaded a neighboring university, fighting its male students and ripping the clothes from three women, was probably relieved at the form this new rebellion took. Administrators, however, would learn that this new challenge to their authority was much more serious than the panty raids had ever been.

Panty raids were in the tradition of carnival, not of revolution. In their violence and exuberant sexuality, campus panty raids subverted middle-class social mores and defied the authority of adults. Yet the participants did not seek to alter the hierarchies of power or the existing institutional controls over sexual behavior. Even though the raids were relatively contemporaneous with the Kinsey report on women and the founding of *Playboy,* they were not the opening salvos of the sexual revolution.

Those who disputed the doctrines of *in loco parentis,* however polite, were engaged in revolution. They directly questioned the systems of sexual controls and supervision that governed their lives and the legitimacy of the authority to which they were subject. They sought permanent change. These direct challenges were very different from the eruptions (panty raids, whether drunken rampages or fraternity high jinks) and evasions (furtive fumbling in back seats, climbing through dormitory windows after curfew) that had characterized the struggles of the previous decade. In a fashion that was rarely evasive, students in the 1960s and early 1970s questioned authority and demanded rights. Yet in many ways the protests against sexual controls on campus were often *less* confrontational than the panty raids had been.

Stories of the struggles over the system of sexual controls on college campuses are commonly told as part of a larger narrative in which American youth storm the barricades of adult authority, demanding freedom from a repressive order. That narrative is incomplete at best. The students who opposed *in loco parentis* doctrines found significant support among members of the faculty and administration and significant opposition among their peers. More fundamentally, youth and the administrators who sought to manage them often met on common ground. For while the student activists who demanded that parietals be abolished and extracurricular supervision ended wanted to *diminish* the role of deans and counselors in their lives, they made the arguments in much the same terms that those administrators had used to justify *expanding* their role and power. The new administrators of "student life" in the postwar universities claimed the task of fostering "growth" and "maturity" in students, of preparing them for life in their democratic nation.⁶ These very premises created openings for student claims that were, in most ways, a logical extension of the doctrines of personal maturity and democratic citizenship so popular in universities in the Cold War years, not a rejection of them.

In the debates over sex and its control on college campuses in the 1960s "both" sides often used the language of liberal humanism and of a therapeutic ethos. Sex itself was often decentered, attached to or subordinated to concepts of civility, responsibility, citizenship, and individual growth. As in the case of the deans and the psychiatrists, the administrators had championed doctrines that eventually diminished their own power to control students' sexual behavior. They handed youth the tools with which to dismantle the system. When youth's challenge came in the language and the logic of the administrators themselves, it was exceptionally difficult to withstand.

—

The rapid expansion of American universities after World War II created conditions that made students' attacks on the practice of *in loco parentis* (and thus on the rules meant to control students' sexual behavior) possible. In this case, federal government actions that addressed social issues not even remotely associated with sex would have a crucial impact on Americans' sexual behavior and mores. The G.I. Bill, which subsidized college tuition and living expenses for veterans of World War II, set off a boom in university enrollment. More than one million men (and a few women) took advantage of the program in the 1940s, bringing the nation's total number of college and university students to an unprecedented 2.7 million. KU's enrollment, like that of most state universities, shattered record after record in those years. The semester that began shortly after the atomic bombs fell on Japan found 3,750 enrolled, 470 of whom were veterans. By the next autumn 5,754 veterans were enrolled and total attendance reached 9,130.⁷ Throughout the United States, universities scrambled to provide housing, classrooms, and instructors, and students found themselves sleeping in gymnasiums and Quonset huts and attending standing-room-only classes. Having precipitated this crisis with its largesse, the government became increasingly involved in managing it. Federal grants and loans paid for new college dormitories and classrooms to accommodate the new students.

This postwar boom was not a short-term challenge. Enrollments continued to rise at a shocking pace for almost four decades, again in large part because of federal initiatives that encouraged college education. The Cold War prompted a flow of money into American universities, much of it to fund basic science and defense-industry research, which seemed ever more important to policymakers and taxpayers in the post-atomic world. When the Soviet Union launched Sputnik in 1957, pulling ahead of the United States in the "space race," Americans resolved to strengthen the nation's commitment to education, especially in the fields of science and technology. Education was defined as a key weapon in the Cold War, necessary to prepare children to compete with other nations on the battlefields of technology and economics and to defend democracy and capitalism against the threat of Soviet communism. The National Defense Act of 1958, passed in reaction to the launching of Sputnik, and later the Higher Education Act of 1965 poured money into American universities.

Well-funded universities had no trouble finding students. The front edge of the baby boom did not turn 18 until 1964, but well before that group swelled the student population, large numbers of America's youth were choosing to go to college instead of directly to work. College was the path to a white-collar job, a middle-class life. Rising aspirations combined with the availability of funding to bring ever more students onto the campuses. The G.I. Bill had begun a trend. It was during the 1960s that universities saw the greatest growth in student numbers: from 3.6 million in 1960 to 8 million in 1970.[8]

In the postwar years, the social aspects of college life were more complicated than in earlier times, largely because the expanding student population was increasingly diverse. To today's eyes, the student body at KU would probably appear quite homogeneous—thousands of young white people, with a very small number of African Americans or other "non-whites," as the census category read then. But though the diversity wasn't racial, it was quite real to those who experienced it. Both class and geographic mobility had a striking impact on the student population. A great many of the new students came from families that had never before dreamed of college education. And in 1947—unlike 1927 or 1937—KU students came from every county in Kansas, from every state except New Hampshire (including the Territory of Hawaii, which for some reason appears in the "other countries" category in the registrar's tally), and from 27 foreign nations.[9]

The University of Kansas, like other American universities, was in the process of re-creating itself to meet the challenges of social and economic change. As universities increasingly articulated a research mission, they also claimed a new educational mission. They embraced the task of educating students to function in a new world. The new technocrats and bureaucrats and corporate employees they were producing for the strongest and most affluent country on earth needed to be mobile, less invested in a local or regional culture, less provincial, less *narrowly* religious, less *culturally* ethnic, even less prejudiced against those unlike themselves. They were to be socialized into the norms of the postwar white middle class and its quest for social and economic improvement. As the dean of students at KU wrote in the early 1960s, "discipline" was sometimes necessary "to correct or modify in individuals or groups attitudes brought to the campus from other cultures," because these attitudes conflicted with the middle- (or professional) class values the university attempted to instill in its students.[10]

Such concerns were widely expressed; university and college administrators compiled detailed statistical portraits on the growing diversity of their student populations and wrote dozens of position papers and policy statements on its implications. An article in the *Journal of College Student Personnel,* for example, discussed the widely held opinion that "colleges have a duty to supervise student morals because the college, especially in a society with so much social and geographic mobility, is one of the chief centers for teaching certain nonintellectual skills." The author, who was in fact making a case against *in loco parentis,* argued that these nonintellectual skills were "by and large, the folkways of the intelligentsia, the professions, and the upper classes. The stark fact is that the range of acceptable behaviors in those worlds is broader, or at least more 'liberal,' than in the quarters from which many of the students are recruited and to which college officials are sensitive."[11]

The cultivation of appropriate manners and mores for the professional class was not the sole extracurricular purpose claimed by universities. Cold War rhetoric pervaded discussions of academic mission, well beyond the obvious issues of scientific and technological education. In a world possibly poised on the brink of nuclear annihilation, with large portions of its population susceptible to the appeals of fascism (as demonstrated by the experience of World War II), with democracy and capitalism seemingly under threat from an expansionist Soviet Union, the stakes were high. Many of those who had been adults during the terrible years of global conflict in the 1930s and 1940s believed that much depended on the strength and resolve of a new generation of Americans. How could the nation foster the "democratic personalities" that gave America its strength? How could it create new leaders, and a "mature and responsible" citizenry?

In the 1950s and 1960s universities claimed a key role in this process. In 1962 the president of the national College Personnel Association, William G. Craig, explicitly linked the goals of American universities to President Kennedy's "program for action in the 60's" as described by the Commission on National Goals. In recent decades, Craig argued, "with the nation's new status in world affairs, the preservation of basic freedoms and responsibilities at home become increasingly important. Our way of life depends upon a renewed faith in and extensive use of democratic methods, upon the development of more citizens able to assume . . . extensive responsibilities in matters of social concern."[12]

Presidential addresses are prone to overstatement and exaggerated claims, but this rhetoric was very much in keeping with more modest discussions of the role of the university: students frequently were cast as "future citizens" in whom the values of responsibility, maturity, and citizenship must be fostered. This approach found its way into university lobbying efforts and mission statements as well. The 1958 Annual Report of the University of Kansas embraced a "humanistic philosophy of the dignity of the individual; avoiding coddling but assisting students to a more responsible, self-directing and productive end."[13]

—

With large and still growing student bodies, with immense and expanding expectations of university functions, the old administrative structures rapidly became insufficient for American universities. New administrators—professionals—were required to manage the logistics of student life and to oversee that avowed process of "assisting students to a more responsible, self-directing and productive end." In 1963 Laurence C. Woodruff, dean of students at KU since the late 1940s, emphasized Americans' high expectations of their universities in an article for the Lawrence *Journal World*. The American public, he explained, expected the university to serve "not only in loco parentis for their students but as 'all things to all people.'" Building steam, he catalogued those expectations: to "house the student, feed him, watch his finances, oversee his moral and social development, provide a broad recreational and cultural program, and be concerned with his emotional and physical health problems as well as his intellectual development and maturity." The "inevitable result," he concluded, was the "phenomenon of the personnel dean," a new administrative official who took a holistic approach to student education. At KU, student personnel officers insisted that the "educational experience" of students was not restricted to the classroom but consisted of "all of the impacts of the University upon the student through the twenty-four hour day."[14]

Deans of men and deans of women had been around for decades, but their roles were changing in conjunction with new notions of educational mission. In the 1950s and 1960s many colleges and universities sought deans with professional degrees in student personnel work, and expected them to fit into a larger administrative structure that oversaw all aspects of "student life." One can see the changes at KU clearly: in 1953 an administrative reorganization created a new position, dean of students. This dean supervised the deans of men and women, as well as the housing office and student financial aid. A committee on student personnel practices was established the same year. In this reorganization and its aftermath, these deans and other "student personnel workers" claimed a larger role and higher status within the institution. According to KU administrators of "student life," the chancellor, in order to "fulfill the complete educational responsibility to the student," relied on "professional specialists" who were "fully as competent professionally in their areas as are the faculty members employed to assist the student in achieving academic growth." Insisting that university education was a "twenty-four hour a day growth process," not just "academic stimulation," the new administrators positioned themselves as parallel to—and equal in importance to—the faculty.[15]

And so, justified both by the postwar student population explosion and by Cold War fears, personnel administrators carved out a significant domain within the university. But in claiming their own importance they were also asserting the centrality of students. The university they spoke of was not the faculty-oriented institution with twin missions of teaching and research, but an institution organized around the complete education of the nation's youth—a mission in which personnel administrators claimed equal status with the faculty. And while these administrators attempted to meet a myriad of student needs, the overarching rationale they claimed—fostering personal growth and responsibility—quite logically led them to encourage students to take greater roles in the governance of the university, especially in their lives outside the classroom.

Thus, while KU's women students were subject to carefully detailed and often stringent rules governing their comings and goings during this period, these rules were both made and implemented by the women students themselves.[16] Beginning in 1948 the Associated Women Students (AWS) met biannually to determine the rules under which women students would live; a student disciplinary committee heard cases and punished infractions. This was less of a transfer of power than it might appear. University administrators were fairly confident that the AWS would not do more than tinker with the rules, and in any case, both the dean of women and the university chancellor had to sign off on their legislative efforts. The AWS motto certainly suggests that the group took its limit-setting and disciplinary role quite seriously:

> Associated Women Students
> Of which you are a part
> Works to protect your privileges
> With your best interests at heart.

The AWS regulations were published in a handbook usually entitled "Wise Words for Women." In constant emphasis that the rules were by and of the women, not just for them, the handbook is written in the first person plural—an inclusive, not a royal, we: "None of us look our best in the remnants of last night's lipstick and bobby pins, so we have certain 'visiting hours' for men callers at our houses."

Much of each year's handbook was devoted to etiquette and dress, clearly aimed at instilling uniform "appropriate" behavior in a diverse population. This section of the book dispensed with the inclusive "we" and instead set out rules. "What about that array of forks and spoons?" the 1959 version asked, and answered: "Just remember to start at the outside and work toward the plate." "Introductions aren't hard if you know some easy rules to follow," said an early 1960s edition, and: "A lady does not carry a lighted cigarette while walking." "'Casual' is the word for class dress, but this does not mean slacks or bermudas. Slacks and bermudas are NEVER worn to class, to the library, or to downtown stores," insisted the 1964 handbook, while an earlier version offered a complete table of what "We wear" to classes, teas and receptions, and out-of-town games. And finally: "Love is wonderful! But there is a time and place for everything . . . Don't flaunt your affections in public places. It certainly won't help your reputation, and it is unattractive and embarrassing for others." Concern about respectability underlies most of these prescriptions, demonstrating the continuing importance of reputation in controlling women's behavior.

The student handbook at Haskell Institute also used concepts of respectability and reputation. "The Haskell Code," which the handbook noted was "developed by Haskell students," specified that "the extent to which Haskell students may properly show their affection in public is hand-holding, but petting is not respectable." Respectability, here, has a dual purpose, as the "code" concludes: "The actions and manners of a person away from Haskell has a great bearing on Haskell. We should show that Haskell has taught us good behavior and remember that we represent the Indian race." This officially sanctioned code demonstrated the Haskell administrators' commitment to the forced assimilation of native students into a middle-class culture. In practice, because administrators assumed that teaching respectability—and maturity—to these students was a formidable task, Haskell students were subject to strict regulations and draconian penalties. Male and female students had not only curfews but bed checks, and violations were punished not by loss of social privileges but by additional work duties, usually twenty extra hours for a first offense. A Haskell custodian (not Native American), asked by a reporter in 1965 if these rules were not too strict for college students, replied: "Man, are you nuts? If we let these kids run loose, by Spring this campus would be overrun by little papooses. It's all we can do to keep them out of the bushes now!"[17]

Both Haskell and KU attempted to instill notions of respectability, but KU students were never subject to such demeaning stereotypes or such strict regulation. Curfews for women at KU were generally fairly liberal: by the end of the 1950s weekend curfews were usually midnight or later, with several "late permissions" also available. In contrast, in 1965 Haskell was still conducting nightly bed checks for men and women at 10:00 on week nights and 10:30 on Saturdays and Sundays. As rules relaxed at KU, however, the rules got ever more complicated. Awareness of different levels of maturity in 18-year-old freshmen and 22-year-old seniors led students and administrators to institute different curfews for under- and upper- class-women. Attempts to accommodate study hours and promote regular class attendance dictated one set of hours for week nights, another for Friday and Saturday, and different hours yet for Sunday. There were hours for finals week, hours for orientation week, individual late permissions, group late permissions, men's calling hours, hours for women in men's houses, quiet hours. Penalties were imposed for violating any of these curfews, as well as for not following proper sign-out procedures.

The shifting maze of rules began to appear more and more arbitrary to the students. It didn't seem fair that the senior who was on the verge of flunking out could stay out as late as she wished while the straight-A freshman had to sign in by 11:00. It didn't necessarily make sense that a woman could face disciplinary measures for coming home at 11:05 Thursday evening but could stay out until 1:30 A.M. on Friday. The logic for having such rules was undercut by the very flexibility of the system.

While the parietals system became more responsive to student needs and desires over time, penalties for infractions remained heavy. The students who had responsibility for administering punishments were often harsher in disciplining their peers than administrators might have been. They quite regularly took weekend privileges away from women students who arrived a minute or two past dorm closing time. Once KU's dean of women was called upon by the student officers of a sorority to discipline two members who were deemed incorrigible; upon investigating, the dean discovered that their sin was being between one and three minutes late for curfew three times.[18]

The use of students to adjudicate cases and determine penalties was a common administrative tactic in American universities. Administrators frequently enlisted student leaders or student organizations to help maintain order and control on campus; the rapid growth of fraternities in the early part of the century was partly predicated on such administrative assumptions.[19] But the dean of women at KU did not promote student oversight simply as a front for administrative control, allowing her to distance herself from the dirty work of day-to-day discipline. She and many of her colleagues justified student participation in rule making and discipline as a way to foster qualities of maturity and responsibility in youth. At KU and elsewhere administrators were sometimes at the forefront of change, pushing students to assume more individual "responsibility" for their daily lives.

KU was the second university in the nation to have a senior key program for women students. Beginning in the fall of 1960, a senior woman had no official "closing hours," but could sign out a key to her residence and return when she wished. This plan was passed by the rules convention of the AWS, but the initiative behind it, as well as the clout to get it approved by the chancellor and board of regents, came from the dean of women, Emily Taylor. Throughout her eighteen-year tenure at KU, Dean Taylor advocated equal rights for women and publicly stated that her job was to promote independence and responsibility among her students. Her sales pitch for allowing senior women freedom from curfews was in keeping with these goals: student delegates to the rules convention, she wrote in a letter to the parents of each senior woman, believed that "senior women were sufficiently mature to accept personal responsibility" for their actions. The new key system implied no change in "standards of propriety," she said bluntly, attempting to deflect the most predictable criticism. Instead, it reflected the university's faith in the "maturity and judgment of our senior women," who had given the university "every reason to believe that they will use their freedom of decision judiciously."[20]

Initiatives such as the senior keys, couched in terms of "maturity" and "responsibility," shifted attention from the "moral" justifications for oversight (controlling sexual behavior) and presented greater freedom of action as a positive step toward the larger educational goal of social maturity. Certainly all parents did not accept the shift from propriety to maturity at face value: one mother wrote Dean Taylor that peer pressure would certainly lead daughters to request a "very dubious moral permission," for in the case of senior keys, "such unrestrained liberty can well become license, and will definitely impair the reputation of KU."[21] But over and over again, with successive classes of students and their parents, the issue of dormitory closing hours was presented in terms of students' personal responsibility for their actions and not in terms of behavioral control. It was in the fall of 1965, five years after the inauguration of the key program for senior women, that student protest about parietals—and about the other ways the university exercised control over students' nonacademic lives—became a major campus issue. Perhaps ironically, the first storming of the barricades at the University of Kansas was accompanied by the battle cry "Responsibility!" The language of the student life administrators and educational theorists had been co-opted by the students.

In November 1965 the *University Daily Kansan* ran a front-page article under the headline "Student Freedom Movement Gains Momentum at Meeting." The first sentence, with a breathtaking conflation of the headline's "freedom" with "responsibility," read: "A push for greater student responsibility at KU was sparked last night at an open meeting of Students for a Democratic Society." The accompanying cartoon illustration portrayed a mass of students, women with lacquered I-sleep-in-curlers mid-

1960s hair, men in coats and ties. Their features were uniformly serious, even grim. Across the top flew a banner: "Student Responsibility." A placard to the left proclaimed: "*We* have the right to be citizens too"; a placard to the right demanded: "Abolish closing hours."[22]

The national organization to which the KU chapter of Students for a Democratic Society (SDS) belonged was still small in the spring of 1965, with fewer than 1,500 members in 52 chapters across the nation. Since its founding in 1960, members had participated in various movements for social justice. In 1965 the national SDS organization began to focus its attention on the Vietnam war. That November, the same month in which the KU chapter launched its movement for student freedom/responsibility, national SDS staged a protest against the war that drew 30,000 people. The KU chapter also organized against the war, sponsoring a discussion led by the SDS activist Todd Gitlin, from Harvard University, in October 1965. But it was the twinned issues of parietals and university control of students' nonacademic lives that captured the attention of the KU campus and demanded the greatest share of attention from the fledgling SDS chapter in Lawrence. Because SDS championed an ideal of participatory democracy and rejected hierarchical leadership, there was little direction from the national organization to local chapters. Lawrence's SDS chapter had autonomy to define its own issues.[23]

The SDS chapter at KU pursued its concerns about student rights and university authority under the name "The Student Responsibility Movement," and not everyone involved belonged to SDS. But KU's SDS, in its position papers, its journal, and its public meetings, worked to equate the terms "freedom" and "responsibility," arguing that the university's *in loco parentis* stance hindered "the individual's quest for maturity in a free society." Arguing specifically against parietals for women at the first SDS assembly, a senior from Garden City, Kansas, asked the rhetorical question: "Are [women] going to be adults, or are they going to be cripples, plodding along on the crutches of the University? Are they going to be citizens now, or are they going to be thrust upon a complex world at the sudden moment when the sheepskin is placed in their hands and told: 'Now—you're an adult.'"[24]

The arguments of KU's SDS were couched in existentialist terms— "the role of moral agent"; "genuine independence"; "choice."[25] This language combined well with the administrative language of responsibility and shared with it some basic assumptions. The terms employed by the Student Responsibility Movement also betray the movement's roots in the philosophy department, whose graduate students and junior faculty (and at least one faculty spouse) were, at least initially, the most visible members of the movement. They pushed the debate over parietals (one that most students understood as a debate about the sexual freedom and conduct of women students) toward a discussion of the role of the individual in the larger world. In the second issue of the *Kansas University Students for a Democratic Society Journal,* the graduate student John Garlinghouse virtually ignored the immediate issue of women's hours. Noting, somewhat disingenuously, that he did not intend to address the fact that "a high school dropout selling cabbage in a supermarket" had rights and freedoms denied university students, he shifted ground to argue that the problem was not with the specific rules but with the "whole atmosphere they create":

> Ours is a complex world, fraught with dangers and inconsistencies. It has its Vietnam . . . its Budapest, its Algeria . . . To cope in any way with these problems, the universities must produce independent, responsible human beings. If an individual entering a university is socially a fetus, another four years in an incubator will not help him. He will be no more than a senseless automaton . . . [The university] only defeats itself when it attempts to incubate its students. Both our society and we, ourselves, sell ourselves cheaply when we allow it to do so. If we do not act soon, and constructively, to remedy this situation, we can pass into history confident that our children and our children's children will be set upon by our very same problem. In some form. At some time. With progressively more horrible implications.[26]

In passages such as this one the issue of gender tended to disappear. The tendency is worth noting, for, after all, the local issue that led to such global speculation was parietals—a set of rules that applied to women students only, not to their male counterparts. However, the women who spoke or wrote for the record kept gender front and center, even to the point of shifting focus from the individual to the collective. One female undergraduate told a *Kansan* reporter that she had a dream of hundreds of KU women gathering at the hour of curfew, "in plain sight for the University to see, but refusing to be herded [inside] like cattle." The most visible woman in this initial debate, the one who wrote key articles for the *Journal* and gave the major speech at the SDS meeting, centered her arguments in existential philosophy and psychology. Identified only as "Mrs. Donald Emmons," she was the wife of a young assistant professor in the philosophy department. "At the very core of becoming a human being is assuming the role of moral agent," she wrote. "Women," however, "are not encouraged to think of themselves as persons with lives to choose. They are regulated in the most minute aspects of everyday existence—a method well used in Nazi concentration camps to disintegrate the personality." Conceding that closing hours for women were "generous" ("I should think that most could not keep them and stay in school"), she nonetheless concluded: "The thing that is wrong with them is that they are imposed." The university, she maintained, prepared women better for lives as "cocker spaniels" than for "self-actualizing" adulthood.[27]

As gender was only inconsistently visible in these movement writings, it is not surprising that the issue of sex—the control of which most students, parents, and administrators had traditionally assumed to be the point of women's curfews—was almost invisible. In discussions of "moral choice" we sometimes catch a glimpse of it, but the object of such moral choice might just as well be cheating on exams for all the articles specify. The writers refused to treat sexual mores as a separate and more important category of moral choice, instead implicitly arguing that individuals face a whole array of moral choices in their everyday lives, and that sexual behavior was not the most significant of those.

Nonetheless, much of the opposition to their demands centered on the issue of sex, so proponents of "responsibility" occasionally attempted to counter such charges. In "A White Paper on Student Rights," circulated by the new "University Party" before the spring student elections, the candidates tried to make the issue appear ridiculous: "'Bacchanalia!' comes the cry to the background chorus of 'How Ya' Gonna Keep 'Em Down on the Farm After They've Seen KU?' The obvious assumption is that, freed of restrictions other than those of law, the average student will become some kind of satyr." Instead, the candidates asserted, more freedom would lead to "*less* bacchanalia." Such comments were rare, however, for both the administration and the student responsibility movement avoided discussions of sexual morality. The dean of women stated categorically that parietals were "not related to moral issues," a statement the *Kansan* rendered as "Rules Not Meant to Curb Morals." However, while the shared language of individual maturity and responsibility shaped much of the debate among one set of students and administrators, the issue of sex control continued to structure the unfolding events.[28]

—

The Student Responsibility Movement received a great deal of attention on KU's campus. While the SDS chapter could claim only a few dozen members in 1965–66, its focus on university authority over students' nonacademic lives engaged a much larger number of students and prompted many articles in the *University Daily Kansan*. And as the movement appealed to administrators on their own terms, stressing the development of responsibility and maturity, they could not ignore or easily refute its logic. As a sign of how seriously the administration took the protests, when a small group of students drafted a lengthy list of questions about university policy, KU's provost, James Surface, who received the list—without warning—on a Friday, worked through the weekend to provide detailed answers by the beginning of the following week.[29] This exchange, which was chronicled in great detail by the *Kansan*, focused on the legitimacy of university authority over students. The questions suggest a more legalistic turn of mind than the earlier philosophically based demands: "What is the University's definition of '*in loco parentis*'?" "What is the legal justification for discrimination against women?" "What are the 'accepted standards of social conduct' to which students are expected to adhere," and are they "codified in state law"?

Surface answered the questions carefully, including those he characterized as "'when did you stop beating your wife' type of questions." *In loco parentis*, he said, was not a term employed by the university itself, but had its Kansas origins in a State Supreme Court case mounted by local merchants against the student union. One of his main points was that the university did not only regulate students' lives but also served as a buffer for them against the outside world. He repeatedly cited the number of student thefts from the university bookstore that were handled without police interference, seeming not to realize that students did not see illegal actions such as theft as parallel to the right to decide what time to return to their dormitories.

The provost answered questions about women's hours straightforwardly. Women had different rules than men because "they need more protection and security. It would be dangerous to have women's housing unlocked. Men can take care of themselves." The "legal justification" for such "discrimination," he wrote without changing the terms used in the question, was "the same as for all the rules. It lies with the chancellor and the board of regents." Knottier questions about the "accepted standards of social conduct" received vague answers. He quoted the student handbook: "The University assumes that its students are basically honest and adequately familiar with the commonly accepted code of right and wrong. It seems unnecessary, therefore, to enumerate the countless 'thou shalts' and 'thou shalt nots' upon which our society is founded." In terms of sexual behavior, "The University adheres to the laws of the land, which, in general, prohibit co-habitation outside of wedlock and deviate behavior."

After meeting with Surface, the students told the *Kansan* reporter they were "deeply impressed" with his "candidness and apparent sincerity," but found the university policies he described disturbingly "arbitrary." They followed up with a second set of questions pointing out legal and logical inconsistencies: "Isn't discrimination against women contrary to the Civil Rights Act of 1964?" "If the law of the land relating to sexual behavior is university policy, why does the university expel pregnant coeds?" And how did the student handbook's statement that "college students are assumed to have maturity of judgment necessary for adult responsibility" square with detailed regulation of students' nonacademic behavior? The authors of these questions hammered at the legal status of the university's disciplinary authority, insisting that students did not give up their rights to due process merely by matriculating at a university.

Even before this exchange, the chancellor's office and the board of regents had sought clarification of their own positions. Beginning soon after the Student Responsibility Movement's opening salvos, they checked legal precedents and requested the Council on Student Affairs to draft a report that would both detail the sorts of authority exercised by the university over its students and explain from whence that authority derived. As similar protests had erupted throughout the United States, there had been much discussion among university presidents and their boards of regents or trustees about the legal position of universities. Such discussion was not just about whether they had the legal right to act *in loco parentis,* but about what sorts of liabilities that role implied. KU officials read, annotated, and filed articles speculating on the legal status of students and the dangerous implications of *in loco parentis.*[30] But in their commission to the Council on Student Affairs they sought an immediate guide to local action.

Both documents prepared in 1965 by the Council on Student Affairs, the legal (based on a 1956 statement from the Kansas attorney general) and the administrative, supported the university's right to impose standards of conduct on its members. However, in demonstrating that right, they traced power back through the chancellor to the board of regents to the "People" or "taxpayers" of the State of Kansas. Such advice had limited utility for administrators, who more and more self-consciously based their claims to authority upon their professional expertise and on the national mission of "the university." Few administrators in postwar America believed that the local knowledge of state taxpayers should dictate university policy so directly. And in the case of Kansas, most students, faculty, and administrators at the state university were less socially conservative than the majority of the "People" who lived in the state. Thus questions of legitimacy generated by the Student Responsibility Movement were not easily resolved.[31]

—

It was in this climate of uncertainty—and possibility—that the Associated Women Students met in 1966 to draft the rules under which women students at KU would live for the following two years. The AWS was largely responsible for the proliferation of rules about women's hours that was typical of the latter stages of parietal systems. At each biannual convention it had voted more freedoms for women students, but had anchored them in an ever more complicated system of rules, penalties, and exceptions. The 1966 convention, following closely upon the highly visible actions of the Student Responsibility Movement, would break with that tradition. In the context of the raging debate over university control of students' lives, some delegates asserted that the AWS charter allowed them to *make* the rules, not just to fine-tune them.

What is most striking about the Associated Women Students meeting that convened on March 12, 1966, is how far from agreement these young women were. They did not simply disagree on what rules were appropriate or how to implement them; rather, different groups approached the issue from what seem today to have been radically different understandings. The "responsibility" faction was well represented, mainly by delegates from "scholarship halls," where students from Kansas attending KU on academic scholarships lived, and by married women, who had only limited representation in the rules convention. Those who were involved in the Student Responsibility Movement had lobbied hard in advance of the meeting, writing signed editorials in the *Kansan* and circulating a copy of the New Left activist Tom Hayden's "Student Social Action" (1962), to which they added a handwritten title, "In loco parentis," and a request: "Please pass this on so that more KU women will *stop* and *think* about *their AWS* constitution & the regulations under which we live." (A copy was passed on to the chancellor's "Student Protest" files.)[32]

A second group, drawn primarily from the large and powerful network of sororities on campus, maintained that the purpose of women's hours was to control sexual behavior. While the rhetoric and actions of both administrators and student protesters had subordinated the issue of sexual mores to one of responsibility in this debate, these delegates insisted that the key issue was the sexual morality, or "standards," of women students. They strongly supported a system of administrative supervision to help women "set their standards." A third group (sometimes overlapping with the "morality" delegates) skirted the "standards" argument but held to a gender-specific line: hours were necessary for the safety of women students; because women were different from men they required different regulations.

The convention quickly came to a boil around one question: Should closing hours be abolished for all women students? The language of the delegates' arguments tells us at least as much as does the outcome of the convention.

The "responsibility" argument presented no surprises to anyone who had been reading the *Kansan* in the preceding weeks and months. It was less elegantly argued, certainly ("We are responsible to our actions for ourselves," stated one delegate), and lacked philosophical and legal foundations. Sometimes it sounded like a simple claim: we're old enough/mature enough to take care of ourselves. Quite often, these delegates seemed to be arguing that they had successfully internalized the "generally accepted standards of propriety" and thus didn't really need external compulsion.[33] They didn't frame their arguments around the importance of sexual freedom for women—a wise strategic decision but also one in keeping with their larger concerns. These delegates placed themselves squarely in the context of a continuing public debate about maturity, democratic citizenship, and women's roles in American society. Their comments at the convention were amplified through association with the Student Responsibility Movement of the previous fall.

The "responsibility" delegates' various motions to abolish closing hours were countered by delegates working with highly gendered notions of sexuality. It was the antiprogressive, sorority-dominated faction that raised the issues most explicitly. They insisted that the rules and regulations *were* about morality, real or perceived. Arguing that KU must not adopt "open closing" for all undergraduate women, the Gamma Phi Beta delegate explained: "When you come to the university, your freshman and sophomore years, you are away from your folks and this is when you truly determine your standards. I truly believe that we need to impose some rules on freshmen and sophomore women. It is too easy to disregard whether things are right or wrong." A Chi Omega delegate urged the convention to think of the "philosophy involved": hours were necessary so that women could "set their standards."[34] In direct opposition to the "responsibility" argument, these women portrayed rules as the *means* to moral grounding and responsible conduct.

Delegates from scholarship halls rejected this line of reasoning, venturing to "suggest the idea that closing hours do not determine the moral standards on campus." But the "morality" delegates were working with another concern that was still a reasonable one in 1966: reputation. "Public Image," the Gamma Phi Beta delegate sputtered incoherently: "Run around free or do what ever we would like to." The Pi Beta Phi delegate, in more measured tones, said: "To go to this extreme now is hurting not only ourselves but it is hurting the other women we go to school with." In much of American society a woman's "reputation" still determined, in significant ways, the sort of life she could expect to lead, for it affected her marriage prospects. While this seems the most antediluvian of the arguments here, it is worth noting that the most progressive "responsibility" delegate capped her argument by claiming that "many women are contemplating marriage ... if you are contemplating marriage you are capable of deciding your own hours."[35]

Most of the "morality" delegates were willing, in a form of compromise, to go along with the arguments of the third group, which took the position that the very term "closing hours" should be changed to "security hours" to "get rid of a lot of connotations" and emphasize the protective aspect of the regulations. But the language in which these delegates made their point is convoluted and betrays tensions within their seemingly coherent reasoning. The Pi Beta Phi delegate argued, in a paragraph that fairly deconstructs itself:

> We have to realize what we are talking about. If we continue to pass these proposals, we will find ourselves with NO closing hours. We are here to learn, and the reason women have closing hours is because

there is a difference between men and women. Women must be protected. A woman cannot be out on the streets at night . . . I feel women have no place being out on the streets at night. Two women were attacked by men. Therefore, I think this brings us to the point that if we do vote on no closing . . . the sophomores have no place [being included with upperclasswomen who have no curfew]."

100

Security was a compelling issue for many delegates, but some recognized that the security rationale worked against the system of graduated privileges, in which seniors and sophomores were not subject to the same rules. "Seniors have been out after the hours of closing [for years]," noted a scholarship hall delegate, whose criticism emerged in slightly confused form: "We cannot say that two years of difference will not make them any less desirable."[36]

The debate was heated, and the delegates could not reach a satisfactory solution in the allotted time, so the convention reconvened the following week. The president of the AWS made an impassioned, though obscure, appeal: "You are vested with the confidence of your group . . . in setting standards conducive to learning . . . you are vested with the confidence of the people of Kansas to make all of this possible. Let us not make a mockery of this convention . . . let us not surrender in slavery . . . let us not seek power and destroy our freedom . . . let us build together, responsible and free, a community." The delegates debated the difference between "honorable" and "acceptable" behavior, agonized over whether it was their place to "legislate morality," and finally took what they saw as decisive action: they voted to eliminate mandatory curfews for seniors, juniors, and second-semester sophomores.[37]

While not complete, this was the most significant step in the overthrow of the parietals system, which would end entirely in three more years. Coverage in the *Kansan,* while "objective," supported the liberalization of rules and the actions of the convention, though someone undercut the textual message by putting a photo of a cat, with the caption "CATASTROPHIC—a sleepy feline observed most of the demands for liberal women's rules at the AWS convention Saturday," right in the middle of the front-page article.

The *Kansan*'s coverage highlights the level of disagreement among students. Under the headline "Student Opinion Varies," the reporter quotes Sara Paretsky, the future author of detective novels and a scholarship hall delegate to the convention, who said flatly that "there is a real feeling among the majority of women that they need more freedom," and Linda Adamson, a sophomore, who argued, "Students are here to get an education, and hours can only help you. Most girls don't know how to regulate their lives. That's why there are so many illegitimate births."[38] No matter how much some spoke of "responsibility," the subtext remained sex.

Men's reactions to the proposals were also mixed, though the *Kansan* characterized them as a "reserved yes." With no sense of irony, Jon Putnam, a junior (who, as a man, was not subject to any closing hours), told a *Kansan* reporter that he opposed any plan ending curfews for junior women: "The senior key is an earned privilege. Their work is fairly behind them. Juniors and second semester sophomores are still working for a degree. This is what they are here for. A degree is of tantamount importance to all other activities on campus, including dating."[39] Perhaps he feared that without external constraints women's libidos would lead them astray, or perhaps he assumed that most women's desire for an "MRS. degree" was stronger than their desire for a B.A. In any case, he did not seem to think it strange that male students did not have to "earn" the privilege that women were seeking.

The criticisms and the celebrations of the AWS action were premature, for the rules passed by the convention did not automatically take effect. They were, in fact, merely recommendations to the small AWS Senate, which then made recommendations to the administration. Having taken bold action, the convention delegates found themselves in limbo for two months, waiting to see what would happen. There was much behind-the-scenes maneuvering, as Kansas newspapers adopted outraged tones to report what was, in fact, not a dramatic change for a university that already had senior keys.

As the administration Council on Student Affairs considered the AWS rules, the university mental health personnel decided to weigh in, on the grounds of their "responsibility . . . to promote mental health generally." Their statement is so carefully balanced that at first it is hard to tell what position they are taking: "The building of inner controls regarding behavior is a desirable goal at the individual as well as the community level," their statement asserts. "It is evident that mixed feelings regarding rules and authority are experienced by both the students who live by these rules and those whose function it is to administer them." But by the end of the letter the mental health personnel have made a commitment: "Having a satisfying sense of personal freedom and the concomitant responsibility are both essential factors in the maintenance of good mental health. It appears to us in the Mental Health Clinic that the recently proposed changes in living rules for women students, which are being considered by the Council on Student Affairs, are a step in the direction of helping students obtain these goals."[40]

In the end, the AWS convention's new rules were altered. In secret meetings, the AWS Senate reinstituted hours for sophomore women. This action provoked much anger and a sense of betrayal, but it was legal according to the written regulations.[41] Many students were doubly frustrated because it was not clear who was really responsible for the changes. Was it fellow students? Or was it the "administration"?

A note from the chancellor to the president of the AWS Senate suggests that the changes were dictated by the administration. Chancellor Wescoe wrote, in apology, that although he would have preferred to delay the release of the revised regulations to the newspapers "until the Senate had been given the opportunity to see them first," he had decided that he should announce them before the *Kansan* stopped publishing for the semester. Otherwise, he explained, it might have looked as if he had timed the release to avoid student comments.[42]

But another partial and indirect answer appears in the University Party's platform for student elections that same spring term. Calling upon "our University community" to "establish the University of Kansas as a national leader in the recognition of students as free, mature individuals who yearn to be responsible for their own acts, and who seek the experience of full citizenship as the best education of all," the platform praised the AWS convention (not the Senate) as "courageous" and further critiqued the practice of *in loco parentis* at KU. But in a brief preface signed by the candidates, this oppositional document (which found its way into the chancellor's "Student Protest" files), offered an interesting caveat to their strongly worded call for change. While some important administrators "fully sympathize" with students' demands for freedom from supervision, the writers noted, these administrators are "constrained," and thus remain "publicly unresponsive."[43]

How were they constrained? The chancellor's "Correspondence" file for that year is crammed with letters from parents and other citizens of Kansas. Many are accompanied by clippings of highly negative articles from local newspapers about the doings at KU. Virtually all treat women's hours as a means for controlling sexual behavior, and *every* letter opposes change.[44]

"We have always been so proud of the good control and regulations pertaining to women students at KU," wrote an alumni couple. "If the AWS proposal is approved the KU students could retrogress to the low level of some of the eastern schools. We spent some time in the Boston area and were appalled at the decaying morals of the students." "An angry mother" wrote: "Thought the AWS might be interested in planning a nursery for their next project. Just what does the Dean of Women plan for students to do in Lawrence after one o'clock in the morning? . . . If the children are going to manage the school, I wonder if there is any need for the administrative officers." One writer, looking back to the events of the fall, labeled the SDS "communist" and quoted J. Edgar Hoover. More temperate correspondents adopted the language of freedom and responsibility, arguing that freedom must be grounded in law, or in this case, rules. Several threatened to withdraw their daughters; several threatened to stop giving money. "Why, it's like letting the tail wag the dog!" complained a woman from Wichita who had gone to high school with the chancellor. "Why not let the parents and/or taxpayers who foot the bill have a voice in this. . . ?"[45]

A state university ignores such sentiments at its own peril. "Youth" and "Authority" were not the only actors in struggles over the control of sex at the University of Kansas. Another major player—as the legal and administrative memos had emphasized—was "the People," or "the taxpayers," the citizens of Kansas who footed the bills and voted for the state legislators who determined KU's budget.

In this case, university administrators did not oppose student activists; they offered them limited support while managing the public image of the state university. This controversy really marked the end of the university's attempt to provide surrogate parenting through its rules and regulations. The entire parietal system disappeared over the next three years, without fanfare or public controversy but with the full support of the administration. Chancellor Wescoe wrote to a Leawood, Kansas, woman who had protested the change in hours: "I am one who believes, as the father of a mature young woman who is a student in the University, that when a young woman reaches the age of 20 or 21, she is entitled to some respect and, as well, to some freedom." And the dean of women, whose actions in establishing a senior key system in 1960 lend credence to her later statements, told a reporter in 1973:

Relaxing parental rules removed a windmill to fight. We could pay attention to the larger issue—sex discrimination. I believe in equality, and our sole function is to produce as many autonomous adults as we can—not to keep them adolescents. If you can tell a boy you don't like that you have to be home on time, you don't have to make the decision. If you don't have to be in on time, you have to make the decision. A dean of women typically tries to keep her students in their place. I try to tell them their place is wherever they choose.[46]

But—and it is a large but—these administrators were not endorsing sexual freedom. Their support was predicated on student claims to responsibility, which they understood as extensions of the progressive doctrines embraced by student personnel workers in the postwar university. On these grounds, strengthened by concerns about the university's legal position concerning *in loco parentis,* university administrations removed themselves from the business of monitoring women students' hours. Sex was always the subtext in debates over restrictive curfews, and everybody knew it. But sex was not the issue on which this policy was decided. "Responsibility" was, and for some, women's equality with men. By the time a significant number of students started to publicly demand sexual freedom, whether in word or in deed, the administration had already bowed out. *In loco parentis* was dead. There were no real barricades to storm. "Responsibility" had paved the way for "Freedom." Once again, widely accepted beliefs in American society—in this case, the need to produce mature youth, capable of sustaining democracy in the Cold War world—inadvertently paved the way for a sexual revolution.

4

Prescribing the Pill

A girl's face filled the huge poster. She looked hip but not too far out as she stared, wide-eyed, sticking her tongue out at the camera. In the center of her tongue was a tiny white pill. Another poster was less subtle. In psychedelic pink, green, and orange, it showed the Pill's daisywheel case surrounded by copulating couples in different sexual positions.[1] These posters hung in Lawrence, Kansas, and in dorm rooms and apartments throughout the country. By the late 1960s, posters like these offered America's most unconventional youth a celebratory—and incendiary—shorthand for sexual freedom.

American women went "on the Pill" in the 1960s. The oral contraceptive tablets that most Americans called simply "the Pill," were approved for contraceptive use by the FDA in 1960. By early 1969 eight and a half million women were using the Pill; their numbers had grown by about one million each year from 1961.[2] Every day for three weeks out of their monthly menstrual cycle, millions of women popped the tiny tablet through the foil package that fit into the daisywheel container that somewhat resembled a compact—if one didn't know better. The high hormonal doses of the early oral contraceptives had pronounced side effects, which mimicked pregnancy: breast tenderness, weight gain, some nausea. But the Pill was more than 99 percent effective, in no way dependent on the direct cooperation of the woman's partner, and completely separate from the act of sexual intercourse. A great many women were willing to accept some side effects in exchange for freedom from fear of pregnancy. By giving women greater

105

control over their sexual and reproductive lives, this new contraceptive technology helped change the meaning and experience of sex in America.

The great majority of the women who went on the Pill in its early years, however, were not the young single women who lived "the revolution." Most were married. And while birth control within marriage was a highly charged issue for Roman Catholics (complicated by the fact that the Pill became the single most widely used contraceptive method among married Catholic women, surpassing even the Church-approved rhythm method), most other Americans did not see the use of the Pill within marriage as especially controversial.[3] Nonetheless, by the mid-1960s the Pill symbolized the revolution in sex, and little of what appeared in America's mass media was as celebratory as the posters featuring the Pill. Theologians, social scientists, pundits, and advice columnists wrote about "The Pill and Morality"; a flood of articles, studies, and forums addressed the question "Does the Pill Promote Promiscuity?" In America talk of the sexual revolution inevitably turned to talk of the Pill, and discussions of the Pill often centered on its possible effects on America's sexual mores.

Largely because of its symbolic role, the Pill frequently appears in discussions (both then and now) as a sort of *deus ex machina,* bringing about the sexual revolution. In 1968 a no less distinguished figure than Pearl S. Buck, writing for the mass market in *Reader's Digest,* linked a crisis in sexual morality to the Pill: "It is a small object—yet its potential effect upon our society may be even more devastating than the nuclear bomb."[4] This technological determinism, captured so clearly in Buck's analogy to the bomb, is not unusual in Americans' attempts to explain social change, but it overlooks a key fact. The Pill was not simply a new technology available in the free marketplace of postwar America. It had to be prescribed by a physician.

Doctors, then as now, controlled access to oral contraceptives. And at that time only a small minority of physicians would prescribe birth control pills to women who were not married. Most believed, along with a large majority of the American public, that it was wrong for unmarried women to have sex. Thus, before the Pill could play *any* significant role in the sexual behavior of America's unmarried youth, something had to change. Unmarried women—in large numbers—had to have access to oral contraceptives. How did single women get the Pill?

Once again, revolutionary change in Americans' sexual mores and behavior was made possible inadvertently, in this case by efforts to deal with social and political problems that had little directly to do with American youth's claims to sexual freedom. The Pill did not become available to single women because they raised their voices and demanded the right to sexual freedom and control of their own bodies. Instead, it became available to them as a byproduct of two political movements that were at the heart of Sixties liberalism and its attempts to ameliorate the difficult social problems that plagued America and the world.

One of these movements was driven by concern about population growth, both international and domestic, which reached near-panic proportions in the United States during the 1960s and early 1970s. The other, Lyndon Johnson's Great Society, used federal funds and programs to attack the causes and consequences of poverty and racism in the United States. Neither set of efforts, by any stretch of the imagination, was intended to foster a sexual revolution. However, these two movements helped make the Pill available to single women, in large part by providing rationales for prescribing contraceptives that did not employ a language of morality. Only after this change, and with the development of a strong and increasingly radical women's movement, did large and visible numbers of young, unmarried women begin to publicly claim access to the Pill. These women rejected both the policy-driven concerns about population growth and social welfare and the parallel "moral" framework that centered around the question of whether the Pill promoted promiscuity, insisting, instead, that the key issue was a woman's right to control her own body.

—

Senate Chamber, Topeka, Kansas, March 11, 1963. At 1:30 P.M. the Kansas State Senate was called to order, and Chaplain Walls began the invocation: "As usual, Eternal Father, we pause during this moment to acknowledge Thee, and then, as usual, we forget Thee when we return to our work." It's not clear whether the chaplain was generally so cynical or whether he was making a particular point, for that day the Senate was to vote on legislation allowing public agencies to distribute information about contraceptives to Kansas citizens. Senate Bill 375 stemmed largely from the intense lobbying efforts of Patricia Schloesser, M.D., head of the state division of maternal and child services, who was motivated by a frightening vision of unrestrained world population growth. She had been quite effective in her lobbying, for the Senate voted unanimously in favor of the measure. The

House vote the following April, however, was close enough to require a roll call. The representatives from Douglas County, in which Lawrence was located—Odd Williams (businessman) and John Vogel (farmer, stockman), both Republicans, both Lawrence residents—supported the bill.[5]

Those who were most immediately affected by this legislation, the heads of local public health departments, understood its limitations. While it was now legal for public institutions to offer birth control and contraceptive information to citizens of Kansas, the legislature had offered no mandate for them to do so. More important, the legislature had offered no funding. Without money for birth control services, the change in law had little practical impact. Medical personnel in the employ of the state could now discuss contraceptive options with their clients or patients without running afoul of the law, but that was far from the full-scale birth control clinics some public health workers favored.

Among the most vocal and vehement advocates of birth control in Kansas was the director of Lawrence's public health department, Dr. Dale Clinton. Clinton, encouraged by the new legislation, did everything in his power to take advantage of the freedom it offered. He fully intended to set up a birth control clinic. But funding was a major obstacle. Clinton investigated public-private partnerships, even flirted with the idea of private funding for a state-run clinic, but reluctantly concluded that both those solutions violated the health department's mandate and Kansas law. Despite Dr. Clinton's best efforts, public birth control services remained on hold for two more years, awaiting state or federal funding.[6]

Dr. Clinton's sense of urgency was not due to the demands of his clientele, the Douglas County taxpayers. Like Dr. Schloesser, Clinton believed that the world population explosion was a greater threat to public health than any contagious disease or environmental hazard. Throughout his thirteen years (1960—1973) as chief public health officer for Douglas County, he vigorously promoted contraceptive use and measured his department's success largely in the number of birth control pills it prescribed or dispensed.

Dr. Clinton's commitment was extreme, but his understandings were fully in keeping with mainstream thought in public health. In 1959 the professional organization for public health workers, the 20,000-member American Public Health Association (APHA), had adopted a resolution that called for attention, at "all levels of government," to "the impact of population change on health." And in 1963 the APHA called population growth "one of the world's most important health problems" and began lobbying government officials for action.[7]

On January 3, 1965 (one day after Dr. Clinton published a letter in the Lawrence *Journal World* warning that "the ever accelerating wild rate of population growth" was the world's "most serious health problem"), President Johnson pledged in his State of the Union address "to seek new ways to use our knowledge to help deal with the explosion in world population and the growing scarcity of world resources."[8] In April, Senator Gruening of Alaska introduced a bill that led to the funding of birth control programs through the Department of Health, Education, and Welfare. Earlier, the Office of Economic Opportunity (OEO) had funneled some money to family planning programs under the "local option" policy that allowed community groups to initiate welfare programs. (Initially the OEO did not allow its funds to be used for contraceptives for unmarried women; that restriction was lifted in 1966.)[9] The federal government's decisions to spend taxpayers' money on public family planning programs were not based on concern about women's reproductive health or a wish to promote sexual freedom. Rather, the funding was a result of the confluence of alarm about the "population problem" and increased federal involvement in programs intended to alleviate the effects of poverty in the United States.[10] Limiting the number of children born to poor women (or allowing poor women to avoid unplanned and unwanted pregnancies) was a priority for these programs.

The political implications of linking Johnson's Great Society (with its strong focus on poverty) and population control were as apparent at the time as they are today. In the early twentieth century many advocates of birth control had worked closely with the eugenics movement, which sought to limit childbearing among people the eugenicists deemed genetically and racially inferior and so preserve the dominance of white, Anglo-Saxon Americans. Those uncomfortably close links between the birth control movement and the eugenics movement were not so far in the past. In the mid-1960s a few highly visible and radical black activists began to claim that the Pill was an instrument of genocide targeted at blacks by a racist government. (Significantly, these accusations came from men, not women.)[11]

The politics of the Johnson administration's War on Poverty and welfare programs were complicated, at best, and those who attempted to implement policies struggled with opposition from widely divergent sources. In the case of birth control, the administration faced both the suspicions of targeted groups such as poor African Americans *and* voters' reservations about the costs of burgeoning social welfare programs. Thus policy-oriented organizations took on the issue of contraception and poverty directly, with both the American Public Welfare Association and the American Medical Association supporting, in 1964, the availability of contraceptives to, respectively, the "economically deprived" and "private or tax supported health service patients." The American Association of Public Health consistently focused on the dangers of world population growth, an argument that was more compelling to Americans who rejected the idea of "benefits" for the poor and underprivileged. But throughout the 1960s, authors also attempted to demonstrate that contraception for America's poor was fully in keeping with "broadly democratic principles of equal opportunity for all." Birth control, one prominent activist wrote in an attempt to shift the grounds for suspicion, should not be the "special privilege" of the "well-to-do."[12]

Many Americans, however, drew connections between birth control and antipoverty programs that were exactly what government agencies had tried to avoid. For example, when *Good Housekeeping* sampled its 20,000-member "consumer panel" in 1967 on the question "Should Birth Control Be Available to Unmarried Women," its editors discovered that the negative responses (significantly, a strong majority) were based on "moral" arguments, while the affirmative responses were "practical." An Arizona woman wrote: "It would eliminate many dollars in child-welfare payments." A more vehement response came from a woman in the Midwest, who supported birth control for unmarried women because "I deeply resent having to deprive my family of privileges I cannot afford because I have to pay support for others not of my choosing." Governmental policy also addressed this issue directly, if not always successfully. When state and then federal monies were allocated to family planning in Kansas in the spring of 1965, the funding was accompanied by a directive from the Kansas Department of Social Welfare. It advised public family planning clinics to exhibit "due regard for the individual rights and beliefs of the recipients" and warned against giving clients the impression that public assistance checks were contingent upon accepting birth control.[13]

Once the Kansas legislature made funding available, Dr. Clinton moved quickly and Lawrence's health department began to offer contraceptive services—something fewer than 20 percent of local health departments in the United States did at that time. Clinton, however, was decidedly uninterested in the professional debate about birth control for the indigent and the related directives. Though the framework provided by state (and eventually federal) guidelines indicated an implicit, but clear, association of these programs with services for the poor, Clinton made it equally clear that his birth control clinic was not "indigent-oriented," nor did he consider it the appropriate site for clinical medicine. He did not intend to focus on the poor, and he did not mean to provide women (of any income level) with health care. Instead, he intended to combat the scourge of unrestrained population growth by offering contraceptives to any and all.[14]

This definition of mission would raise questions of constituency and clientele. Kansas's laws restricting birth control, in effect from 1870 through 1963, had applied only to public agencies. Even before 1963 a married woman in Lawrence had ready access to birth control if she could afford a private doctor. When the Pill became available for contraceptive purposes in 1960, Lawrence doctors had begun prescribing it to married women. Its use increased quickly. In August 1962, in order to append local information to some Associated Press articles on the possible dangers of the Pill, the Lawrence *Journal World* sought estimates of how many Lawrence women used oral contraceptives. Dr. Clinton ventured 300, but the reporter got estimates from other doctors and pharmacists that ranged up to 3,000. Clinton responded to the higher estimate as a challenge to his authority, calling it "ridiculously high," but then backpedaled in support of what he had recently called a "wonder drug." "A drug like this," he said, "could increase tenfold in two weeks. It's something people have been waiting for for the past 15 years."[15]

As private doctors in Lawrence were already meeting the needs of their patients, the health department, naturally, would draw a from a different constituency. Married women who could afford private doctors were more or less out of the pool. Who was left? Those for whom medical fees were too expensive. Of the 7,399 families recorded in the 1960 Census, approximately 20 percent had annual incomes under $3,000 (the median family income in Lawrence was $5,427, and a large number of the town's poor families were African American). Clearly there were married women for whom a private doctor was at least a stretch, if not prohibitively costly.[16]

There was also another constituency, one that the state and federal governments had not intended to target: unmarried women. And because of the University of Kansas and Haskell Indian Junior College, Lawrence had a disproportionately high number of young, unmarried women.[17] The Kansas legislature had mandated access to contraceptive information and services only for *married* women 18 years and older. Parental permission was required for women under 18, no matter what their marital status. But the legislature also provided a back door to access: any woman might receive contraceptives at a public clinic if she was "referred to said center by a licensed physician." Clinton interpreted this law in the broadest terms. He was a licensed physician, legally authorized to make such referrals. Thus, as he made clear in newspaper interviews and public talks, any woman who wanted birth control might receive her referral at the clinic itself, at the time of her appointment.[18] With virtually no exceptions, women seeking contraceptives at the health department came away with the Pill.

—

In 1966, soon after Clinton initiated his birth control program, the city of Lawrence became embroiled in a major controversy about the Pill. The controversy was not based in religious opposition to birth control, as was typical in much of the United States, for Lawrence had very few Roman Catholics. Instead of arguing about *whether* the Pill should be prescribed, Lawrence citizens argued about *how* the Pill should be prescribed.

In the spring of 1966 a small group of Lawrence residents, primarily nurses and wives of KU faculty and administrators, formed the Douglas County Family Planning Association, which was loosely affiliated with the national Planned Parenthood organization. One key member was Reverend John Simmons, a minister with the United Campus Christian Fellowship at KU; the first president was Mrs. Aldon (Betsy) Bell, the wife of the dean of the School of Liberal Arts and Sciences. The group's first meetings, at Trinity Episcopal Church, were to hear Dr. Dale Clinton discuss birth control techniques. Perhaps not surprisingly, this group of volunteers was motivated by concern about population growth. Mrs. Bell told a *Journal World* reporter: "There is increasing need to face the problem of overpopulation. The world now is adding one million more people each week, and unless private physicians, the public, volunteer health agencies, medical centers and government agencies assume the responsibility of meeting this crisis, the population explosion will outstrip the world's capacity to feed its people and will cause pressure of educational costs, jobs, crime and revolution."[19]

It was an aggressive notion of responsibility the group called upon: not equal opportunity for all, not freedom of access, but proselytizing for contraceptive use. They worked to recruit support from Lawrence's Ministerial Alliance, and, in a more assertive move, they decided to send mailings to each woman who had a child at Lawrence Memorial Hospital, offering to come to her home and counsel her about contraception. More than 4,000 married women in Lawrence, Mrs. Bell estimated, needed information about birth control. Many of the volunteers who joined the group did so because they wanted to bring this information to low-income, less educated married women who could not afford private doctors, but in working through the churches and the only hospital in town, they were not narrowly targeting poor women. (Significantly, while this group focused on class in their discussions and plans, race was never mentioned in any written documents, even obliquely.)

Initially, the group affiliated with Planned Parenthood attempted to collaborate with the health department. They offered to provide publicity, education, and counseling and then refer women to the health department for contraceptives. But Dr. Clinton said no, both to that proposal and to a subsequent request to use health department facilities temporarily for an independent clinic. He saw an encroachment on his turf and his hackles rose. Perhaps a man of different temperament would have welcomed the assistance. After all, his vehemence on the issue of population control was matched, at least in tone, by these crusading volunteers. They should have been on the same side. To Clinton, however, it was not only a question of territory but of proper authority and of philosophy. He claimed the authority of the state, not the implied reciprocity inherent in a rhetoric of physicians' responsibility and patients' needs. The public health department's mandate was to maintain the health of the community, not to treat individual patients. Clinton saw birth control as a central part of that mission only because he believed rapid population growth threatened the health of the community, and of the nation and the world. General health care was the province of physicians and patients, not public health officials. Just as the health department gave children vaccinations but not treatment for sore throats, Clinton intended to offer women contraceptives but not general reproductive health care. He didn't want the two functions confused, as they would be if a family planning clinic, with its emphasis on general reproductive health and education, operated in conjunction with the public health facility.[20]

Despite Clinton's refusal to collaborate, the idea of a family planning clinic was not dead. These were resourceful people; they found another site and doctors willing to volunteer their time. By late February a birth control clinic was operating out of the Lawrence Community Nursery on alternate Monday nights. The clinic showed two films (*Population Ecology* and *Planned Families*), a social worker offered counseling, and a doctor did the physical examinations and prescribed contraceptives. Dr. Clinton, though he never explained why, saw the new clinic as a challenge to his health department even though the clinic's organizers said the two organizations were organizationally and philosophically distinct. In an attempt to undermine the legitimacy of the new clinic, Clinton put up a sign at the health department proclaiming it the "Official Planned Parenthood Office." The *Journal World* documented every skirmish, and so made the availability of birth control increasingly visible to Lawrence residents.

In January 1967 both Clinton and his would-be allies in population control made their cases before the public in the *Sunday Outlook* section of the *Journal World*. Here, Clinton failed to set the agenda. His complicated explanations of the "regulatory v. service" dyad did not capture the imagination of the *Journal World* reporter. Instead of exploring the differences in authority and purpose that were so important to Dr. Clinton, she focused on how the two groups treated the women who came to them for contraceptives.

The difference between the two organizations, simply put, was that the family planning clinic offered women education about birth control options and required a physical examination, while the health department did not. Mrs. Bell explained that her group believed information and examinations made women "more comfortable" about birth control. Dr. Clinton argued that required examinations frightened women away. Most women do not want to "go through the ordeal" of an exam, he claimed. "Our job is simply to give them what they ask for . . . and we do not attempt to educate the women."[21] Women walked into the health clinic, spoke briefly with Dr. Clinton, and walked out with a prescription, or with the pills themselves. At the family planning clinic, before a woman was given a prescription for the Pill, she received information about various contraceptive options, had a physical examination, learned about the threat of population growth, and was counseled by a social worker. The contrasting ways in which the two organizations treated the women who came to them suggested very different understandings of the physical, social, and emotional significance of "going on the Pill." By early 1967 the differences between the two groups had been clearly drawn, and what remained was for the women of Lawrence to vote with their feet.

—

While Clinton and the Planned Parenthood group struggled, a different sort of controversy had begun at the university. The question was whether the University Health Service should prescribe the Pill to unmarried women students. This debate, unlike the conflict between the Planned Parenthood–affiliated group and the health department, centered around issues of morality. It was precipitated by a 1966 forum on the topic: "Should unmarried undergraduates be given birth control information and/or materials through Watkins Hospital [the student health service]?"

The panelists were three: Rev. Simmons, the campus minister who had helped form the family planning clinic and who focused on sexuality counseling and birth control in his ministry at KU; Father Falteisch, chairman of the moral theology department at St. Louis University and a Roman Catholic priest; and Dr. Raymond Schwegler, director of KU's student health service. According to coverage by the *University Daily Kansan*, Simmons argued that population control was desperately needed. Father Falteisch agreed, and suggested that the Church was moving toward accepting the "responsible use" of contraceptives as legitimate, though not for the unmarried. In the context of 1966 America and their respective churches, both men of the cloth took liberal to progressive positions. The hard line, however, came from the man of medicine.

Dr. Raymond Schwegler was, in his own way, as quirky and stubborn as Dr. Clinton. He had grown up in Lawrence, graduated from KU, and returned to Lawrence in 1935 after obtaining both an M.D. and a Ph.D. at the University of Minnesota and serving a stint as an instructor of gynecology in Mississippi. Dr. Schwegler was no stranger to public controversy. In 1937 his father, dean of the school of education at KU, had been publicly denounced as a Nazi sympathizer for allegedly making anti-Semitic remarks. The cloud remained through the war years, while Raymond Schwegler Jr. served in the Army Medical Corps. Schwegler, an obstetrician, delivered about half the babies in Lawrence in the 1950s, "when the world was quite fertile," but in 1956 he suffered a health breakdown that left him unable to practice medicine for two years. In 1958 he left private practice and joined the KU health service. He had become its director shortly before this controversy, in 1965.[22]

The *Kansan* described Dr. Schwegler, then about 60 years old, as a "small, white-haired man" with a soft voice, but he certainly never minced words. Watkins would not, Schwegler insisted, give contraceptives to unmarried students "under any circumstances." "I know this is old fashioned, mid-Victorian, and the *Kansan* will cut us to ribbons," he is quoted in the *Kansan* as saying, "but I don't want to do it and my staff backs me completely." Rev. Simmons pushed, arguing that unless premarital intercourse was grounds for expulsion, Schwegler's policy was unfair. Schwegler replied: "We'd have trouble keeping the student population up [if we expelled students for premarital intercourse]. But Watkins will not contribute to the recreational activities of the campus." When a student asked about the possibility of a "rebel doctor," Schwegler deemed it impossible: "All the doctors are handpicked—by me." He continued: "If I had somebody over there who I thought was as far out as some of the teaching faculty, I'd fire him. I want a conservative hospital that can be respected."[23]

The 1966 forum on birth control prompted a flood of letters to the *Kansan*. The letters contained no dire predictions about the earth's future if population growth continued uncontrolled. Instead, students used a language of morality to dispute Schwegler's stance. But most of the letters did not discuss *sexual* morality. The writers' concerns were framed in existential terms, in keeping with the campus-wide debate over rules for women the previous spring.

The first response to Schwegler published in the *Kansan* was a long, carefully reasoned letter from an graduate student from Iola, Kansas. His language suggests roots in the Student Responsibility Movement. Noting that the health service did provide the Pill to married women, he argued that by so doing the administration had defined the issue as moral, not medical. Thus, he said, the question was "Who should make the moral decision, the university or the students themselves?" Another graduate student (from Gettysburg, South Dakota) questioned the "the irresponsible use of the concept 'morality' as employed primarily by the 'anti-pill' proponents." Morality, he insisted, existed only in a situation in which there was "opportunity for choice." Without "free access" to contraceptives, students were not making a moral—or immoral—choice about premarital intercourse. Instead, their choices were constrained by fear or coercion.[24]

The "anti-pill" faction was represented by only one letter. The writer, a male sophomore from Nebraska, argued that because the university was a "public servant," it must follow the "doctrines of the society." He warned that premarital sex would be likely to increase if single women could get the Pill, for without fear of pregnancy, "restraining factors would be few and far between." Reaching for an analogy, he asked: "If the possibility of punishment for murder were eliminated," would there not be "a substantial increase in the number of murders committed every year?" Subsequent writers questioned his logic, his psychological stability, and his sexual adjustment. And this young man wrote back to reaffirm his stand, noting, for the record, that he was not sexually frustrated, that he was married, and that his wife was on the Pill.[25]

What was largely missing in this flurry of letters was a statement embracing sexual freedom—an affirmative voice. While all but the Nebraska sophomore agreed that the Pill should be available to unmarried women at the health service, most of the writers shifted the focus away from sex in making their arguments. Only one, a man who was already a highly visible and outrageous member of Lawrence's growing counterculture, inverted the moral hierarchy, rejecting the "artificial hangups" of guilt and the dictates of a society that spent so much of its resources on war and destruction: "All they want to do is go to war," he wrote.[26] The others, who used a framework of "morality" to debate single women's access to the Pill, fit comfortably within the larger argument about "responsible" and "mature" decisions that had been constructed by the Student Responsibility Movement as well as by some members of the administration. While their central claim—that the university should provide contraceptives to unmarried women students—was quite radical, their arguments were not. These were not yet the voices of revolution.

In the forum and in the ensuing debate, there were no arguments centering around the rights of women to control their own bodies. In fact, only two women participated in this public debate, and their names do not appear, effaced in the signatures "Mr. and Mrs. James Cooley" and "Mr. and Mrs. Angus Wright" (all seniors from Salina, writing together).[27] Why didn't women speak out in the paper? After all, the debate was about women's choices—it was not men who might go "on the Pill."

Women did not write because the stakes for them were so high. Discussions about morality and the Pill in the larger society did not center on the morality of existential choice, but on the immorality of premarital sex. In the February 1967 *Good Housekeeping* poll on unmarried women and the Pill, respondents made comments such as: "I truly pity a generation growing up with the morals of alley cats"; and "Making birth control available to unmarried girls to me would mean lowering our moral standards and destroying our culture."[28] These women were not policymakers or experts; they weren't even especially sophisticated observers. But their voices represent a different sort of authority. These are the voices of mothers—mothers of the sort whose daughters went to state colleges in the Midwest. The *Kansan* was a student paper, but news of a daughter's making public claims about her right to birth control was very likely to travel fast and to travel home.

It would be a mistake to assume that these voices of "traditional morality" were provincial leftovers, out of touch with dominant beliefs or with the "modern" views of experts. Writings in the *Journal of the American College Health Association, School and Society,* and the *Journal of School Health* at the time were equally emphatic about the evils of premarital sex, although in a different sort of language. The director of the Princeton health service, acknowledging that he was largely saved from this dilemma because his was a men's college, warned against prescribing contraceptives to unmarried women, as "the student's unconscious mind might interpret such prescriptions as a signal from 'authority' giving permission for sexual freedom."[29]

Another health services director devoted much of an article entitled "Problems of Married College Students" to what he called "pseudo-marriage," that is, unmarried couples living together. While this sort of relationship allowed students to avoid guilt about premarital sex, he explained, it was nonetheless wrong because it "violates the custom of our land." Quoting Samuel Clemens, he proclaimed: "Laws are sand, customs are rock. Laws can be evaded and punishment escaped, but an openly transgressed custom brings sure punishment." And a physician at the Ohio State University health service drew a "cause and effect relationship between mental health and promiscuity" (she didn't actually mean that mental health caused promiscuity; the correlation she drew was the opposite). Ending on a light note, she, like the midwestern sophomore, made an unfortunate analogy to sex: "It is all a bit like cars—some choose a new one and break it in with loving care; others buy from a used car lot—it is just as nice and shiny but you are not sure what problems the previous drivers have left you."[30]

Mass-circulation magazines and professional journals would not have devoted so much space to debates over premarital sex if there had been no audience for them. And it is clear from these articles that significant and relevant portions of the U.S. population, in the mid-to-late 1960s, still strongly disapproved of premarital sex. Nonetheless, these are essentially prescriptive discourses. What of the students themselves?

In the spring semester of 1964 the "Roles of Women" committee of the Associated Women Students (AWS) surveyed its constituency. Presented with descriptions of behavior ("using race as one basis for choosing your associates"; "showing disrespect for those in authority"; "wearing short shorts in town"; "feeling very angry with someone") students were asked to judge each item. Categories were "morally or ethically right," "generally acceptable," "generally unacceptable," and "morally or ethically wrong." The instructions emphasized that each student should indicate what was right or wrong "for *you*." More than 1,900 women completed the survey.

Questions about sex provoked the strongest responses. Significantly higher percentages of women students disapproved of "mixed swimming parties in the nude" than of using an exam "which has been illegally obtained." Only 64 percent of the respondents thought it wrong to choose "associates" based on race, while condemnation of premarital sex was almost universal. Freshmen and seniors agreed on this issue, with 86 percent of freshmen and 83 percent of seniors indicating that premarital sex was wrong even for engaged couples. In fact, most of the respondents (77 percent of the freshmen and 68 percent of the seniors) rated premarital sex with a fiancé as "morally or ethically wrong," not merely as "generally unacceptable." Even stronger was the students' disapproval of sexual intercourse when the couple was not engaged to be married. A striking 91 percent of both freshmen and seniors labeled it unacceptable or wrong. Only 2 percent of each group deemed premarital sex for those who were not engaged "morally or ethically right."

These numbers are clearly not an accurate guide to behavior. It is extremely unlikely that 98 percent of KU senior women were virgins. But almost all of them either believed premarital sex was wrong or believed they should *say* it was wrong. As the survey was anonymous and student-conducted, the easy explanation—fear of adult authority—is not sufficient.[31]

Tracing the public discussions of sex within the university community makes it clear that students also saw their peers as sources of danger. As is obvious from the AWS survey, young women were not unanimously in favor of sexual freedom. The AWS debate over women's hours in 1966 also demonstrated how seriously many women students took the issue of sexual "standards" and reputation. Men's attitudes certainly contributed: national polls revealed that most young American men still wanted to marry a virgin, and many men quite forthrightly divided women into two categories—the kind one married and the other kind.

As the issue of sexual morality provoked nationwide debate, conservative groups targeted campuses for anti–"free love" campaigns. Though most of the ministries on the KU campus were progressive in their stances on sexuality, the national organization Campus Crusade for Christ used overheated rhetoric about sin and promiscuity and "free love" in its KU campaign and found a significant following among students. Other conservative voices were also heard on campus. In 1967 a student union forum offered three professors addressing the question "Is Free Love a Bargain?" As suggested by the title, the answer was no. This forum was dominated by a professor of English, who accused the audience of coming in search of "some rationalization for the sex you've indulged in." Students definitely were having sex, whether or not they conceived of it as "free love." But in such a climate, with the threat of moral condemnation from peers and authorities alike, few students wished to make public their private decisions about sex.

In 1967, following the "Is Free Love a Bargain?" forum, an unmarried woman finally wrote to the editor of the campus newspaper, claiming her right to both sex and the Pill: "I take the Pill because I'd rather express my love than repress it. I'm not promiscuous, but once in awhile I meet a 'special' guy. I've seen too many girls on campus totally disregard school for several weeks as they suffer anxiety over a missed menstrual period . . . If a girl takes one chance a year, that's enough to warrant taking the pill." Countering the Campus Crusade rhetoric, this woman wrote: "The 'Christian' way is not the only way in my opinion. If I'm destined for Hell as you think, then I'll be condemned for something I believe in 100 per cent."[32]

Her letter, which had begun, "I'm a woman and I'm glad," employed a feminist language, emphasizing women's right and capacity to choose. It was a powerful and affirmative statement. But it was unsigned. An editor's note below the letter read: "Contrary to established editorial page policy, we are printing this letter without signature." All letters, no matter how controversial their claims, required signature—except this one. A woman's claiming her right to sex and the Pill was understood as a whole different category of risk.

1. Fewer than 24,000 people lived in Lawrence in 1950. Massachusetts Street, the main thoroughfare, was within walking distance of the University of Kansas and served as the shopping district for both the town and the surrounding rural area.

2. A dance at the Dine-a-Mite tavern, 1943. Although these couples look quite respectable, many of Lawrence's citizens worried that bars and taverns like this one, which served the defense workers and servicemen who poured into Lawrence during World War II, would foster sexual immorality.

3. World War II had disrupted the usual patterns of life in Lawrence, and returning veterans like this one came home with new ideas and experiences that further challenged the social customs of this small town.

4. "9000 Students Make a Crowd," announced the University of Kansas news bureau in 1947. The G.I. bill flooded the campus with students, and postwar prosperity fed rapid population and economic growth, tying the town more closely to a national culture and economy.

5. A "Coke date" at the KU student union, 1946. Official publicity photos like this one portrayed exceptionally wholesome dates, but in fact administrators found it difficult to set and enforce rules for the rapidly increasing number of students, now drawn from more diverse backgrounds than before the war.

6. Attempting to manage the student body, university administrators used elaborate sets of rules, including curfews that applied to women students but not to men. The rules were listed in an official handbook for coeds, along with tips on etiquette and proper attire. This illustration appeared in the 1947 "Campus Cues."

Abide by rules and regulations
While here to get your education.
It simplifies your work and play
To toe the mark from day to day.

7. Students at Haskell Institute, which enrolled Native American students in secondary and post-secondary curricula, were subject to strict rules governing behavior, including 10 p.m. bed checks.

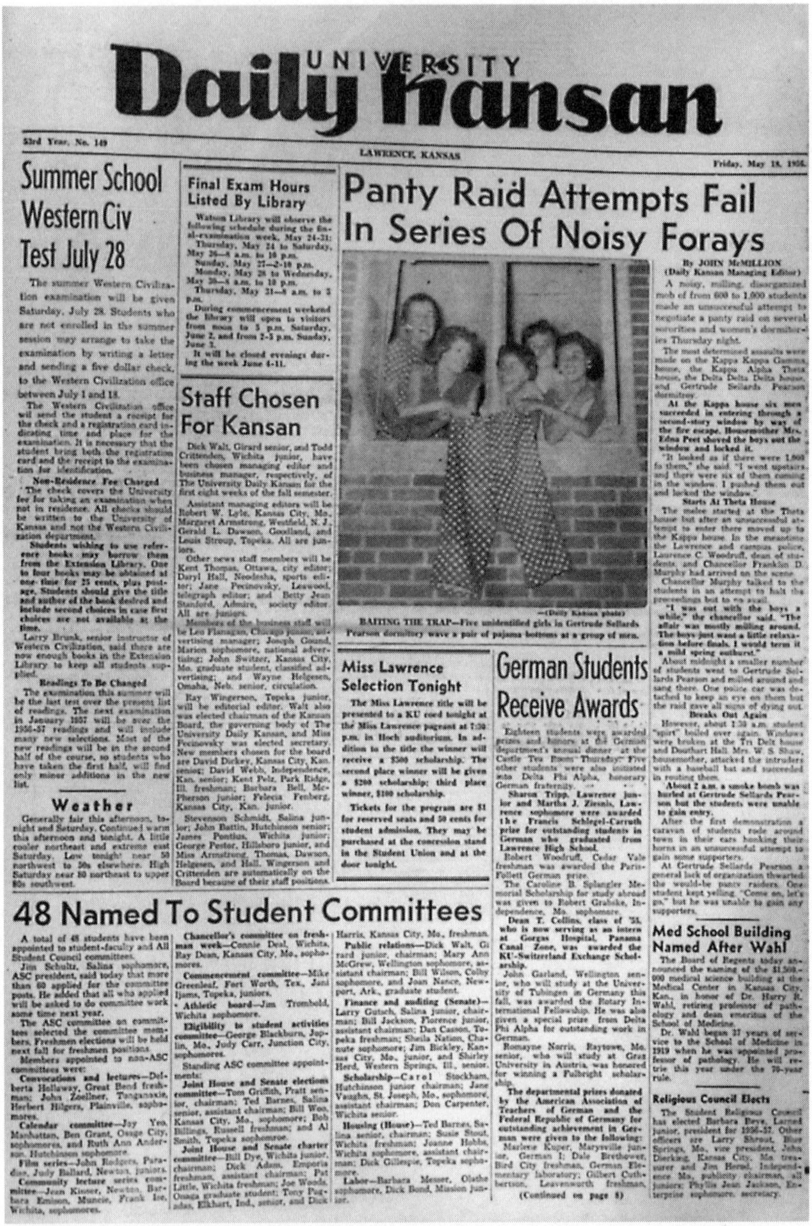

University Daily Kansan

53rd Year, No. 149   LAWRENCE, KANSAS   Friday, May 18, 1956.

Summer School Western Civ Test July 28

The summer Western Civilization examination will be given Saturday, July 28. Students who are not enrolled in the summer session may arrange to take the examination by writing a letter and sending a five dollar check, to the Western Civilization office between July 1 and 18.

The Western Civilization office will send the student a receipt for the check and a registration card indicating time and place for the examination. It is necessary that the student bring both the registration card and the receipt to the examination for identification.

Non-Residence Fee Charged — The check covers the University fee for taking an examination when not in residence. All checks should be written to the University of Kansas and not the Western Civilization department.

Students wishing to use reference books may borrow them from the Extension Library. One or four books may be obtained at one time for 25 cents, plus postage. Students should give the title and author of the book desired and include several choices in case first choices are not available at the time.

Larry Brunk, senior instructor of Western Civilization, said there are now enough books in the Extension Library to keep all students supplied.

Readings To Be Changed — The examination this summer will be the last test over the present list of readings. The next examination in January 1957 will be over the 1956-57 readings and will include many new selections. Most of the new readings will be in the second half of the course, so students who have taken the first half, will find only minor additions on the new list.

Weather

Generally fair this afternoon, tonight and Saturday. Continued warm this afternoon and tonight. A little cooler northeast and extreme east Saturday. Low tonight near 50 northwest to 60s elsewhere. High Saturday near 80 northeast to upper 80s southwest.

Final Exam Hours Listed By Library

Watson Library will observe the following schedule during the final-examination period, May 24-31:

Thursday, May 24 to Saturday, May 26—8 a.m. to 10 p.m.
Sunday, May 27—2-10 p.m.
Monday, May 28 to Wednesday, May 30—8 a.m. to 10 p.m.
Thursday, May 31—8 a.m. to 5 p.m.

During commencement weekend the library will open to visitors from noon to 5 p.m. Saturday, June 2, and from 2-5 p.m. Sunday, June 3.

It will be closed evenings during the week June 4-11.

Staff Chosen For Kansan

Dick Walt, Girard senior, and Todd Crittenden, Wichita junior, have been chosen managing editor and business manager, respectively, of The University Daily Kansan for the first eight weeks of the fall semester.

Assistant managing editors will be Robert W. Lyle, Kansas City, Mo., Margaret Armstrong, Westfield, N. J., Gerald L. Dawson, Goodland, and Louis Stroup, Topeka. All are juniors.

Other news staff members will be Kent Thomas, Ottawa, city editor; Daryl Hall, Neodesha, sports editor; Jane Pecinovsky, Leawood, telegraph editor; and Betty Jean Stanford, Admire, society editor. All are juniors.

Members of the business staff will be Leo Flanagan, Chicago junior, advertising manager; Joseph Cloxad, Marion sophomore, national advertising; John Switzer, Kansas City, Mo., graduate student, classified advertising; and Wayne Helgesen, Omaha, Neb. senior, circulation.

Ray Wingerson, Topeka junior, will be editorial editor. Walt also was elected chairman of the Kansan Board, the governing body of The University Daily Kansan. Miss Peasinovsky was elected secretary. New members chosen for the board are David Dickey, Kansas City, Kan. senior; David Werts, Independence, Kan. senior; Kent Pelz, Park Ridge, Ill. freshman; Barbara Bell, McPherson junior; Felecia Fenberg, Kansas City, Kan. junior; Stevenson Schrandt, Salina junior; John Battin, Hutchinson senior; James Pontius, Wichita junior; George Pestar, Hillsboro junior, and Mara Armstrong, Thomas, Dawson, Helgesen, and Hall. Wingerson and Crittenden are automatically on the Board because of their staff positions.

Panty Raid Attempts Fail In Series Of Noisy Forays

By JOHN McMILLION
(Daily Kansan Managing Editor)

A noisy, milling, disorganized mob of from 600 to 1,000 students made an unsuccessful attempt to negotiate a panty raid on several sororities and women's dormitories Thursday night.

The most determined assaults were made on the Kappa Kappa Gamma house, the Kappa Alpha Theta house, the Delta Delta Delta house, and Gertrude Sellards Pearson dormitory.

At the Kappa house six men succeeded in entering through a second-story window by way of the fire escape. Housemother Mrs. Edna Peet shooed the boys out the window and locked it.

"It looked as if there were 1,500 to them," she said. "I went upstairs and there were six of them coming in the window. I pushed them out and locked the window."

Starts At Theta House — The melee started at the Theta house but after an unsuccessful attempt to enter there moved up to the Kappa house. In the meantime, the Lawrence and campus police, Lawrence C. Woodruff, dean of students and Chancellor Franklin D. Murphy had arrived on the scene. Chancellor Murphy talked to the students in an attempt to halt the proceedings but to no avail.

"I was mad with the boys a while," the chancellor said. "The affair was mostly milling around. The boys just want a little relaxation before finals. I would term it a mild spring outburst."

About midnight a smaller number of students went to Gertrude Sellards Pearson and milled around and sang there. One point a car was detached to keep an eye on them but the raid drew all signs of dying out.

Breaks Out Again — However, about 1:30 a.m. student "spirit" boiled over again. Windows were broken at the Tri Delt house and Dearfoot Hall. Mrs. W. S. Shaw, housemother, attacked the intruders with a baseball bat and succeeded in routing them.

About 2 a.m. a smoke bomb was hurled at Gertrude Sellards Pearson but the students were unable to gain entry.

After the first demonstration a caravan of students rode around town in their cars honking their horns in an unsuccessful attempt to gain some supporters.

At Gertrude Sellards Pearson a general lack of organization thwarted the would-be panty raiders. One student kept yelling "Come on, let's go," but he was unable to gain any supporters.

BAITING THE TRAP—Five unidentified girls in Gertrude Sellards Pearson dormitory wave a pair of pajama bottoms at a group of men.   —(Daily Kansan photo)

Miss Lawrence Selection Tonight

The Miss Lawrence title will be presented to a KU coed tonight at 7:30 p.m. in Hoch auditorium. In addition to the title the winner will receive a $500 scholarship. The second place winner will be given a $250 scholarship; third place winner, $100 scholarship.

Tickets for the program are $1 for reserved seats and 50 cents for student admission. They may be purchased at the concession stand in the Student Union and at the door tonight.

German Students Receive Awards

Eighteen students were awarded prizes and honors at the German department's annual dinner at the Castle Tea Room Thursday. Five other students were also initiated into Delta Phi Alpha, honorary German fraternity.

Sharon Tripp, Lawrence junior and Martha J. Zironis, Lawrence sophomore were awarded the Francis Schlegel-Carruth prize for outstanding students in German who graduated from Lawrence High School.

Robert Woodruff, Cedar Vale freshman was awarded the Parie-Follett German prize.

The Caroline B. Splangler Memorial Scholarship for study abroad was given to Robert Graboke, Independence, Mo. sophomore.

Dean T. Collins, class of '25, who is now serving as an intern at Gorgas Hospital, Panama Canal Zone, was awarded the KU-Switzerland Exchange Scholarship.

John Garland, Wellington senior, who will study at the University of Tubingen in Germany this fall, was awarded the Rotary International Fellowship. He was also given a special prize from Delta Phi Alpha for outstanding work in German.

Romayne Norris, Raytown, Mo. senior, who will study at Graz University in Austria, was honored for winning a Fulbright scholarship.

The departmental prizes donated by the American Association of Teachers of German and the Federal Republic of Germany for outstanding achievement in German were given to the following: Marlene Kuper, Marysville junior, German I; Dale Brethower, Bird City freshman, German Elementary laboratory; Gilbert Cutkomp, Leavenworth, freshman,

(Continued on page 8)

48 Named To Student Committees

A total of 48 students have been appointed to student-faculty and All Student Council committees.

Jim Schultz, Salina sophomore, ASC president, said today that more than 60 applied for the committee posts. He added that all who applied will be asked to do committee work some time next year.

The ASC committee on committees selected the committee members. Freshman elections will be held next fall for freshman positions.

Members appointed to non-ASC committees were:

Convocations and lectures—Delberta Hollaway, Great Bend freshman; John Zsellner, Tanganaxie, Herbert Hilgers, Plainville, sophomores.

Calendar committee—Joy Yeo, Manhattan, Ben Grant, Osage City, sophomores, and Ruth Ann Anderson, Hutchinson sophomore.

Film series—John Rodgers, Parsons, Judy Ballard, Newton, sophomore; Jean Kissner, Newton, Barbara Emison, Muncie, Frank Ice, Wichita, sophomores.

Chancellor's committee on freshman week—Connie Deal, Wichita, Ray Dean, Kansas City, Mo., sophomores.

Commencement committee—Mike Greenleaf, Fort Worth, Tex., Jane Ijams, Topeka, juniors.

Athletic board—Mary Jo Trumbold, Wichita sophomore.

Eligibility to student activities committee—George Blackburn, Joplin, Mo., Judy Carr, Junction City, sophomores.

Standing ASC committee appointments:

Joint House and Senate elections committee—Tom Griffith, Pratt senior, chairman; Ted Barnes, Salina senior, assistant chairman; Bill Woo, Smith, Topeka sophomore.

Joint House and Senate charter committee—Bill Dye, Wichita junior, chairman; Dick Adam, Emporia senior, assistant chairman; Pat Little, Wichita freshman; Joe Woods, Osage graduate student; Tony Pogalden, Elkhart, Ind., senior, and Dick junior.

Harris, Kansas City, Mo., freshman.

Public relations—Dick Walt, Girard junior, chairman; Mary Ann McGrew, Wellington sophomore, assistant chairman; Bill Wilson, Colby sophomore, and Joan Nance, Newport, Ark., graduate student.

Finance and auditing (Senate)—Larry Gutsch, Salina junior, chairman; Bill Jackson, Florence junior; assistant chairman; Dan Casson, Topeka freshman; Sheila Nation, Chanute sophomore; Jim Bickley, Kansas City, Mo., junior, and Shirley Herd, Western Springs, Ill., senior.

Scholarship—Carol Stockham, Hutchinson junior chairman; Jane Vaughn, St. Joseph, Mo., sophomore, assistant chairman; Don Carpenter, Wichita senior.

Housing (House)—Ted Barnes, Salina senior, chairman; Susie Stoud, Wichita freshman; Joanne Hobbs, Wichita sophomore, assistant chairman; Dick Gillespie, Topeka sophomore.

Labor—Barbara Meuer, Olathe sophomore, Dick Bond, Mission junior.

Med School Building Named After Wahl

The Board of Regents today announced the naming of the $1,500,000 medical science building at the Medical Center in Kansas City, Kan., in honor of Dr. Harry R. Wahl, retiring professor of pathology and dean emeritus of the School of Medicine.

Dr. Wahl began 37 years of service to the School of Medicine in 1919 when he was appointed professor of pathology. He will retire this year under the 70-year rule.

Religious Council Elects

The Student Religious Council has elected Barbara Bova, Leroni junior, president for 1956-57. Other officers are Larry Shrout, Blue Springs, Mo., vice president; John Dierking, Kansas City, Mo. treasurer and Jim Hovel, Independence junior, publicity chairman, all juniors; Phyllis Jean Jackson, Enterprise sophomore, secretary.

---

8. Almost every spring during the 1950s, panty raids erupted on campuses throughout the United States. The sex researcher Alfred Kinsey dismissed them with the comment "All animals play around," but most university administrators took them seriously, especially after some developed into full-scale riots in 1952.

9. A civil rights march, Lawrence, 1964. Lawrence was a full participant in the events that rocked the nation in the 1960s.

10. In 1969, a Vietnam war protester's sign plays on the KU cheer "Rock Chalk Jay Hawk, Go KU." The Jayhawk is KU's mascot.

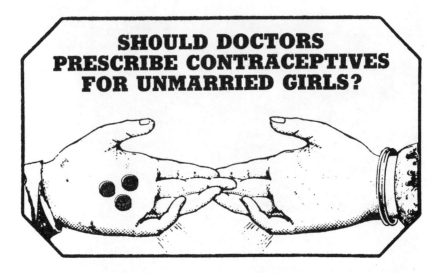

SHOULD DOCTORS PRESCRIBE CONTRACEPTIVES FOR UNMARRIED GIRLS?

11. A headline from the *Ladies' Home Journal* in 1968. Although a majority of Americans believed physicians should not prescribe the Pill to single women, Lawrence's public health department dispensed birth control pills to any woman who requested them.

12. By 1966 a highly visible counterculture community had emerged in the town. Here, members of different cultures cross paths on Lawrence's main street in 1970.

13. In the early 1970s the counterculture's public embrace of drugs and freer sexual mores created tensions with Lawrence's conservative townsfolk.

14. A Lawrence Chamber of Commerce meeting, 1970.

15. KU students dance at the Red Dog Inn, 1967.

16. Gay Liberation dances began in Lawrence in 1970 and attracted participants from throughout the region. This poster is from 1973.

17. A standoff at the Rock Chalk Café, 1970. In the spring and summer of 1970 violence erupted in Lawrence. Two confrontations between young people and police—one near Lawrence's Afro House and the other in the center of the "hippie" district—left two young men dead.

18. A Lawrence *Journal World* photographer captured the aftermath of the second fatal shooting.

19. Detail from "The Crank Case," back cover of the women's liberation issue of *Vortex*, 1970. This special issue of Lawrence's main underground paper featured disturbing images of sexual degradation and exploitation, prompting protest from all directions.

20. In the summer of 1970 some members of Lawrence's counterculture portrayed a community focused around sex and drugs and asked in the *Oread Daily Review*, "dis is a Revolution?"

WE ARE OUT TO LET YOU LOVE THE ONE YOU WANT

the lawrence
GAY LIBERATION FRONT
FRIENDSHIP AND GOOD TIMES

Political action; Education; Raps;
Dances, Parties; Activities
Counseling Service...

meetings:
7:30 PM
MONDAYS
UNION

Office B-112 UNION 864 4089   Write: BOX 234 Lawrence

21. The possibilities for gay men and lesbians in Lawrence improved dramatically during the sexual revolution, thanks in part to the Gay Liberation Front, whose members promoted the message "Gay is good." This ad appeared in the KU student newspaper in 1972.

22. Many young men and women, like this couple studying together in 1966, insisted that they needed to understand each other as "people," not as "potential dates." While such changes appear modest compared with countercultural images of sexual freedom, their cumulative effect may be the revolution's most significant legacy.

That this woman remained anonymous and was allowed to do so by the *Kansan* editorial board in violation of its policy, that women's voices were so conspicuously silent in the previous year's debate on the Pill, that 91 percent of the women students surveyed *said* they believed premarital sex to be "ethically or morally wrong"—all this is strong evidence that it wasn't only the prescriptive voices of adults denying the legitimacy of the culture of youth. Even within student culture, there was a gulf between public claims and private behavior. For the women of KU were having sex. And they were, in increasing numbers, on the Pill.

121

Actually getting the Pill could be complicated, however. When a young, single woman sought a prescription for contraceptives in the 1960s, she was making a statement about her sexual status. Virgins didn't need birth control pills unless they did not plan to remain virgins much longer. Even if a woman felt perfectly comfortable and confident about her sexual status and relationships, in attempting to get the Pill she had to make that status, to some extent, public. When a single woman went to a doctor to request any sort of contraceptive device, she risked refusal, embarrassment, even lectures on morality and appropriate behavior. Some women bought cheap rings and tried to pass them off as wedding bands. Others claimed they were coming in for a "premarital exam," with the wedding pending. Still others complained of menstrual cramps or heavy bleeding and came away with the Pill, prescribed to "regulate" their periods. But many doctors, especially those in small towns and university communities, saw through such pretexts and often treated young women with suspicion. Single women were not guaranteed, by law or custom, access to birth control.

In communities across the nation, information networks developed to warn women away from some doctors and steer them toward others who were more sympathetic or more lax. At the end of the decade Lawrence High School's "underground" newspaper, *Freedspeak,* ran a notice: "NEED BIRTH CONTROL PILLS?? See Dr. Clinton at the Douglas County Health Clinic at 7th and New Hampshire." Even earlier, in 1966, the university newspaper had run a series on the Pill, including articles entitled "The Pill: Social Phenomena," "Pill Hard to Get in Lawrence," and "The Pill and How to Get It." The news was largely discouraging. One article quoted Dr. Margaret Clark, a private physician in Lawrence, who said, "I give prescriptions to married women and to girls who come in and show me they are getting married. But to unmarried women? Heavens no!" She told the

Kansan reporter that three or four unmarried women asked her for birth control pills every week, but she always turned them down.[33]

Doctors at the KU Medical Center, in Kansas City, were more willing to offer the Pill, though several anonymous women testified that doctors had simply handed them samples and said to return for a prescription when they turned 21. One woman told the story of a doctor who gave her the pills, but "stress[ed] the dangers of promiscuity." As this anonymous "coed" explained to the *Kansan* reporter, the doctor told her about a patient of his who had gotten the Pill because she was "going out with this one guy so steadily and hadn't even thought about him telling anyone else." But he told someone he worked with that "his girl was taking pills," and the other man took her out. When she wouldn't go to bed with him, he beat her up.[34]

The *Kansan* articles were generally straightforward, presenting the problem of "getting the Pill" in a factual but generally supportive manner. But woven throughout is the subtext of danger, of difficulty. It would take time before a story like that one was greeted with anger, rather than reported as, essentially, a possible side effect of the Pill.

—

As women learned through informal networks, alternative newspapers, and the completely mainstream *Journal World,* the quickest, cheapest, and least complicated place to get birth control pills in Lawrence was the public health department. The university student health service refused to "contribute to the recreational activities of the campus," in its director's colorful words, and many students worried about having such information about their sex lives in what were, after all, official university records at the health service. What might seem a clear case of doctor-patient confidentiality was potentially blurred by the doctrine of *in loco parentis,* no matter how tattered it might have become.[35] And private doctors in Lawrence were unpredictable at best. The volunteer clinic was open only two nights a month, and simply could not serve large numbers of women. Also, with its heavy involvement of people connected to KU, and its emphasis on education and counseling, it didn't offer KU women or other young single women the anonymity and confidentiality many sought. So, in the face of such limited alternatives, the unmarried women of KU, and of Lawrence, turned to Dr. Clinton.

The number of women obtaining oral contraceptives at the public health department grew dramatically from year to year, and the vast majority of the new patients each year were KU students. The patient load closely followed the academic year. In 1971, for example, there were only 44 new patients in August, but in September, with the beginning of the fall semester, there were 300. That year the Lawrence–Douglas County health department served 8,529 birth control patients and dispensed or prescribed almost 38,000 months of pills.[36]

Those totals are amazing at a clinic with a single physician, especially since Dr. Clinton also served as director of the entire county health department. Clinton was proud of his clinic's efficiency, referring to it as a "low-cost, high-volume operation." The volume, however, was very much dependent on the specific form of birth control distributed. If you believed, as Dr. Clinton did, that gynecological examinations were a necessary component of general health care but not a precondition for using oral contraceptives, the prescription (or the pills themselves) could be handed across a desk after a few basic questions. Unlike the diaphragm, which several Lawrence doctors considered inconvenient and "messy" to fit, the Pill could be prescribed without any encounter with a patient's reproductive organs. And (again unlike the diaphragm) women did not have to be shown how to use the pills. No time-consuming practice was required; the time the doctor spent on education could be minimal. The Pill was a wonder drug not simply because of its effectiveness for women but also because of its possible convenience for those who prescribed it. Women went to the health department and walked out a few minutes later "on the Pill." Stories of young women who were offered virtual armloads of free pills and told to pass them on to their friends still circulate today. According to the rumor mill, Clinton always erred on the side of generosity in dispensing birth control.[37]

The Planned Parenthood–affiliated clinic took a very different approach. Prescription of the Pill was contingent upon not only a physical examination but also a time-consuming process of education and counseling. These procedures necessarily limited the number of women the all-volunteer bimonthly clinic could serve. It was gradually overwhelmed by demand. The clinic, which had opened in early 1967, closed its doors permanently on the first day of 1970. Though it had been founded to serve low-income residents of Lawrence, the president of its sponsoring group explained, it had been used almost exclusively by KU students (she did not say whether they were married or single). Many of the volunteers were frustrated by what they saw as a misdirection of resources, and upon closing the clinic the directors sent a letter to Dr. Schwegler at the student health service and to the chancellor arguing that the university must take responsibility for its students' birth control needs instead of allowing students to overwhelm community resources needed by and for a different population.[38]

Proposals to provide birth control to students had been on the table at KU for several years. In the fall of 1967 the newly formed Independent Student Party (composed partially of SDS members) had raised the issue as part of its broad program stressing "student responsibility." "Contraceptive Information" did appear as a line item on the agenda (entitled "Campus Problems for Consideration") of the Committee on Student Affairs in late 1967, but no action was taken. In 1970, after the closing of the Planned Parenthood clinic, a student group approached top-level administrators about the health service's birth control policies. The administrators responded sympathetically, promising that two upcoming vacancies at Watkins would be filled with doctors who would prescribe the Pill without using marital status or "morality" as criteria. This never happened. KU was not out of step with other American campuses, however. In 1970, 53 percent of American college health services offered no gynecological care to women students, and 72 percent did not prescribe contraceptives (to single *or* married students).[39]

Birth control information and referrals became more easily available at KU by the end of the decade, even if administrators refused to take the official step of *furnishing* contraceptives to single students. The dean of women's office, which had long provided low-profile counseling and assistance to women with problem pregnancies, began a high-profile attempt to provide birth control information to interested women students. The dean of women, Emily Taylor, told a reporter for the *Kansan* that birth control was a matter of a woman's "personal control over reproduction." Another important source of information was the Lawrence chapter of Zero Population Growth (ZPG), which was founded in 1970 at a time when there were only 3,000 ZPG members in the nation. Centered in the biology department at KU, Lawrence ZPG sponsored speakers, engaged in political lobbying, and ran a birth control information line for Lawrence and Douglas County.[40]

Neither of these programs could have operated without consent from the highest levels of the administration. At the same time, neither of these programs was likely to provoke as much outrage among the taxpayers of

Kansas as would an official policy guaranteeing contraceptives to unmarried women. While there were active and powerful opponents of the provision of birth control to single women at the university, there were also important advocates among the administration, the faculty, and even the campus ministries. Together, these people gradually made the university more responsive to students' needs for birth control while attempting to avoid the public controversy that bolder action might provoke.

125

—

Thus far, the story of the Pill in Lawrence, Kansas, has been one of elite-managed, gradual change. The Pill became available to a large number of young, unmarried women through the actions of a set of local elites, including civic-minded matrons, doctors, nurses, social workers, and university personnel, none of whom intended to promote sexual freedom, much less revolution. There were factions and groups with different approaches, but in the early stages of their efforts they all avoided discussions of morality and called upon the world crisis of population growth for legitimacy.

Until the 1970s Lawrence's youth also fit into this model of gradual change. While thousands of young women went on the Pill during the 1960s, public acknowledgment of that private behavior lagged behind. The accretion of private acts did change social and sexual mores, but gradually, and usually without direct confrontation. These young people found practical allies among adults who saw contraceptives as a tool in their struggle against the population explosion. Most of these young women took the pills provided under this rubric and used them to have sex without getting pregnant. The two groups were working with different interests and motivations, but to most of the young women it didn't really matter, so long as they could get the Pill. For all of the stridency of conservative voices in Lawrence, the trend toward birth control for the unmarried, though gradual, was generally progressive. While the Pill may have been revolutionary in its results, it was not especially revolutionary in its introduction.

In the late 1960s and early 1970s the process of elite-managed, gradualist change began to intersect with other movements that were clearly more revolutionary in intent. The Lawrence counterculture became increasingly visible and vocal in its rejection of both established authority and "traditional" sexual mores. Even before 1967, when the Summer of Love in the Haight-Ashbury section of San Francisco drew national attention to "hippies" and to American youth culture's public embrace of drugs and sex,

Lawrence had its own small countercultural community. This set of inter-secting groups existed on the fringes of the university, put out small poetry magazines and the first of Lawrence's several underground newspapers, and openly flouted the mores of respectable Kansas society. Lawrence's coun-terculture grew exponentially in the late 1960s and was a critical source of revolutionary challenges to the established sexual order. However, Lawrence's hardcore countercultural types were not involved in the early struggles over the Pill, even though many of the young women centered in that culture took it. In an indirect way, Lawrence's counterculture provided context for the debates by publicly adopting a doctrine of sexual freedom, but there was no direct challenge to either the moral framework or the population control agenda that structured institutional policies until the Lawrence women's movement began to make demands.

In the early 1970s the women's movement captured the Pill, in both its symbolic and its physical manifestations. Women in Lawrence—and not only young women—interrupted the process of gradual change within the paradigms of population control and sexual morality and offered, instead, revolutionary claims about gender equality, cultural authority, and sexual freedom.

By 1972 any woman in Lawrence—married or unmarried—could obtain birth control pills, free if necessary. This had been true, and widely known, for at least five years. But it wasn't simply access to the Pill that was at stake. It was the nature of the access, and the meaning attributed to it, that angered some women. In 1972 two different groups of women in Lawrence challenged the medical men who controlled access to the Pill.[41] Though the two groups used different methods and different vocabularies (fittingly, as they represented different generations), both made claims based on the rights and needs of women themselves and not on those of the larger society. In so doing they stepped outside the discourses of morality and of the population problem and centered the debate over access to the Pill in a discourse on women, rights, and freedom.

By the end of the 1960s, throughout America, women were beginning to speak out against the discrimination and oppression they saw in virtually all aspects of society. The women's movement, or "women's liberation," touched a chord of recognition in many women and provoked vehement opposition in others. By no means was the women's movement a consensus effort in the United States, and even many of its supporters found little in common. The National Organization of Women's (NOW) advocacy of

126

equality in the workplace was a far cry from the violent language and imagery of the Society for Cutting Up Men (S.C.U.M.). But women's voices were raised, and it was increasingly difficult for anyone to avoid confronting the issues that these women were talking and writing about.

The women's movement in Lawrence was no more unified than the national movement. Lawrence's diverse women's groups varied in nature and purpose. Participants were highly aware of the national scope of the movement, and situated themselves among different strands, sometimes with official or semi-official national affiliations. A Women's Liberation Front was formed in mid-1968. KU's dean of women, Emily Taylor, was a NOW-style feminist who lobbied for political legislation and university policies supporting equal rights for women. Her office had supported a form of liberal feminism on campus, including a commission on the status of women, and had served as a center of action for some women students and administrators throughout her tenure.

On the other end of the continuum, women in Lawrence's large and diverse counterculture had begun to draw connections between the oppression of minorities and the oppression of women. The women of *Vortex* (the most important underground newspaper) published a women's issue in 1970, and soon afterward the *Lavender Luminary*, a lesbian paper, appeared. W.I.T.C.H. (Women's International Terrorist Conspiracy from Hell) emerged briefly as a local group. Consciousness-raising groups formed. In Lawrence, women were talking with other women about their lives, and those conversations would have repercussions in the world they inhabited.[42]

Women's liberation was a controversial subject and a difficult practice, for not even the women most committed to it agreed on means and goals. But there was a deep-seated and powerful belief in Lawrence, shared by thousands of women from many walks of life, that the time for change was at hand. So when the famous feminist activist and author Robin Morgan came to speak at KU in early February 1972, the overflow crowd spilled out of the huge union ballroom.

Morgan's talk was scheduled as part of a series called the Minority Opinions Forum, which brought controversial speakers to campus in that controversial era. Morgan was a radical feminist, and she spoke and wrote with articulate rage as she detailed the oppressions of women in contemporary society and called women to action. One woman who heard the talk that night remembers it as "not always [so] radical . . . she called Marx a good Jewish boy." In fact, it wasn't anything in particular that Morgan did or said, but instead the energy of that assembly that precipitated action.[43] In an open forum following Morgan's speech, women spoke with a sense of urgency, and they discovered other women who had been working on similar issues at the university: women's health care, child care, affirmative action, a women's studies program. Not all the women who came together after Morgan's talk were newly awakened to political action. Some had been active for years in the civil rights and antiwar movements, and they knew how to orchestrate political protest.

The next night about seventy-five women, including university employees, faculty wives, and undergraduate and graduate students, several of the women accompanied by their children, met again and resolved to occupy a campus building and issue a set of demands. Calling themselves the February Sisters, twenty women and children entered the East Asian building (chosen primarily because one of the women had access to a key) at 6:30 P.M. on February 3. Others who remained outside the building distributed leaflets detailing the group's demands, including full health care for women students, a federally funded child care center on campus, an end to discriminatory employment practices at KU, more women in high-level administrative positions, an affirmative action program, and a department of women's studies.

Chancellor Chalmers was informed of the occupation by an anonymous phone call (to his bridge party); he initially ignored the call, but by 8:00 P.M. the University Senate Executive Committee was meeting and it was clear the occupation was being taken seriously. Negotiations continued through the night, with the Sisters receiving strong support from some key women administrators and faculty members. When the Sisters emerged from the building early the next morning, they had won commitments from the administration on a substantial portion of their demands, including the women's health program.

They followed up their demands with carefully researched proposals. In their document on health care, while they drew heavily on the authority of the American College Health Association's 1970 report on birth control, they also couched their argument in language echoing the American tradition of rights and freedoms. "We, the February Sisters," their proposal for a human sexuality clinic began, in an invocation of the U.S. Constitution. Arguing that "control of her reproductive functions is a fundamental right of every woman," the Sisters insisted: "The University cannot view the action proposal . . . as a request for additional privileges, but rather as a demand to recognize right [sic] which have been neglected."⁴⁴

The Sisters' demands were fueled by outrage at continuing transgressions. By not covering the cost of pap smears in the student health insurance, the university was refusing to acknowledge women's sexual and reproductive organs as legitimate parts of their bodies. Women who requested gynecological exams at Watkins were sometimes refused and often lectured on "morality"; women who sought birth control were also frequently subjected to "morality lectures," even when presenting themselves as seeking "premarital" exams; a married woman might have to see three or four doctors before finding one willing to give her contraceptives. Basically, the Sisters argued, women were not treated with respect. This, they stated in their strongest language, "we consider . . . to be dehumanizing and an affront to the dignity of the woman involved."⁴⁵

It was not simply the right to access these women claimed. Women had developed a network of information, and with a little resourcefulness, expense, or persistence a woman could provide for her gynecological and contraceptive needs. More important, these women were rejecting the frameworks of sexual morality and population control that had governed access to contraceptives for more than a decade. The February Sisters condemned the ways that many Americans used concepts of sexual morality to deny women's autonomy and dignity—a fairly obvious and expected critique—but also criticized the efforts of population control groups. Organizations like ZPG were "dangerous," a Sister argued in the *Kansan,* because they sought to "subvert Women's Liberation to [their] own ends." Birth control was not about population, she wrote, but instead "a woman's issue involved with the concept of a free woman." These women understood that rationales for contraception based on population control, no less than those based on morality, left room for comments like the one made by the irritated director of student health, Dr. Schwegler, who said that he did so many pelvic exams he sometimes felt like he worked in a whorehouse. The February Sisters and their allies meant to provide a new framework for prescribing the Pill that centered around the needs of women themselves and left no room for such demeaning and disrespectful remarks.⁴⁶

After the actions of the February Sisters in February 1972, Watkins student health center officially began prescribing the Pill to unmarried women. Somewhat ironically, the following month the Supreme Court ruled that women could not be denied contraceptives on the basis of marital status.[47]

—

The struggles over the Pill in Lawrence were not yet over, however. Even though Watkins offered contraceptives, students still sought the quick access to birth control and the relative anonymity offered by Dr. Clinton's clinic at the public health department. In 1972 the health department drew 2,100 new birth control patients, down only 300 from the previous year, before Watkins' policy had changed. Birth control was second only to salaries in the department's budget. In the fiscal year 1971–72 the health department spent $16,916.43 for contraceptives. Slightly less than half of that sum was supplied by the state.[48]

In August 1972, however, the Kansas State Department of Health cut off funding for Clinton's birth control program. The state agency received its funding from the Department of Health, Education and Welfare (HEW), and it came with federal mandates. These mandates committed doctors to follow a specified procedure in prescribing the Pill, including performing a complete physical exam, pap smear, visual exam for cancer, tuberculin test, hemoglobin, and urinalysis. Clinton, who adamantly believed that public health departments were not appropriate sites for clinical medicine, refused to perform these tests. E. D. Lyman, the state director of public health, cut Clinton's funding. Lyman explained: "We accepted funds from the Federal Government on certain terms. They are more than just guidelines, they are contractual terms."[49]

Clinton argued his position in a September meeting of the public health committee of the town's Board of Health, which oversaw his department's functions: "The 'guidelines' name many irrelevant procedures which the patient must endure before she is given her birth control supplies . . . The 'comprehensive services' appear to be simply a mechanism for diverting birth control funds into other activities, using birth control as a carrot (or whip)." Referring to the procedures elsewhere as "roadblocks" and "hassles," Clinton argued that HEW was attempting, through the state departments of health, to convert local public health departments into free comprehensive clinics. Comprehensive medical services for the indigent were not his mandate, he insisted, and he would continue to provide birth control as before, funding it through donations from patients, not to exceed $1 per woman each month. Dr. Schwegler, the director of KU's student health service, who was also serving as chairman of the public health committee, told the *Journal World* that he was "irritated as a private citizen" over the state health department's action. Clinton prevailed with Lawrence's Board of Health, and his refusal stood. Though the local clinic lost a $12,000 federal grant, it was soon running a $10,000 surplus from donations by birth control patients.[50]

HEW not having provided a sufficient "carrot" or "whip" to move this local institution, Clinton's health department returned to its former balance of supply and demand. If there was no philosophical agreement between provider (who addressed the population problem) and consumers (who overwhelmingly wanted free or inexpensive birth control pills without accompanying lectures on morality, even if in the guise of "counseling"), there was a remarkable efficiency in their transactions. But here, once again, the powerful paradigms of population control and morality would be challenged by a woman's voice.

In this case the challenge was not ideological or even fully coherent. Following the cutoff of state funds for birth control, a Lawrence woman named Petey Cerf launched an attack against Dr. Clinton. Birth control policy emerged at the center of the ensuing fight, but it was not the only issue involved. More than anything else, it seems, Cerf was angry at what she saw as Clinton's arrogance.[51]

Petey Cerf's attack would turn the county health department inside out, revealing the fault lines of gender and class in Lawrence. Cerf was not acting as an avowed feminist. She was of an earlier generation of women, old enough to be the mother of most of the February Sisters. She was extraordinarily competent, involved in public affairs, with a long history of activism in Lawrence. Despite her lack of feminist rhetoric, her campaign against Clinton, coming as it did in the midst of the struggles over women's liberation, was understood as a challenge to male authority. And because this small local struggle intersected with changes on the national level, as a direct result of her efforts the Lawrence–Douglas County health department would be completely remade along another model.

Mrs. Cerf had been involved in the feud between Clinton and the Douglas County Family Planning Association (the Planned Parenthood affiliate) in 1966. After that confrontation she had written a letter of protest to the president of the Board of Health about Clinton and his policies, but had received no answer. This time she made her letter public, sending it to the *Journal World* and to the *Kansan*. In this letter she criticized Clinton's "omission" of "certain safeguards" in prescribing the Pill, and suggested that women might have died as a result. Cerf also wrote to the University of Kansas board of regents, warning that Clinton was endangering the health of KU's women students by prescribing the Pill without performing necessary tests.[52]

Clinton, who participated regularly in national conferences on birth control, in fact believed that the Pill was absolutely safe. He had promoted it with a messianic zeal for a full decade. From 1962, when the thalidomide tragedy had raised fears about analogous problems with the new pill, Clinton had rejected all medical cautions. After the journalist-activist Barbara Seaman's influential book, *The Doctors' Case Against the Pill* (1969), raised public awareness of the dangers associated with oral contraceptives, Clinton wrote angrily to the *Journal World:* "[There is] not one scrap of hard evidence that the pills . . . have any discernable effect of cancer, blood clots, or any serious illness." He concluded: "Perhaps we should take pregnancy off the market until all the known and presumed hazards have been more thoroughly investigated."[53] Even in 1972, after the links to blood clotting had been widely discussed in professional journals, including a major article in the *American Journal of Public Health*, and in popular magazines ranging from *Good Housekeeping* to *Vogue* to the *New Republic*, Clinton insisted that one reason he did not intend to perform "irrelevant" tests was that they "falsely implied that birth control was dangerous." The health department was obliged, he explained to a special meeting of the public health committee called in the wake of Cerf's charges, "as part of its educational function, to debunk medical fallacies." Clinton's assertions did not mesh with what Lawrence citizens were reading in national publications.[54]

The controversy continued. By December Mrs. Cerf had compiled a detailed report, "One Woman's Evaluation of the Douglas County Health Department Program," which she presented at the December meeting of the public health committee. The room was crowded, as eighty or more "critics and defenders" of Clinton "clashed" (the *Journal World*'s terms) for over two hours. The minutes of the meeting record generally dismissive comments toward Cerf from male members of the board. One noted that Cerf "was not fully qualified to make medical judgements on the actions of Dr. Clinton" and that "her data were probably somewhat distorted." Another said that Clinton was doing "a good job"; still another that Clinton was giving people "more than their money's worth." The sole woman board member to speak said she thought the screening of birth control patients would be a "good idea."[55]

Dr. Schwegler, as chairman of the committee, attempted to smooth things over by officially welcoming increased community input. But Cerf did not let this die. She organized a bus tour to other health departments in the region for Lawrence officials and managed to get the *Journal World* to run a three-part special series on the health department. The contest between Clinton and Cerf had, by this time, produced sound bites. Clinton: "What our patients want is birth control—family planning is a semantic catch-all." Cerf: "Birth control pills should not be handed out like bubble gum."[56]

With continued publicity, Lawrence officials and citizens took sides. There was a clear gender division. Most (male) physicians, including Dr. Schwegler, supported Clinton. The League of Women Voters, which had been sending an observer to Board of Health meetings every month for decades, gave advice and support to Cerf. The women of Penn House, a multiracial group that offered assistance to Lawrence's low-income residents through participatory programs and community initiatives, distributed a statement agreeing with Cerf's evaluation and criticizing the Board of Health: "We were astounded," they wrote of the earlier meeting, "to see supposedly well educated intelligent gentlemen rise to take a very defensive and non-constructive position." And finally, a long letter to the editor from a woman with no connection to either Cerf or Clinton appeared in the *Journal World.* She told of asking two physicians in town their opinion of the health department. Each had offered, instead, "a verbal lambasting of Mrs. Cerf's audacity." This woman said she saw it as her "duty" to point out that "Mrs. Cerf is not an idle housewife who seeks to irresponsibly stir up trouble. The woman has done her homework on this matter." The language, particularly "audacity" and "idle housewife," suggests the role of gender in this struggle, as does the fact that Cerf's public support came overwhelmingly from women and Clinton's from men.[57]

Though he still had significant support in Lawrence, Clinton announced his resignation on March 8, 1973—without further comment. Dr. Schwegler, speaking on the record, named Mrs. Cerf as the proximate cause, noting that "the pressure of a handful has forced us [the Board] into a very ugly situation."[58] And indeed it had, for without Clinton the health department lacked not only a director but a physician. Its operations were at a standstill.

At the public health committee meeting following Clinton's resignation, a group of Lawrence doctors pushed to rehire him. One had canvassed fifteen local doctors and had found not one willing to consider the job. All agreed that replacing Clinton would be quite expensive; he had been making a meager $21,372 a year. The board proposed offering him up to $50,000 to return to the post. "Clinton was the hardest working health officer we've had in Douglas County in 50 years," one said. "I don't think we can ever find one man to do the job that Dr. Clinton did."[59]

The meeting was primarily notable for its gender divisions. Several male doctors made slighting comments and jokes about Cerf and her supporters, prompting a series of women to rise and rebut the criticisms. The female city commissioner told the male doctors it was "unfair" to characterize critics of the health department as "troublemakers." Dr. Schwegler then summed up the crisis at the department with yet another telling figure of speech: "At the moment we're trying to hold our pants up with the belt buckle broken."[60]

In the end, the doctor who predicted they couldn't find one man to replace Clinton was right. The Board of Health, with much internal and external dissension, hired two women. Mrs. Kay Kent, hired as administrator of the department at a salary of $15,948, had a master's degree with an emphasis on community health from Boston University School of Nursing. Dr. Ginny Levene, who was hired as a half-time physician for $9,200, held a master's and doctorate of public health from the Johns Hopkins University School of Medicine.[61]

Under the leadership of Kay Kent, the health department instituted the procedures mandated by federal guidelines and thereby regained federal funds. Dr. Clinton's efficient birth control operation became a comprehensive family planning clinic, more generally concerned with women's reproductive health. In 1974, the first full year of Kent's administration, birth control patients dropped from the 8,528 of Clinton's final year to 3,746. The number of pap smears done rose from Clinton's 12 to 1,505. New patients from KU were referred to Watkins, where Schwegler refused to compile statistics. And by 1978 there was an average wait of four weeks for an appointment at the health department's birth control clinic.[62]

Cerf had successfully challenged the authority of the male doctors. The changes that ensued, though prompted more by economics than by ideology, would significantly alter the institutional structure and function of the clinic. The struggle between Cerf and Clinton was given its specific shape by local, contingent factors—most powerfully, by the two strong-willed individuals who clashed over the issue of birth control. Nonetheless, the struggle and its outcome were also shaped by national circumstances. It was the existence of federal funding and associated guidelines for prescribing oral contraceptives that provided Cerf with her opening to challenge Clinton. After Clinton's resignation, it was possible to hire Dr. Levine and Mrs. Kent only because of large-scale changes that brought more women into the professions; significantly, both had been trained in highly respected private universities that drew students from across the nation.

Mrs. Kent's health department offered far superior reproductive health care to the women of Lawrence, married and unmarried, than had Dr. Clinton's. Her assumption of the directorship and her continuing success in that position despite powerful initial opposition, like the battle that had paved the way for her appointment, were moments of women's triumph in a fundamentally sexist milieu.

It would be a mistake, however, to read this story simply as the triumph of women over male authority. Clinton was a complex figure, and he played a complicated role in the politics of birth control in Lawrence. He displayed a marked indifference to the reproductive health of individual women. His passion was population control—but because of that passion he provided birth control pills to many young women. He gave the Pill straightforwardly, without lectures on the dangers of promiscuity or comments on the patient's moral character. Marital status, he said, was not "one of the medical criteria."[63]

Young women who took the Pill Clinton prescribed had sex without fear of pregnancy. They obtained the Pill simply by request, without the demeaning act of lying about an impending marriage or the purchase of a cheap gold ring at a drugstore. They were, by and large, grateful.[64] By prescribing the Pill, Dr. Clinton—inadvertently—facilitated the sexual revolution in Lawrence and changed the lives of thousands of young women and their partners. It is ironic that his resignation was caused by other Kansas women who acted from outrage over his neglect of women's reproductive health.

5

Revolutionary Intent

Sex, Drugs, and Rock 'n' Roll. Make Love, Not War. Free Love. Gay Lib. The Myth of the Vaginal Orgasm. By the late 1960s America was alive with calls to sexual revolution.

A great many Americans, the ones to whom Richard Nixon successfully appealed as "the silent majority" at the end of the decade, were horrified by these public demands for sexual freedom. Young women on the Pill, young men with long hair who chanted "Make Love, Not War" or even worse, praised the liberating power of "fucking in the street"—these were not disenfranchised youth from the margins of American society. Some of America's most favored children, those upon whom the very future of the nation seemed to depend, were rejecting adult authority and traditional morality. Their words and deeds shocked a nation already rent by conflict over the war in Vietnam and by the increasing violence of America's struggles over race. No less a word than revolution seemed adequate to describe the crisis in public life.

Though the revolutionary claims to sexual freedom seemed sudden to many Americans, changes in sexual behavior had been gradual—even evolutionary. Every fumbled caress in the back seat of a car, every homosexual encounter, every condom in a wallet, every diaphragm or coca-cola douche or birth control pill used outside marriage, every struggle over sexual boundaries, had cumulatively changed America's sexual landscape. Though the sexual (mis)behavior of millions of individuals remained hidden from view in a society that imposed real penalties for violating its sexual codes, each transgression against the "accepted standards" of sexual behavior had widened the gulf between "private" and "public," or between what the sexologist Alfred Kinsey called the "covert" and "overt" sexual cultures.

In this gradually widening chasm the sexual revolution took root, nurtured by the large-scale social and economic transformations of postwar America. Social and geographic mobility, which detached people from local beliefs and traditions, fostered change in sexual behavior and mores, as did the rise of national culture, which penetrated local, insular communities. Efforts to promote democratic citizenship, as well as concerns about individual rights, free speech, poverty, and world population growth, all played largely unintended roles in reshaping America's sexual code. But it was the self-conscious, purposeful, radical claims of the late 1960s and early 1970s that transformed the accretions of decades—all the secret transgressions and unintended byproducts— into "the sexual revolution."

The sexual revolution was never a single, coherent movement. The violent and misogynistic rape fantasies that represented sexual liberation in some of the underground newspapers produced by countercultural communities in the 1960s fit uneasily with contemporary efforts (often within those same communities) to transcend traditional sex roles and so remake love. Many who championed sexual freedom were hostile to gay liberation and to the personal and political desires of gay men and lesbians. X-rated movies did not seem at all liberating to many of those who sought liberation. "Living together" was not the same thing as "free love," no matter how often the mass media confused the two. This "revolution" was an amalgam of movements and impulses joined in the chaos of that era. They were often at odds with one another, rarely well thought out, and frequently without a clear agenda, but they shared a powerful impatience with the hypocrisy and repressiveness of the sexual status quo.

It is not possible to make sense of the sexual revolution without sorting out its different strands. At the same time, it is crucial to remember that people did not experience the various strands of the revolution as separate and discrete. America seemed in revolution because of the combined force of these divergent impulses, not because of any single set of acts or beliefs. Everyone and everything that claimed to be part of this revolution, or that was so identified by critics and pundits, lent its weight to the rest. In the mass media, college girls on the Pill and the drug-suffused and truly promiscuous sexuality of the Summer of Love were conflated and joined in a seamless web labeled "sexual revolution." The whole was greater than the sum of its varied parts, especially because Americans, quite correctly, saw the sexual revolution as one facet of the whole panorama of social upheavals and crises that were shaking their society to its very foundation. America felt itself in revolution. A story of sexual revolution, local or national, cannot be told in isolation from the tumultuous events of the era that gave it birth.

—

In the last years of the 1960s the most powerful nation in the world was in crisis.[1] Caught in the quagmire of the Vietnam war, America failed to confront the limits and consequences of its power. And far from the firefights of Vietnam, the United States itself had become a battlefield, with complicated conflicts portrayed in stark terms: youth against their elders, blacks against whites, women against men, "hippies" against "traditional American values." There were tanks in the streets of America, charred and desolate blocks in cities that had remained untouched in the global conflagration of World War II. This time, however, America was at war with itself.

By late 1968 the war in Vietnam had become a painful and divisive fact at the center of American life. More than half a million American troops were deployed in Vietnam. The nation's war dead already numbered more than thirty thousand. Tens of thousands of American families had lost a loved one. Hundreds of thousands more waited anxiously for the return of a son or a husband, and others worried over the draft, lottery numbers, and deferments. President Lyndon Johnson reassured the country that there was "light at the end of the tunnel," but after the Tet offensive in early 1968 few had faith in that promise. The trusted CBS anchorman Walter Cronkite was much more compelling when he concluded that America was "mired in stalemate" in an unwinnable war.

Since 1965, when large numbers of American ground troops had first been sent to Southeast Asia, many Americans had questioned the morality or the legitimacy of the nation's role in the Vietnam conflict. Their motivations varied. Some believed the involvement was poor foreign policy; others were pacifists; still others centered their opposition to the war in larger critiques of American capitalism and of domestic inequality. Most of these protesters were not young radicals bent on revolution. One of the most active and vocal antiwar organizations was the eminently respectable Clergy and Laymen Concerned About Vietnam. By 1967 a broad spectrum of Americans actively protested the war.

By 1968 the nature of the protests had begun to change. Some very visible antiwar leaders began to use a rhetoric of violence. Some radicals moved beyond criticism of America to public support for America's declared enemy. "Ho, Ho, Ho Chi Minh, Viet Cong Are Gonna Win," chanted protesters, alienating many of their moderate fellows. The president of the United States was repeatedly greeted with the refrain, "Hey, hey, LBJ, how many kids did you kill today?" In August 1968 antiwar protesters gathered in Chicago during the Democratic National Convention. As delegates chose their party's candidate for president, national guardsmen with fixed bayonets guarded the streets of Chicago. In scenes of chaos and violence, police beat protesters—and reporters and bystanders—bloody and senseless. The protesters chanted: "The whole world is watching."

If not the whole world, most of America saw those scenes. Even in the country's poorest and most isolated communities, a large majority of families had televisions. About 89 million Americans watched the violence in Chicago. But this doesn't mean they all saw the same thing. Americans were bitterly divided over what had happened and why, but most came down on the side of "law and order." Even though by 1969 a majority believed involvement in Vietnam was a "mistake," a national opinion poll found that 69 percent of the American public also believed that antiwar protesters were "harmful to American life."[2] Ronald Reagan, then governor of California, had a standard joke for public appearances: hippie protestors, he said (conveniently ignoring the housewives and clergy and businesspeople who also marched against the war), "dress like Tarzan, have hair like Jane, and smell like Cheetah." More seriously, bumper stickers read: "America: Love it or Leave it."

The Vietnam war was only one factor in the fragmentation of America. Race was another. Though national legislation newly guaranteed civil rights, the obstacles to full equality seemed, to many, more obvious and intractable than ever. Many Americans had been affected by the moral power of the civil rights movement, the vision of a just society offered by leaders like Martin Luther King Jr., and the courage and conviction of African Americans who risked their lives to claim rights that most European Americans took for granted. Fire hoses being trained on children during civil rights protests in Birmingham, Alabama, along with countless other scenes of racist violence, caused many to question the status quo. Young people, especially, were moved to take action. In the summer of 1964 more than a thousand white students joined black volunteers in Mississippi on a "Freedom Summer" project to register African Americans to vote. Civil Rights organizations like the Congress of Racial Equality (CORE) and the Student Nonviolent Coordinating Committee (SNCC) garnered national support and membership, but old ways of life and old hatreds died hard. Change was slow, in the North as well as in the South.

Frustrated, many African American activists began to reject what they saw as white-dominated organizations and the gradualist tenets of nonviolence. The integrationist dreams of the early civil rights movement were increasingly replaced by angry shouts of "Black Power," and by separatist visions that included armed resistance. By the late 1960s it had become painfully obvious that "race" was not just a southern problem, as cities throughout the nation exploded in flames. In 1965 Los Angeles's black ghetto, Watts, had burned for six days and six nights following a confrontation between white police officers and a young black man they had pulled over for a traffic violation. In 1967 race riots or rebellions took place in 167 cities; three square miles of Detroit burned, and 43 people were killed, most by National Guardsmen. After the assassination of Dr. Martin Luther King Jr. in 1968, rage and sorrow spilled into violence. In more than 130 cities black ghettos burned. Television cameras captured the devastation, with scenes of young men throwing Molotov cocktails and grinning looters filling shopping carts and rampaging through streets, smashing and burning as they went. Fear gripped the nation. Parents kept their children home from school, and even in white suburbs far from the burning ghettos some residents barricaded their houses for safety against the riots they were watching on TV.

To some young people, raised in relative affluence, imbued with a Kennedyesqe democratic idealism, and concentrated in the peer cultures of colleges and universities, both the Vietnam war and the long history of racial discrimination served as indictments of America. Some of those men and women embraced radical politics, reinvigorating America's left and attempting to practice "participatory democracy" through organizations like Students for a Democratic Society. By the late 1960s, however, the "Movement," as it was called, had itself splintered and fragmented. Some turned to violence in pursuit of ever more revolutionary goals. It was a small number of people who made bombs and embraced a doctrine of revolution "by any means necessary," but in the eyes of many Americans those few tarred the rest of the Movement with their violent rhetoric and acts.

At the same time, government officials were increasingly ready to use force against protesters. Tear gas was used on campuses throughout the country. Governor Reagan sent the National Guard in full battle gear to clear "People's Park" adjacent to the Berkeley campus. Reagan said flatly: "If it takes a bloodbath, let's get it over with. No more appeasement."[3] In May 1970 Ohio national guardsmen fired more than sixty times into a crowd of about two hundred students protesting America's invasion of Cambodia. Four lay dead. All over America, once again, rage and sorrow turned to violence. Campuses shut down. Buildings burned. Angry students confronted armed troops. Two more students were killed, this time by white Mississippi state troopers firing into a dormitory housing black students at Jackson State College. Most Americans blamed the demonstrators.

Many, perplexed and upset by the divisions that seemed to be tearing their country apart, blamed "the generation gap." Ignoring the fact that most young people were not "radicals" or "hippie protesters" and overlooking the many protesters and critics who were not young adults, they framed the conflict as one of youth against their elders. That version stemmed, in part, from the tactics of "youth" leaders such as the 29-year-old Abbie Hoffman, who warned: "Don't trust anybody over thirty." Nonetheless, a small but highly visible portion of America's young did very publicly and explicitly reject mainstream culture, which some of them summed up in the shorthand term "Amerika." These men and women considered themselves members of a counterculture and struggled to create new communities and forge a culture that rejected materialism and practiced love, not war. The drugs and sexual experiences that were often integral to these cultural experiments outraged many of their fellow citizens.

By the late 1960s America's "youth culture" had come to *look* very much like the counterculture. Long-haired boys and braless girls. Psychedelic music. Pot. Sex. Certainly not everyone fit this mold, but these were the markers of belonging, of being "hip." The counterculture and its style purposely violated the tenets of "respectability." As countercultural style (not always fully associated with its ideological substance) became mainstream youth culture, the styles and behavior that challenged the notion of respectability became increasingly widespread. Those adults who had to manage and control young people, such as high school principals, focused on outward signs: long hair on boys was "disruptive." Such thinking led to many indefensible violations of civil rights, but the instincts behind them were right. Those at the leading edge of the counterculture were cultural radicals who meant to shock and disrupt every bit as much as the political radicals did. By the late 1960s, in fact, the two groups were intertwined and difficult to distinguish. "Total Assault on the Culture," proclaimed one hero of the "conspiracy."

In the summer of 1970 a young man in Lawrence, Kansas, wrote an open letter to his parents, which he published on the front page of the mimeographed underground paper, the *Oread Daily*. "WE ARE A SPOILED GENERATION," he began.

> We have always been comfortable and had everything we really wanted. We are an idealistic generation. YOUR GENERATION IS THE ONE WHICH HAS TRIED TO Surround yourselves with securities and absolutes . . . and so when our idealistic generation wanted to improve upon your absolutes . . . you became defensive of your absolutes. We became defensive of our idealism. And we became *FRUSTRATED!* And we became *ANGRY!* And we are a spoiled generation . . . and your absolutes will *NOT* survive . . . And what becomes of you . . . when they have finally stripped you of . . . absolutes—it's a psychic survival . . . and our standard of sanity is not yours; and our psyches are becoming strong to survive your oppression. You think us crazy—WE ARE! WE ARE CRAZY, HAPPY, DOPE FIENDS, QUEERS, REVOLUTIONARIES, YOU NAME IT! AND I'M YOUR SON, AND I'M CRAZY AS A LOON![4]

America was at war on many fronts.

—

The battles of the sexual revolution in Lawrence cannot be separated from the conflict that suffused the nation. Because battles over sex took place as part of—and in the context of—fundamental struggles over America's culture and its future, the claims and counterclaims of both revolutionaries and their opponents took on greater urgency. Sex was an incendiary issue in itself, but the larger crisis of the age intensified actions and reactions alike. The people of Lawrence were full participants in America's conflicts, and across the political spectrum Lawrence's citizens understood sexual revolution as just one part of an "age of revolution." As these Kansans struggled over the war, and race, and the future of the nation, they created the field on which the battles over sex would be waged.

The confrontations of the Sixties were particularly explosive in Lawrence. People read titillating stories about hippies in national magazines and watched ghettos burn on television, but they did so with no sense of complacency. The streets of Lawrence were tense, its small-town atmosphere explosive. The presence of the university had propelled Lawrence into direct participation in the violence of the age, for the relatively liberal atmosphere and cultural opportunities offered by the university had helped make Lawrence a "congregation point" for many people who did not "fit in" elsewhere, creating a fairly large community of cultural and political radicals. These people, in general, were not welcomed by the townsfolk. For even though KU made Lawrence's radical communities possible, the tensions and conflicts centering around them were not restricted to the campus. In fact, when it came to radical action, KU students ran a poor third to the hippie/freaks who congregated in Lawrence and to African American high school students and their families. Through much of the turbulent era, cries for revolution coexisted at KU with fashion shows for women students and a fraternity-sorority system that could have been lifted from the mid-1950s. But by the end of the 1960s, with National Guardsmen in the streets, everyone in town was enmeshed in the struggles of the age.

While it was certainly because of the university that Lawrence became a regional center for radical politics and cultural experiment, geography had a lot to do with Lawrence's version of the Sixties as well. It was on the "silk route" for drugs, as one former "merchant" wrote later. Huge quantities of drugs passed through the town, moving from both coasts and up from Mexico. "Baghdad on the Kaw," some called Lawrence, with considerably more irony than the *Journal World* had summoned during World War II when it worried about "Reno on the Kaw." Political and cultural radicals alike knew Lawrence was an oasis in the long drive across the country on I-40. Movement people talked about "Highway 40 SDS," for many passed through Lawrence on the trip from coast to coast. Hippie caravans and hitchhikers stopped off for days or weeks in that safe haven on the edge of the West's plains and mountains. "Lawrence was like on the Oregon trail for hippies," someone recalled. And Lawrence people traveled, too—out to California and New York; up to Omaha and Madison. And back. Lawrence was a crossroads.[5]

A vibrant counterculture had grown up in Lawrence by the mid-1960s. Hippies claimed public space and created their own versions of institutions. There were hippie farms and dope fields, and one sociology graduate student lived outside of town in an unheated tepee through the long Kansas winter. But Lawrence proper also had to cope with this new community. Not far from the KU student union was a big old house, painted white (and thus called "The White House") where some members of the counterculture lived—or crashed—and partied. The Rock Chalk Café (really a bar) was a hangout; its owners sold out in disgust after watching their clientele of fraternity boys be replaced by long-haired freaks. Too often things got violent, and they worried about the drugs.

And drugs were everywhere, abundant and cheap. Before 1964 a small number of "bohemians" experimented with peyote and mescaline, but Lawrence's drug scene began to coalesce in the spring of 1965, when the first acid (expensive at five to fifteen dollars a hit) arrived. By 1966 the marijuana plants growing wild in ditches and gullies were being chopped down and used or sold; acid and speed swept through town from the west coast. Some caught "the codeine bug": codeine and beer, and "pow one stoned out zombi stumbling along Oread St.," wrote a contemporary chronicler of the drug scene. By 1968 "the thing leveled out to casual insanity," with cheap acid, psilocybin, cocaine, hash—and good grass from Vietnam and Mexico.[6]

It always surprised visitors from the coasts, not simply the drugs, but the things that happened in Lawrence. In 1966 Ed Sanders (the publisher of *Fuck You: A Magazine of the Arts*) and his band, The Fugs, came out to visit from New York because Sanders was impressed with one of Lawrence's poetry magazines. Walking around town late one night, Sanders encountered another man, completely naked, also walking down the street. The two chatted for a minute, and then each went on his way. As Lawrence people tell the story, Sanders had a revelation: "Well, mercy, the revolution's come."[7]

In the spring of 1968 the Topeka *Capital-Journal* ran a feature piece entitled "A Visit to Kansas Hippieland." The article was sympathetic in its way, assuring Kansas readers that although long hair and "way out" clothes are not unusual among the hippies, "daily baths are an accepted and expected occurrence": "If anything can summarize the Kansas 'hippie,' it is an alienation from some aspect of society and an obsessive compulsion to 'do your own thing.' The 'thing' may be simply sex and drugs, or a genuine desire to expand creative or humanitarian interests." The article's hook, however, was the idea of the heartland. In this Bible Belt midwestern town, the reporter asked, referring to Lawrence, "are Kansas hippies really hippies? Or are they just outside agitators?"[8]

The question had some validity. Kansas hippies and the politicos and poets who preceded them in Lawrence's nascent counterculture belonged to a national culture. What the reporter found in Lawrence were local versions of national phenomena. A short-lived chapter of SDS was formed in Lawrence in 1963, then again in 1964, and yet again in 1965, when the organization's secretary turned out to be an infiltrator from the right-wing Minutemen and the group gained attention through the "Student Responsibility Movement." The *Kansas Free Press* began publishing in 1964—the same year as the *L.A. Free Press*—and one of its editors took a year out to publish the *San Diego State Free Press* before returning to Lawrence. Other underground papers followed, and they "belonged" to the Liberation News Service or the Underground Press Syndicate, reporting on the scene in Lawrence ("dope!") but freely appropriating articles and art from the uncopyrighted underground press around the nation.

And the university was (yes, inadvertently) crucial to the counterculture's development. Some of the major poets of the era spent time "in residence," brought to Lawrence by members of the English department or by the student union activities board. Allen Ginsberg's visit in 1966 was profiled in *Life* magazine. The Black Mountain poets were major influences—Ed Dorn wrote portions of his "Gunslinger" epic in Lawrence, as well as a tribute to "The Great White Dog of the Rock Chalk Café"—and the small poetry magazines *Grist* and later *Tansy* had close connections to Ed Sanders and the East Village scene in New York City.[9] Just like the American Medical Association or the American Historical Association, the counterculture offered its own nationally based identity. It's just that the credentials were different.

But while Lawrence's "community" comprised that not-unusual university-town conglomeration of politics, poetry, protest, drugs, sex, and rock 'n' roll, it was definitely *of* Kansas. A darkly powerful oral history of the "Kaw Valley Hemp Pickers," *Cows Are Freaky When They Look at You*, makes the point: "The love-and-flowers angle of the Haight-Ashbury didn't ever happen here. Kansas hippies came from places like Hugoton, Bird City, Tonganoxie and Ulysses. Just two years before, they'd been driving the square and fighting. They might have been the nastiest guy in Garden City or somewhere. They were not lightweights. Creeps, but not lightweights." While only a portion of the hippies and freaks met that description, an undertone of violence runs through many recollections of the era. Perhaps it was partly the drug business. Pot grew wild in the fertile soil of the Kaw

(Kansas) River Valley. People argued about whether it had been carried up from Texas in the hooves of cattle during the cattle drives of the last century, or whether it was what remained from the hemp midwestern farmers had grown for rope during World War II. It was low-grade marijuana, ditchweed at best—in fact, in his capacity as public health officer, Dr. Clinton reported that he'd had samples analyzed and found no active principle whatsoever. But it could be used to cut the good stuff, and it was a cash crop, there for the harvesting.[10]

In February 1970 the CBS program *60 Minutes* did a show on the Kaw Valley Hemp Pickers. It was a classic case of the straight world missing the joke: the "Hemp Pickers" was not exactly an organization. But Lawrence appeared on national TV in "footage suffused with a vague menace," the pickers portrayed as a "gang of new-age Daltons," guns very much in evidence. The media attention provoked a crisis in the community, but the macho image suited many. It was overstated but accurate enough. Lawrence was not Berkeley or Haight-Ashbury, and those specific local cultures didn't translate well. A be-in scheduled at the university's Potter Lake in April 1968 drew only sixty people to the slightly forced celebration. An attempted university-wide strike in spring 1970 fizzled, prompting Abbie Hoffman—who was there purely by coincidence—to jeer at the "marshmallow strike." (Hoffman alienated practically everyone in Lawrence: he opened his visit with an announcement that he hadn't had a bath in four months, got into an altercation with members of the black student union, and blew his nose into an American flag. He departed with words that are now classic in Lawrence: "This place is a fucking drag, man, I'm going to Dallas.") Instead, Kansas's autochthonic countercultural event was the Big Eat, an annual "drug'n'drink'n'fuck picnic . . . where they smoked, dropped, drank, shot up and competed for most-stoned honors in the Kansas Death March."[11]

Lawrence's counterculture included gentle visionaries and charismatic psychotics and a whole lot of people who, in the spirit of the age, were experimenting with new ways of life. To a great many of their fellow citizens, however, they all looked dangerous as they took over public spaces and visibly "countered" the mainstream culture. In their words and actions (sex not the least of them), the hip community and its self-proclaimed "outlaws" rejected the world so many of Lawrence's people had worked hard to build. The townspeople's concern—and anger—about the hippies and freaks went well beyond provincial fear of difference fed by sensationalist stories in the national media. On home turf, these groups were engaged in a struggle for the future of their town and their nation.

—

Proximity to Interstate 40 was not the only geographic factor that shaped Lawrence's "Sixties." In the nineteenth century, as the United States had expanded steadily westward, the balance between slave and free states had become increasingly problematic. Kansas, too far north for cotton cultivation, survived years of violence as an abolitionist stronghold on the edge of the slaveholding South and entered the Union in 1861 as a free state—"The Free State" was the Kansas state motto. Lawrence, from the mid-nineteenth century, had attracted a population of free blacks and freedmen and women. But in the twentieth century Lawrence's permanent black residents—as was common throughout the country—were much more likely than whites to live in substandard housing, to drop out of school, to be poor.

147

The university, founded in 1866, admitted its first black student in 1870; two hundred African Americans attended KU between 1870 and 1910. But generally progressive attitudes faded with the advent of Jim Crow in the South and a hardening of racial lines in the nation. By 1910 the university was enforcing segregation at concerts, at sports events, and in student housing. When a new student union was built in 1927, it had a separate cafeteria for blacks. Downtown, most restaurants and cafés refused to serve Lawrence's black population. The KU student body voted in 1943 to allow black students to attend university dances, but discrimination persisted both on campus and off. In 1947 several KU students formed an interracial Lawrence chapter of CORE. Twenty-five members staged a sit-in at one of the town's restaurants the following spring. Other students threw them out.[12]

Gradually KU began to provide some leadership. In the mid-1950s Chancellor Franklin D. Murphy threatened to show first-run movies without charge on campus unless Lawrence movie theaters stopped segregating their audiences by race. This tactic worked, and segregation in theaters and restaurants diminished. But in the early 1960s members of KU's Civil Rights Council (CRC) were still battling discrimination by Lawrence businesses, especially private landlords, and facing down discriminatory practices on campus as well. Dormitory assignments were made on the basis of race, as were student teaching assignments for education majors. Fraternities and sororities held the color line with tacit approval from the upper administration, and the university officially approved off-campus housing that denied equal access to black students. In the spring of 1965 members of the CRC, frustrated by years of vague promises and very slow change, occupied the chancellor's office. Though 110 people were briefly arrested and almost as briefly suspended, the CRC won its battle, making significant gains for racial equality on campus. By the end of the 1960s KU, like many American universities, funded an "Afro House" for black students and townspeople and had created a Black Studies department. By the end of the decade, as well, a radical Black Student Union (BSU) had replaced groups like the interracial CRC on KU's campus. BSU members were fond of quoting Malcolm X: "If someone lays a hand on you, send him to the cemetery." Some members bought guns, arming themselves in "self-defense." The BSU worked to promote Black Power not only on campus but also in the black community of Lawrence, fostering a black student union at Lawrence High School and creating town-gown coalitions for radical action.[13]

Many of Lawrence's African-American citizens saw the need for some sort of action, if not precisely the "self-defense" program advocated by the BSU. Economic and social disadvantage and discrimination had not disappeared with national legislation and federal programs. In 1970 Lawrence had 403 "Negro" families, in addition to its African-American students and other single adults. Of these families, 94 were "female-headed" and 108 fell below the poverty line; 51 of the 84 families receiving public assistance were African American.

Efforts to ameliorate poverty became enmeshed in conflict, however, and a multiracial welfare rights organization, developed with federal funding through the Office of Economic Opportunity and assistance from KU, had its building firebombed by a second (all-black) group in what the first group labeled an attempt at extortion. Black high school students, embracing Black Power doctrines, walked out of classrooms in 1968—a move supported by most of their parents and many local church groups. While they were protesting a general climate of discrimination in America, the students' demands were local: mainly they wanted black cheerleaders, a black homecoming queen, and courses on black history. There were vague promises, good intentions, bad faith, and much stalling. Not much was resolved. Emotions ran high. Lawrence was caught up in the racial turmoil of the era, and in its level of conflict, sometimes looked like a city ten times its size.[14]

148

Of course, Lawrence was not only a black-and-white town. There were 154 Hispanic families living there in 1970, and more than half again as many American Indians as African Americans residing there, though most were students at Haskell Indian Junior College. Native Americans were probably more likely to be discriminated against in town than were blacks by the late 1960s. Owners of several taverns flatly refused to serve Indians, citing, as justification, problems with drunkenness. Even though more than half of the Haskell students surveyed in a 1973 poll said they had experienced "prejudice" in Lawrence, a great majority rejected militant tactics and an even greater majority—four to one—disapproved of the tactics and goals of A.I.M., the American Indian Movement. In 1970, as calls for Red Power spread through the nation, Haskell students did not participate in Lawrence's upheaval.[15]

—

The "days of rage" in Lawrence began on Monday, April 13, 1970.[16] Shortly before the end of the school day, a group of about one hundred black students took over the administration office at Lawrence High School. They issued demands that were substantially the same as those black high school students had made three years before: a black cheerleader, a black homecoming queen, black literature courses for all grades, fair elections for school offices. They also demanded that the school hire ten new black teachers, "not those colored teachers we have now." Young men from the university's BSU showed up. When the high school students refused to return to class, the principal called the police, describing the group as "disrupting business and generally raising hell." The next day tensions mounted. Young black men who weren't students appeared on the Lawrence High campus. Stories about their intentions vary, but that day ten students were suspended and four other young men were arrested. A few fights broke out between black and white students the next day, and when police arrived some of the black students scuffled with them. There were injuries, none serious.

That night, however, the arson began. A downtown building was torched in a quarter-of-a-million-dollar blaze. A store was broken into, and the rumor circulated that guns and ammunition were stolen. The situation was worse at the high school the next day, with another confrontation between black students and the police. The school board voted to close the school on Friday to give things a chance to cool down. Meanwhile, someone called elementary and junior high schools with bomb threats. Parents were worried about their children's safety. The police were jumpy. By this time the whole town was jittery and watchful.

Most of the black students stayed home from school on Monday, April 20, and that night black parents walked out of a school board meeting. At 9:13 P.M. someone firebombed the high school administration offices. Firefighters responding to the call were met with sniper fire but managed to extinguish the flames. Shots were fired at several Lawrence businesses and at the Santa Fe Railroad depot. The KU campus had been quiet during all this conflict, but shortly after 10:30 the university's student union began to burn. By the time the 40,000-square-foot building was reduced to a smoldering wreck, Lawrence was officially in a state of public emergency. The governor instituted a curfew, suspended sales of gasoline, liquor, and guns, and sent state highway patrolmen to back up Lawrence's small police force.

At this point Lawrence's freaks and street people got involved. Gathering outside the Rock Chalk Café on the edge of campus, they defied the curfew order. Police were met with a barrage of bricks and bottles. As dark fell, the fires started. Lawrence's most visible hippie house, "the White House" near the Rock Chalk Café, began to blaze. Snipers kept the fire trucks away. An elementary school burned down. The governor sent in the National Guard.

During daylight hours police and national guardsmen searched houses—not in the predominately black section of town, but in the hippie enclave near the university. They violated all manner of due process laws, but didn't find much. Forty-five people were arrested. Six more fires were set that night; streetlights were shot out by snipers. But gradually the momentum receded, and an uneasy truce began. The hip community gathered Saturday, May 2, for the annual "Big Eat."

But events on the national scene interrupted the fragile peace. On Monday, May 4, panicky national guardsmen at Kent State killed four students at a protest over Nixon's invasion of Cambodia. Kent State became the flashpoint for action throughout the nation. Students at 350 colleges and universities went on strike, and protests closed down more than 500 campuses. Governors called out the national guard to quell riots on university campuses in 16 states. Buildings burned, and tear gas lingered long after the crowds dispersed.[17] At KU, where no major organized protest had greeted Nixon's announcement of the Cambodian invasion, students and professors gathered at the burned-out hulk of the union building and marched to the National Guard armory, bearing four coffins.

A new part of the Lawrence community had become engaged. After Kent State, KU students became fully involved in the struggles preoccupying the town. Each day the demonstrations grew larger, though only one night brought significant violence. Members of the university community called on Chancellor Chalmers to close KU, as many other universities had shut down in recognition of the tragedy in Ohio. The governor, however, threatened to send in the National Guard to keep KU open. In the end, after masterly political maneuvering on the part of the administration, KU adopted what was known as the Rhode Island plan. Students might, on the grounds of individual conscience, decline to participate in a university they believed should be closed. As it was already finals week, that meant that they might refuse to take final exams without forfeiting class credit. KU stayed open; the National Guard troops stayed away. The *Journal World* congratulated the administration for a job well done.[18]

As students dispersed when the semester ended that May, Lawrence went into summer mode. Without most of the students, it seemed more like a small town, quiet and slow under the hot summer sun. But the events of the spring had polarized Lawrence. If three-fourths of America's citizens opposed the student protests following Kent State, that same population in Lawrence felt doubly—or even triply—angry. A Lawrence physician, citing the disturbances, publicly proclaimed himself in favor of Kansas's newly liberalized abortion laws: "I think we have a whole generation of unwanted children—hippies, Yippies, drug addicts, outcasts. They are just not with society and I think they were unwanted pregnancies, generally. I think we should do something about this." And in a more practical critique the *Journal World* noted that some KU students and faculty seemed to be "following a case book on, 'How to alienate the public and members of the state legislature.'"[19]

At this point, some of the more politically oriented and astute members of Lawrence's counterculture attempted to organize an alliance between freaks and some university folk modeled after the "Ann Arbor tribe" created in Michigan by the countercultural hero John Sinclair. The Lawrence Liberation Front, as they called themselves, made some headway in establishing productive alliances, though much of their energy was spent trying to cope with the internal fault lines of gender and sexual orientation. They started a paper, the *Oread Daily*. (That its initials were "O.D.," slang for "overdose," did not escape notice.) One of their number ran for sheriff, another for justice of the peace. But barely submerged tensions began to interrupt the usually quiet summer days, and Lawrence became a standard example in state-of-the-nation media reports. The *Los Angeles Times* noted: "The possibility that vigilante groups will take up arms is a feature of life here that bothers many blacks, the large colony of long haired self termed 'freaks' and people on the University of Kansas campus." The *Journal World* (quoting the *Times*) disclosed the existence of a "secret organization" ready to intervene if violence broke out again.[20]

And on the night of July 16, it did. A black man sitting on the porch of Lawrence's Afro House was wounded by buckshot; a white woman not far away was shot in the leg. Gunfire was reported at an elementary school on Lawrence's predominately poor east side, and Lawrence police responding were met with sniper fire. Patrolmen Kennard Avey and William Garret said later that they had pursued two suspects from the scene to the Afro House, and then followed a man and woman who emerged from Afro House and drove away in a Volkswagen. Accounts of the next few minutes vary greatly, but the outline is this: the police car attempted to pull the VW over, and the driver ignored the demand until she accidentally ran up on a curb. Her passenger, Rick "Tiger" Dowdell, a BSU member and Lawrence resident, got out of the car and walked/ran/fled into an alley. Police officer/pig William Garrett followed him. Dowdell pulled a gun/Dowdell had no gun. Garrett fired a warning shot but when Dowdell fired at him the police officer responded with three rounds, one of which killed Dowdell/There was a single shot and Dowdell lay dead in the alley.

Lawrence erupted. On the east side of town a police officer was shot and another's patrol car damaged by shotgun blasts. The house of a district court judge was firebombed, and things started to burn where the hippies and freaks hung out. When patrol cars tried to enter the area they were bombarded with firecrackers, bottles, and bricks. Talk of vigilante action became louder. On Monday night, four days after Dowdell was shot, police used tear gas to disperse a crowd of about 150 that had gathered outside the Rock Chalk Café to watch a brush fire that had been set across the street. Police officers with buckshot-loaded shotguns herded the remaining freaks into the Rock Chalk. When the freaks emerged from the Rock Chalk a little later, direct action recommenced. A few men rolled over a red VW bug in the middle of the street—its owner, the story goes, had asked them to torch her car because she needed the insurance money. This justification was not obvious to the police. They moved in, guns ready. Shooting began. Buck-shot and carbine slugs were found later. And two young men fell, one shot through the leg and the other, an 18-year-old in town to visit his girlfriend and pay a parking ticket, dead on arrival at Lawrence Memorial Hospital. The university bulldozed the White House, symbolic center of sex, drugs, and revolution, and put up a parking lot. It was over.

After violence and death in their own streets, revolution was not an abstract concept to the people of Lawrence. They understood the stakes in the cultural struggles racking America all too well. So as some of Lawrence's people sought a "sexual revolution"—a transformation in which sex was both a weapon of revolution and its subject—their claims of revolutionary intent were not made or taken lightly. In the midst of crisis, Lawrence's people understood that the battles over sex were part of the war over America's future.

6

Sex as a Weapon

In July 1965 the Lawrence chapter's delegate, Eileen Wilcox, returned from the national meeting of the Congress of Racial Equality (CORE) in Durham, North Carolina, with grave concerns. She was upset by the intensifying effort to push whites out of the civil rights movement; she was horrified by the open advocacy of violent tactics; and, most of all, she was angry about the role sex had played in the conference. "Perhaps the most unsavory element in CORE and other civil rights organizations is the sexually motivated minority, i.e., those who use the libertarian atmosphere of the civil rights movement to satisfy their own sexual frustrations," Wilcox, who was white and married, wrote in the *Kansas Free Press*. "People in civil rights organizations are willing to elevate the political, social, and moral tone of our society. Whenever a large group of mostly unattached young men and women get together, a certain amount of sexual promiscuity is expected. It was distressing, however, to note the grossness and blatancy on the part of some of the people inspired by those high ideals and committed to improving society. A few people can do a great deal of harm to the public image of the movement."[1]

In the wake of the Freedom Summer of 1964, as sexual relations took place across racial lines among the volunteers, racial-sexual tensions did disrupt the interracial community of civil rights workers. Some blamed white women, others blamed black men. Many women saw it as less a problem of race than one of gender: when the black activist and Student Nonviolent Coordinating Committee member Stokely Carmichael quipped in 1964, "The position of women in SNCC is prone," his words served as a lightning rod for feminist anger at sexual discrimination and the sexual exploitation of movement women by movement men, black or white.[2] Wilcox's objection, however, belonged to a different tradition. She wasn't concerned about the sexual exploitation of women; she was appalled by the "promiscuity." She was also worried that what she saw as a heedless disregard for sexual morality would compromise hard-won public support for social justice movements.

Some of America's most prominent and committed activists—Tom Hayden, for one—would share her concern, especially when it came to the growing counterculture. Most members of the New Left, who were, in 1965, political but not cultural radicals, did not see sex as a tool of revolution. They sought political solutions to injustice and inequality; sex seemed beside the point. No matter their private sexual behavior, these politically oriented leaders were suspicious of the hip community's embrace of pleasure, believing that the mantra of sex and drugs and rock 'n' roll would only undermine the Movement's "serious" goals. But well before the end of the decade, most of them understood that the cultural revolutionaries were not heedlessly indulging their "sexual frustrations," as Wilcox had believed of her fellow civil rights workers. For no matter how heedless individual couplings might be, the role of sex in parts of the Movement was highly purposeful.

Some very visible portions of America's youth embraced sex with revolutionary intent, using it not only for pleasure but also for power in a new form of cultural politics that shook the nation. As those who threw themselves into the "youth revolution" (a label that arose in the 1960s but did not stick) knew so well, the struggle for America's future would take place not within the structure of electoral politics but on the battlefield of cultural meaning.

For some, sex itself became a moral claim, a way of distancing oneself from mainstream or "straight" society, of inverting the moral hierarchy that labeled war a just pursuit and sent people to jail for making love.

> Is it obscene to fuck,
> or,
> Is it obscene to kill?

asked a poem in one underground paper. All over the country, young people embraced variants of "Make Love, Not War." Lawrence's hip community made the same moral claims, but with a marked lack of faith. On the pages of a late 1969 issue of Lawrence's underground newspaper *Vortex,* a man and woman frolic naked in an autumn meadow. Three photos surround a poem about the goodness of the body ("body good/smell nice") and its potential for redemption:

> all get naked
> all get good.
> See enemy naked
> can't hide
> can't lie
> can't hate naked
> squat
> take shit together
> understand
> look at knees
> and ass
> no fear
> just love
> just naked
> just

In the third photo, aligned with "take shit together," the naked man sits on a toilet (yes, in the meadow), with the woman on his lap. Not sex; the distance between their genitals would satisfy the chaperon at a 1950s high school dance. And the toilet lid is down. But the porcelain toilet in the dry grass compromises the promise of redemption through nature. This community was not naively romantic.[3]

For many who embraced an alternative culture, sex was celebration, liberation from the deadening rules of a society gone badly wrong. John Sinclair, around whom a "community of artists and lovers" coalesced near Detroit, placed sex at the center of his group's "Total Assault on the Culture." "There are three essential human activities of the greatest importance to all persons," he wrote in 1968, " and . . . people are well and healthy in proportion to their involvement in these activities: rock and roll, dope, and fucking in the streets."[4]

His claim was outrageous, and that was partly its point, but it was also an element of a coherent philosophy. "Fucking," according to Sinclair, helped one to "escape the hangups that are drilled into us in this weirdo country"; it helped to destroy an economy of pain and scarcity. Writing in an underground newspaper, the *Sun,* he argued:

> Our position is that all people must be free to fuck freely, whenever and wherever they want to, or not to fuck if they don't wanna—in bed, on the floor, on the streets, in the parks and fields, "back seat boogie for the high school kids" sing the Fugs who brought it all out in the open on stage and on records, fuck whoever wants to fuck you and everybody else do the same. America's silly sexual "mores" are the end-product of thousands of years of deprivation and sickness, of marriage and companionship based on the ridiculous misconception that one person can "belong" to another person, that "love" is something that has to do with being "hurt," sacrificing, holding out, "teardrops on your pillow," and all that shit.[5]

Sinclair was not alone in his paean to copulation. Other countercultural seekers believed that they had to remake love and reclaim sex in order to create a new and honest community, free from the hangups of "Amerika." These few struggled, with varying degrees of honesty and sincerity, with the significance of sex in the world they meant to create.

For some of these people, including Sinclair, sex was not only part of a new philosophy; it was also a weapon against the society they rejected. In the spring of 1968 the revolutionary potential of sex also suffused the claims of the Yippies, who merged political and cultural radicalism as they worked to stage a "Festival of Life" to counter the "Death Convention" (the Democratic National Convention) in Chicago. "How can you separate politics and sex?" Jerry Rubin asked with indignation. The Yippies lived by that creed. Sex was a double-edged sword, to be used two ways. Sex was a lure to youth; it was part of an attempt by the more political strand of the counterculture to tap the youth market, to "sell a revolutionary consciousness."[6] They reasoned that young people drawn by "sex and drugs and rock 'n' roll" would discover a new politics through the practice of freedom. For the Yippies, however, sex was also a challenge thrown in the face of "Amerika."

The first Yippie manifesto, released in January 1968, summoned the tribes to Chicago. It played well in the underground press, with its promise of "50,000 of us dancing in the streets, throbbing with amplifiers and harmony . . . making love in the parks." Sex was a politics of pleasure, a politics of abundance that made sense to young middle-class whites who had been raised in relative affluence, in the world without limits that was postwar America. Sex was also incendiary, and the Yippies knew that well. It guaranteed attention. Thus the "top secret" plans for the convention that Abbie Hoffman mimeographed and distributed to the press promised a barbecue and lovemaking by the lake, followed by "Pin the Tail on the Donkey," "Pin the Rubber on the Pope," and "other normal and healthy games." Grandstanding before a crowd of Chicago reporters, the Yippies presented a city official with an official document wrapped in a *Playboy* centerfold inscribed, "To Dick with love, the Yippies." As a symbolic act, presenting the centerfold did not proffer freedom so much as challenge authority. It was a sign of disrespect—to Mayor Richard Daley and to straight America.[7]

Most of America's youth were not revolutionaries, political or cultural. On the political side, SDS (for example) had only about 100,000 members at its height, and completely disintegrated with the rise of the tiny, violent Weathermen faction in 1969. On the cultural side, few completely "dropped out." As Todd Gitlin wrote in his soul-searching memoir of the Sixties, "There were many more weekend dope-smokers than hard-core 'heads'; many more readers of the *Oracle* than writers for it; many more co-habitors than orgiasts; many more turners-on than droppers-out."[8] Probably only a few thousand committed themselves completely to cultural revolution, but hundreds of thousands lived on the fringes of the counterculture and still thought of themselves as hippies or freaks or heads. By the late 1960s the symbols of countercultural identity had become virtually synonymous with those of youth culture. Just as in the 1920s bobbed hair and "petting parties" and jazz symbolized one's membership in the culture of youth, by the end of the 1960s it was long hair and drugs and rock music and sex. So even though many more young people participated in these "essential activities" as symbols of generational identity rather than as part of a "total assault on the culture," the potency of the symbols lay in opposition to the world of their parents, and that of straight America. As such, sex was more than the private pursuit of love or pleasure. It was the weapon of choice for a generation that was—as everyone knew—in revolt.

—

In November 1966 Lawrence got its first real underground paper, *The Screw*. Saved from vulgarity by "The," which transformed a troublesome verb into "a twisted device for holding things together," as the first editorial statement proclaimed, *The Screw* at first seemed less offensive than its immediate campus predecessor, *Squat.* From 1914 through 1958 KU students had published humor magazines that were university-funded but always on the verge of being banned by the administration. The *Sour Owl,* which was begun in 1914 by the Owl Society, a semi-secret men's honor society, provided dirty jokes and raunchy cartoons for over four decades, occasionally disappearing when it went too far beyond the boundaries of "good taste." In 1956 its coed staff put out an issue that provoked cries of outrage in the *Journal World,* though its mix of tasteless jokes and illustrations was not, on the face of it, worse than usual. KU's dean of students sent an official reprimand to all who played an "active part in this inexcusable publication," complaining that the last issue had been "received with strong disfavor if not downright disgust by the vast majority of sensitive and discerning readers." *Sour Owl's* replacements, the *Bitter Bird* and *Squat,* looked much like the *Sour Owl* ("Squatty Joke: Sigma Chi: 'Do you know what virgins dream about?' Theta: 'No, what?' Sigma Chi: 'I suspected as much.'"). By the late 1950s the campus humor magazines had run out of steam, replaced by national publications like *Playboy* (with special campus subscriptions advertised in the *Daily Kansan*) and *Mad.*[9]

While sex was the obsessive topic of these magazines, which worked very hard to offend, this was sex as dirty joke, sex as key to the eternal war of the sexes. The war the staff of *The Screw* meant to wage was not that of the sexes; for the brief moment between the partial demise of the double standard and the rise of a feminist consciousness in Lawrence's counterculture, sex seemed to be what united, rather than divided, men and women. *The Screw,* as "a serious independent weekly community paper," claimed its purpose was to bring together the "interlocking cliques" of Lawrence's "underground scene," and through "chemicals, . . . Rock, . . . and guiltless sex," to "help blow that *death* out of people's minds." Similarly, when African-American students at Lawrence High School planned a "Black Heritage Week" in early 1970, they also claimed sexual freedom as a means to community. "'Soul: the antidote to puritanism,' is the theme which should be remembered,' said Miss Collins, the [Black American] Club's president," reported the *Kansan.*[10]

Building community through "guiltless sex" demanded public claims to sexual freedom. In 1967, when one could not say "damn" on television and even "mild" nudity was forbidden, *The Screw's* centerfold featured a stylized drawing of ancient Egyptians superimposed over a list of eighty sexual acts, beginning with "The man leaning forward, receiving between his thighs the woman lying on her back, her legs stretched out," moving through "Copulation with a male quadruped," to the final possibility: "Three spintries: a cunnilingator is irrumated."[11] Transcending the repressive traditions of Western civilization? In the tradition of bohemians and beats, these new rebels attempted to define their community not only by celebrating sex but by shocking and offending outsiders.

Another presentation of *The Screw*'s message began: "People in Omaha don't fuck. People in Omaha are too damn old or hung-up to fuck." Of course, "people in Omaha don't know who Paul Krassner is," either. "Do you know who Paul Krassner is?" No? "Ask the librarian; if she doesn't know, pinch her tit." The librarian, like the Yippies' Pope, stood for repression and dried-up sexuality. In a different vein, KU's Black Student Union (in 1970, shortly before the violence began, full of talk about guns) used a language of sexuality to attack whites and white culture. When the BSU attempted to wrest power and funds from Penn House, a multiracial organization of low-income people partially funded by KU, it adopted the homophobic language sanctioned by the Black Panther Eldridge Cleaver. An unsigned article in the BSU newspaper *Harambee* threatened the white director of Penn House, Keith Miller: "This peckerwood faggot and faggots like him have to be treated like mad dogs, and removed from the Black Community by whatever means necessary." *Harambee* also offered "Revolutionary Poetry": "an eye for an eye / a tooth for a tooth / don't worry bout his balls / they al / ready gone," wrote sonia sanchez. "What a white woman got," asked another poet, "except her white pussy / always sucking after blk / ness . . . what a white woman got / cept her faggoty white man / who goes to sleep in her / without / coming." "Pin the Rubber on the Pope." "Pinch her tit." "Peckerwood faggot." This is not about the redemptive power of sex. This is sex as a weapon.[12]

In fundamental ways, the weapon was well-chosen, for sexual explicitness and "obscenity" upset people like little else. "Obscene" language in a poem published in the university-funded *Harambee* prompted employees of the University of Kansas Printing Service to walk off the job in protest.[13] When they contacted the chancellor's office for advice, the employees were told that the university did not practice censorship. If the paper arrived with the proper voucher and paperwork, the printing service was obliged to print it. The employees, who said they feared they would be held liable for printing obscene material, received permission to appeal to the state attorney general for a ruling on the material in question.

While the employees' concerns about litigation and liability may have been reasonable given that the paper was paid for with public funds and many members of the public were suspicious of the goings-on at KU, public comments made by these workers show more complicated motivations. One employee, a KU senior from Lawrence, believed the BSU should have its own newspaper. This particular issue of *Harambee,* however, dealt "with subject matter of obscene words and ideas that not only contradicts human beings but our whole morality. If we print a paper like this then there are not moral or ethical codes to live by." An older man said: "I don't think we have to publish this filth. They talk about cleaning up our streets and cities, why not clean up our speech?" BSU members insisted that the words in question were "functional terms in the black community" and argued that it didn't matter if they were offensive to "white middle class standards." One of the poems began:

> Hey, all you
> white-cocksuckers
> you jive-time
> mother fuckers
> that call your-
> self men.

Attorney General Frizzell ruled that the publication was not legally obscene according to the standards of *Roth v. United States.* In this landmark 1957 decision, sometimes known as the *Fanny Hill* case, the Supreme Court had ruled that for material to be legally obscene it must appeal to a prurient interest in sex, be patently offensive to community standards, and be utterly without redeeming social value. Frizzell allowed that *Harambee* was patently offensive to community standards, "the language employed . . . customarily reserved for the graffiti found in public restrooms." However, he concluded, "by no stretch of the imagination does it appeal to a 'prurient interest' in sex. The effect is probably quite the opposite."

Countless such struggles over freedom of expression went on in America during this era. Compared to actors in many such controversies that involved public funds, both the University of Kansas and the Kansas attorney general came down squarely in support of First Amendment rights. But their decisions are not what is most significant here. *Harambee* was a revolutionary organ. Its writers and editors were in full attack mode, not only in the talk of "peckerwood faggots" and "white-cocksuckers," but in calls to armed revolution. The issue to which the Printing Service employees objected was full of exhortations to violence. "Free All Politicalfl Prisoners" was the caption to a drawing of a gun. "Politics, as Brother Mao emphasizes," one article concluded, "grows out of the barrel of a gun." But it was "motherfuckers" and "cocksuckers" that provoked the visceralfteactions, the condemnations of "filth," not the detailing of who was going to be "offed when the / time comes for the / thing to come down / Bang————————." Sex was a potent weapon, stronger than even threats of violence.

In the underground press the constant use of vulgar and "obscene" words for sexual acts and organs thus assumed a political urgency. "In the 10th minute of the final hour the Daughters of the American Revolution applied lipstick to their cunts and mascara to their pubic hairs," wrote Azrael (who usually did the recipe column—homemade yogurt, bread, cannabis tea—in *Vortex*) in a dismissive aside about the irrelevancy of *Vortex*'s book reviews "in the last minute of the final hour."[14]

The word "fuck" appeared everywhere: the words "FUCK THE DRAFT" scribbled on a small sheet of paper by the future Yippie and Democratic candidate for sheriff George Kimball got him arrested in a 1965 protest march.[15] *Vortex* kept the community apprised of scheduled "Fuck trials": "On January 8 [1969], Ed Aker will stand trial for the nefarious crime of saying FUCK in front of the Rock Chalk . . . January 30, John Brazee will take to the courts in defense of his criminal use of FUCK." And the *Students Free Press* at Lawrence High School accorded great power to this short word. On the cover of the third issue was wild-haired Abbie Hoffman, complete with an admonition to cut out the picture and frame it; several pages later the editor prompted: "If you look closely at the cover picture, you will notice a word on Abbie Hoffman's forehead. (And it isn't *firetruck*.)" The same issue reported that the *Students Free Press* had gotten "state-wide *free* publicity" because a member of the Kansas legislature had attacked it for "peddling smut." Students from all over Kansas had then written to Lawrence High for copies of the paper: "They dig it!" Publicity aside, the author was appalled. "I am beginning to wonder just what these men are doing in Topeka, " he wrote. "Certainly intelligent people don't fall for that crap that four letter words are going to destroy the Country?" And pulling out the standard moral line: "Perhaps four letter words will destroy this nation, but you can rest assured that those four letter words like: bomb, kill, hate, and maim. No one needs to worry about smut when words like these are still in our vocabulary."[16]

The lure of the four-letter word was complex. The transgression was a rush at first: think back to the late nineteenth century, when a glimpse of ankle was sexually charged. Moreover, those in the counterculture valued an earthy authenticity they placed at odds with civility, politeness, and convention. "Fuck" was not polite. But more than anything else, "fuck" got attention. John Thompson, who was arrested for standing at the corner of Bancroft and Telegraph in Berkeley holding a sign bearing his "one-word poem" ("FUCK"—later amended to the active verb "FUCK!") said: "I could walk around this campus for weeks with a sign that said MURDER or SHOOT or KILL and no one would pay the least attention. I write this one little word and BAM, into jail I go."[17] There was power in that word, and not simply because some claimed it was the moral opposite of words like "kill" or "hate." No one would have paid the least attention on Bancroft and Telegraph if Thompson's sign had read "LOVE" or even "MAKE LOVE!" The Kansas legislator would have ignored the *Students Free Press* if the thousands of words complaining about cafeteria food and repressive rules and stultifying classes had not been strengthened by the single word "fuck." Writing "fuck" was the verbal equivalent of throwing a bomb.

"Fuck" was thus the verbal frame used by Lawrence's revolutionary White Panther Party to announce the candidacy of its "defense minister," George Kimball, for Douglas County sheriff. "The youth of Kansas are fed up, are *fucking fed up* with political diatribe . . . George Kimball represents a change." Handwritten below the official announcement was the legend "Rock & Roll Dope FUCKING IN THE STREETS."[18]

In the spring of 1970, with Lawrence in flames, George Kimball had more local countercultural bona fides than almost anyone else. He had come to Lawrence in 1961, when he enrolled at KU on a ROTC scholarship. He dropped out before the end of his first year and spent some time in the East, but was back in Lawrence by 1965. This time he survived less than a full semester at KU before he was kicked out for criminal use of the word "fuck." The full sentence was "FUCK THE DRAFT," written on a piece of paper he displayed at a small protest rally in front of Lawrence's Selective Service Office. For that he was arrested on a charge of "gross public indecency," with bail set at one thousand dollars. This arrest ended his KU career, but he stayed in Lawrence, hanging out at the Rock Chalk, doing some writing and scheming. Along with John Fowler of Lawrence's Abington Bookstore and the poet Charles Plymell, he edited the literary magazine *Grist,* which published work by an eclectic Sixties pantheon of poets and other assorted countercultural folk: Allen Ginsberg, Charles Bukowski, Tuli Kupferberg, Ed Sanders, John Sinclair, Charles Olson, Gary Snyder, Ed Dorn, Kenneth Irby, James McCrary, William Burroughs, even a dreamy nude photo of the poet and Warhol-film actor Gerald Malanga as the "Grist Playmate of the Month . . . suitable for framing to hang on yr bedroom wall." And when the Abington and *Grist* faded from the scene, Kimball moved on to John Moritz's new Tansy bookstore beside the Rock Chalk Café.[19]

Stories abound, some more trustworthy than others. Kimball had smelly feet and a glass eye, which an occasional unwary soul found staring up from the bottom of his beer glass. He wrote a novel "for adult readers" that was published by the Ophelia Press. It was set in Lawrence High School and featured lots of basketball games with (an in-joke) Jim Carroll "scribbling . . . his darned old *Basketball Diaries* . . . whipping his notebook out of his pocket before he reached the bench." And there was a LHS junior girl who thought lines like: "Larry looked *so* handsome in his blue satin warm-up jacket, and I suppressed a passionate shudder when I gazed down at his substantially-bulging white uniform shorts."[20]

In *Cows Are Freaky When They Look at You,* the oral history of Lawrence's counterculture, "Jean Raphael" recalls George ("Hugo") giving her advice: "He said, 'Hey, I hear you write poems. I bet they'd be a lot better if you put more four-letter words in 'em.' He handed me a poem and said, 'Now, see, this is really good. This is politically correct poetry. It says "fuck" here.'"[21] Whether the truth of this memory is metaphoric or literal, "fuck" was a word that determined the directions of Kimball's life.

On July 20, 1970, just minutes before the deadline, 26-year-old George Kimball paid the filing fee of $100.05 and became the Democratic candidate for sheriff of Douglas County. The Democrats had not run anyone against the Republican incumbent in years, and Kimball waited until the last minute so they wouldn't have time to find another candidate. The Douglas County Democrats were livid—and endorsed the Republican.

Kimball, as a Yippie, ran a theatrical campaign. He wore a tin star and brandished a real, if rusty, six-shooter. He had bumper stickers made up with the slogan "Douglas County needs a two-fisted sheriff"—a reference to the incumbent's withered right hand—and when someone complained, he said his own glass eye was fair game. ("Fuck, he can make political hay out of my one eye if he wants to.") When the state attorney general, then a candidate for governor, announced on television that he intended to prevent Kimball from closing down KU (something he'd never said he would do), Kimball called a press conference to announce that the attorney general was a "scurrilous liar" who "harbored a predilection for engaging in unusual activity with livestock." Kimball was attracting a lot of attention. Invited to Wichita to speak to a group of Yippies, he found the local sheriff, Vern Miller, and his deputies already at the rally. Miller, who was running for state office, had promised that his first act as Kansas attorney general would be to "land with both feet in the middle of the drug-ridden hippie community in Lawrence." Before Kimball even began to speak, Miller and the deputies were moving toward the stage. The first time Kimball said "fuck," Miller arrested him on a charge of "violent and obscene language." The arrest made the papers all through the state.

Despite Kimball's outrageous, countercultural appeal, the events of the summer of 1970, with sniper fire in the streets and two young men lying dead, brought the costs of conflict closer to home and made the Yippie theater less compelling. Even most of the hip community had second thoughts about supporting Kimball. In the end *Vortex* refused to endorse him, and some of his best friends decided they couldn't vote for him. On election day Kimball got 13 percent of the vote—and lost every precinct in the county.

However, Phil Hill was elected justice of the peace. Hill was a street person and "dope marketer" who lived in his car in Lawrence's "hippie haven." He (in what the candidates later claimed was a carefully orchestrated scheme) had filed as a Democratic candidate at the same time Kimball filed for sheriff. Justice of the peace was a relatively unimportant office—justices of the peace could perform marriages and hear civil cases claiming damages of less than one dollar—but the filing fee was correspondingly low. Hill's "campaign" was as low-profile as Kimball's was high. Running unopposed, he got the second-highest vote total of any Democrat on the ballot.

With a little encouragement from Kimball, a media circus ensued. Phil Hill, dressed in a borrowed black graduation robe, freely pronounced his judicial philosophy to assembled reporters. His goal, he said, was to establish a "poor people's court." "We've already got one girl who's going to sue her landlord for 99¢ because he called her a prostitute," Hill explained, and added that he intended to impose his maximum 99¢ fine on industrial polluters as well.

Marriage got the biggest play: "We'd like our court to promote sexual liberation. We especially want to see group marriages and we want to do some homosexual marriages. It would be good to get a test case on them." In fact, Hill said, he'd probably charge extra for heterosexual marriages. The *Kansan* ran a photo of Kimball giving Hill a "congratulatory kiss" on the lips, which ended up in the files of the Lawrence Police Department.

Hill, who had told a reporter for the Kansas City *Star* that he intended to continue his career as a dope marketer ("a typical set-up. Involves a lot of accounting") while in office, was the human-interest story of the week. The story, in Kimball's words, "broke in every fucking paper in the country" and beyond. An American missionary in Peru wrote in outrage to the *Journal World* after reading about Hill's election in a Lima newspaper. And then the *60 Minutes* "Kaw Valley Hemp Pickers" segment aired, with Mike Wallace and Harry Reasoner "chuckling over the election of Phillip C. Hill" by the citizens of Lawrence, Kansas.

A few days later the Kansas attorney general ruled that the office of justice of the peace had in fact been abolished in 1968. Phil Hill, along with about fifty other Kansans who held this modest office, was deposed. (The ruling rendered invalid all marriages performed by justices of the peace in the past two years.) Hill, who had never been a particularly prominent member of Lawrence's counterculture, disappeared back into obscurity. George Kimball left the state, his "fuck" charge still pending. He was tried in absentia, fined $250, and sentenced to ninety days in jail. So Kimball stayed away from Kansas.

—

The "hippies" on whom the newly elected attorney general, Vern Miller, had vowed to stomp were a very visible minority of Lawrence's population, their numbers swollen sometimes by high school kids and college students who lingered on the fringes, who bought the dope and read *Vortex* and shopped at Sandalwood and the Magic Circus. A poll at the University of Kansas in 1971 suggested that 69 percent of KU students had smoked pot, compared to the findings of a national Gallup Poll—undoubtedly more rigorously conducted—that more than 40 percent of college students had done so. Lawrence, many who were there remember, was one of the most drug-oriented towns in the United States. And while the local "K-pot" was pretty awful, there was a lot of good stuff (and not just pot) moving through town, at perhaps the cheapest prices in the country.[22]

Like many towns and cities with large and concentrated populations of young people, Lawrence had a lot of trouble with the new culture that had sprung up in its midst. The university both contributed to the counter-culture's growth and moderated some of the reactions against it, but many local citizens were horrified at what they saw. In the summer of 1969, a year before the violence began, a group of "concerned citizens and businessmen" met with the city manager to discuss ways to improve law and order in Lawrence. Thirty-eight men were involved, representing the American Legion, the VFW, Noon Optimists, Noon Cosmopolitans, the Lion's Club, Knights of Columbus, and Jaycees. Their careful comments about "civil disorder and unrest," however, arose from the same impulse as a letter in the *Journal World* complaining that Lawrence was being taken over by "low life white trash."[23]

Too often such concerns have been dismissed solely as small-minded provincialism. That was undoubtedly part of it, but by no means all. There were some pretty unsavory characters running around Lawrence, including a few of the type that led Ed Sanders to describe the counterculture as a "valley of plump white rabbits surrounded by wounded coyotes." As one of Lawrence's "top dealers, quantity and quality" told a *Vortex* interviewer, "Dealers on the whole you know, uh, are not . . . for the most part you run into pretty, uh, unreasonable, uh, dishonest . . . . theives. Theives."[24] But neither the worst elements of the counterculture nor the worst fears of the straight world fully explain the tensions in Lawrence. For Lawrence's straight citizens were not just looking at Flower Power and imagining degeneracy and danger. Members of Lawrence's hip community actively represented themselves that way. It was like saying "fuck." Dangerous, vulgar, obscene—it was all a carefully crafted image, not without some substance, and if there were many other self-representations and realities produced by the varied groups who merged into an uneasy community, the ugliest ones were among the most powerful. While many of these images show a fine sense of irony and self-mockery, it's doubtful that more than a few hundred of Lawrence's people were completely in on the joke.

For all the endless repetition of "fuck," it was not words but images that most forcefully rendered sex a weapon against straight culture. *The Screw* and *Vortex* and the other publications that emerged from the hip community on the outskirts of Mt. Oread were heavy on the graphic impulse, printing everything from freehand doodles in the margins to elaborate illustrations and comics. "Those Fabulous Furry Freak Brothers," a comic strip about two pot-befuddled hippies plagued by Norbert the Narc, appeared frequently in *Vortex,* as in dozens of underground papers throughout the nation. But Lawrence had a lot of local talent, too, and these artists drew members of their own community, not generic representations of hippies and freaks.

S. Clay Wilson, one of the most famous of the classic underground comic artists, had landed in Lawrence for a couple of years in the mid-1960s, midway between New York and San Francisco. As Steve "Chopper Pilot" Wilson, he embarked on the instant-myth-making process that engaged so many of Lawrence's "deviate subculture" (Wilson's words). His bio for *Grist* read: "Steve Wilson!!/ is a graduate of the University of Nebraska and one-time resident of the Lower East Side. He was run out of New York by the East Village Other. An associate of the evil J. Gary Brown, he now rides his Hog through the streets of Lawrence in search of stray snatch."[25]

Wilson's more recent account of those days is that he tried New York and hated it, so he moved to Lawrence, where he found steady pay as a model in the KU art department, drew his comics, and bridged several of the "interlocking cliques" that *The Screw* was so concerned about.[26] His intricately rendered (Hieronymus Bosch comes to mind) versions of the people who would call themselves the River City Outlaws or the Kaw Valley Hemp Pickers are drawn from brutish biker culture, not the realms of peace and love. In a drawing called "Dirty Earl's Hamburger 'n' Shake Shack," a Wilson self-portrait takes the foreground in aviator glasses and cowboy hat, gun tucked into belt: "This blue steel .44 isn't just part of my costume motherfucker." Balancing this figure is an obese biker: "I've got to take a brute crap." And at the top of the drawing, rising from the welter of bikes and bikers, a woman prattles on:

I'VE BALLED LEROY
I'VE BALLED HANK
I'VE BALLED GEORGE
I'VE BALLED WILS
I'VE BALLED MIKE
I'VE BALLED VAL

I'VE BALLED GARY
I'VE BALLED HOWARD
I'VE BALLED WAYNE
AND . . .

"All on their bikes too man," says one of her audience. "Chicks suck," says another. And from the far corner: "And then the dumb bitch decided to get off like she was on the turnpike." This was the cover for *The Screw*'s third issue, the image its staff chose to represent—and to help create—Lawrence's hip community.[27]

169

Within the community, some were aware of the problems of such representations—and realities. The *Oread Daily Review,* a "humorous" and "self-critical" summary of the events of 1970, included a page devoted to the White House, "once a farout, neato, cod hippie—pot partie palace, *Now* a (free) University parking lot, Thanks to the Revolution." Through the open front door is visible a naked woman sliding backward down the staircase bannister, her breasts dangling, her nether regions headed for the erect penis of a waiting man. Another couple of indeterminate gender are having sex on the front porch. The upstairs bedrooms seem to be occupied by larger groups, smoking dope. "Dis is a Revolution?" asks the hairy nude man perched, lotus position, on the front porch railing. Plenty of people asked with him. But for many, the sex and drugs were a purposeful part of the revolution, more important than the protest marches and political analyses. The public representations of sex they crafted were intentionally vulgar and intentionally shocking.

A strange example of this impulse toward vulgarity and shock value is the *Vortex* women's issue from early 1970. Anger over issues of gender and sex had been building within the Movement for some time, with more and more Movement women feeling they were fighting not only an oppressive society but also their male co-revolutionaries. "Fuck your woman so hard till she can't stand up," the Lawrence hero John Sinclair had declared in the White Panther Party Manifesto.[28] A lot of women were finding that version of revolution unacceptable.

In the winter of 1970 a group of women took over New York's influential underground paper the *Rat.* The move was precipitated by Jane Alpert, whose status at *Rat* had been greatly enhanced by her involvement in the bombing of several buildings in 1969. On her way to a benefit for her bombing-trial defense fund, Alpert picked up the latest issue of *Rat* and was repulsed by a brutal S. Clay Wilson cartoon (featuring amputations) and less than amused by the headline "Clit Flit Big Hit" for a story on clitoral orgasm. In a stormy meeting about sexual exploitation, *Rat's* female staff members prevailed, and they began recruiting New York feminists to write for a women's issue. Robin Morgan's contribution, "Goodbye to All That," a rage-filled attack on the exploitative and macho culture of the male-dominated Movement, was one of the most influential pieces of writing ever published in the underground press.[29]

In Lawrence, as in towns and cities around the nation, there were hard talks and explosions following the publication of Morgan's manifesto. And the women of *Vortex,* like their sisters at *Rat,* took over the paper, despite, as they wrote in their editorial column (one month before Lawrence went up in flames), the men of *Vortex,* who "keep hitting us with the fact that we Lawrence 'girls' just don't have the political experience to put out a paper. Not just their experiences, but also the experiences of other women, women who fought for People's Park and women who were beaten in Chicago and returned to kick out the windows. They're right. But knowledge and experience come through struggle and contact, and putting out this paper has in itself been an intense experience of struggle and genuine contact with the political experience."[30]

The *Vortex* women were both angry and tentative, unsure of their positions, not quite in control of their tone. The editorial begins with self-abnegation and apology, but gradually works into a voice of outrage before subsiding once again into a defensive posture: "Ask yourself why sex is used to sell everything from cars to movies to *Playboy* to under ground papers. Just because Madison Avenue doesn't hit you over the head by calling their products cunt cars or clit flicks doesn't mean you're not being exploited. Or just because revolutionary newspapers cum out and call a cunt a clit, doesn't mean that they or you have joined the sexual revolution." And then, immediately, the shift back to the inexperienced good girl tone: "We're not advocating Female chauvinism, Bitch Power, or trying to cut off your boyfriend's penis. We are struggling for recognition for our capabilities, potentialities, and ourselves."

These were women in process, struggling to define their feminism and not certain where they were going. The *Vortex* women, in fact, wrote very little of the "women's issue." Morgan's "Goodbye to All That" is the issue's centerpiece, paired with a response from the White Panther minister of communication, Genie Plamondon: (1) We shouldn't fight each other when there's so much work to do; (2) "I'm not going to join any women who want a genderless society . . . I love to fuck, I love being a woman." But the Lawrence group put the issue together, and its layout, in many ways, speaks louder than words.

The front cover of the women's issue is lovely, a kind of vague vaginal imagery done in a pastel wash (If S. Clay Wilson's cartoon looked like Hieronymus Bosch in line drawing, imagine Georgia O'Keeffe working in blue-green pastels). But the page that offers an overview of "women's liberation" and various feminist groups (NOW, The Feminists, WITCH, Redstockings, the Stanton-Anthony Brigade) devotes a third of its space to a cartoon by Grant Canfield. A woman, clad only in thigh-high boots and gloves, sits on a toilet. The toilet rests on the head of a naked man; excrement drips over his face and shoulders. He's masturbating. It's hard to say which is more erect, his penis or her breasts, but by conservative estimate, if his body were in scale to his penis he'd be twenty feet tall. The cartoon is entitled "Womens Liberation."

The back cover is an unsigned comic strip: "The Crank Case." Two women sit, smoking dope. One is heavy, with hairy legs. Tattooed on her left biceps are a phallus and the words "PRICKS FOREVER." The other, clearly blond even in a black-and-white line drawing, is tall and busty and pretty. Suddenly the pretty one rises and shouts: "I'm sick of it, Edowda Miekunt!! Every magazine shows a bare female ass or tit, but . . . NO CRANKS!" They take it to court, "Judge Crulius Halfman" presiding, and charge the "artists of Amerika" with ignoring the desires of women "by showing NO CRANKS." Weeks drag by, "tension MOUNTS," and finally "the case reaches CLIMAX." Judge Halfman erupts: "I WANT FUCK!" Edowda Miekunt shouts, "Climb on! I Can Dig It!" and kneeling doggy-style, is sodomized by a disembodied "prick." The judge gets the busty blonde, but when she tells him he's a "real bad lay," he reasserts his judicial power: "For that, bitch, I charge you with contempt of court and sentence you to 10 years in bed with the Amerikan pig force." The last frame has our blond heroine spread-eagled on the ground, performing fellatio on one "pig" while another uses his finger for what the *Rat* had called "Clit Flit." "PIG NATION TRIHUMPS again."

This cartoon is a very complicated work, despite or perhaps because of its insistent vulgarity. The artist has included "crank" shapes hidden in (or as) other objects, offering a sort of graphic challenge that, to risk overinterpreting, signals the ubiquity of patriarchy, even in the small details of life. But the blatant "moral" of the story seems to contradict the feminist politics of the issue. Women set out to demand sexual satisfaction, but by the end the woman who took action is spread-eagled and gang raped. "PIG NATION TRIHUMPS again." But not without the women's active complicity. "Climb on!" cries Edowda Miekunt. "Why not?" says her friend. Pig nation does not triumph until the women make it so, through sex. Was the cartoon anti-sex? Anti-women? Or was it primarily a weapon against "straight" society in its language of "cranks" and "kunts"?

Though the women who took over *Rat* never relinquished control, the women of *Vortex* ceded editorial power back to the male editors for the next issue. But their efforts had attracted attention, and claimed a full page of "Feedback" in the next issue. Not surprisingly, the letters frame another unsettling illustration: a woman, nude but for combat boots and helmet, strides toward us, gun blazing in what was surely clear to all as phallic imagery.[31]

The first letter, a full column long, came from a male supporter of women's liberation in Manhattan, Kansas. "Dear Editors:" he began. "I damn well resent the clear insinuation of Canfield's shit-slinging scribble, that a man who supports women's liberation is just an idiot who gets a sexual thrill out of being crapped on by a women . . . As for that excrescence on the back page—you can find stuff better than that on any restroom wall. The art and the consciousness of that masterpiece are both at the same level—somewhere below the scurf on a cesspool . . . It gives no hint that the present condition of our sexual culture is anything more than the 'natural' consequence of biological makeup."

This writer made it clear he didn't believe that women had chosen these cartoons, but he had a point to make that transcended either gender or sex. "Pig nation triumphs throughout that cartoon, not just at the end. Pig nation triumphed when Vortex ran that cartoon, and it will continue to triumph so long as 'underground' papers indiscriminately take anything that offends the old culture as being therefore revolutionary."[32]

"Dear Sisters:" began the letter from a Kansas City Women's Liberation group. "It is difficult to understand how the 'Crank Case' cartoon and the Women's Liberation cartoon . . . could appear in a Women's Issue. Did the guys give you only certain sections of the paper? . . . Publishing cartoons that dehumanize people is part of the sickness of America. Female Liberation does not mean adopting male modes of expression and relations between people." Though somewhat preachy, this letter was gentle and fairly conciliatory toward the *Vortex* "Sisters": "Would it be possible to meet and talk with you?"

Finally, a letter from WITCH (Women's International Terrorist Conspiracy from Hell), positioned directly below the woman warrior, dispensed with the niceties of salutation. "Vortex: Women's Liberation is no longer standing idly by around the country while the so-called underground press makes money off our flesh."

> Lets run it on down. White male underground papers are chauvinist. Sure, we'll "let" the girls have their say, after reminding them that they couldn't possibly equal us in political experience (Did it ever occur to them that just being a woman in America means tasting and "experiencing" political oppression?) Sure, we'll let the "girls" put in some articles on women but we'll put in some groovy, sexy, dirty cartoons which show that we don't really take this women thing seriously. We have a sense of humor, we know that all these women need is a goood fuck. And if they don't get the humor of our cartoon, we'll put in a gruesome, humorless cartoon which shows how it really is—with women dropping shit all over men's ears and shoulders. Goodbye to the chauvinist underground press, Goodbye to their special sale on Charlie Manson buttons, goodbye to their put-down of their female staff, GOODBYE VORTEX.

The *Vortex* women, however, had had complete control over their issue. And they stood by it, even though it meant some fancy footwork around their critics' objections. If nothing else, they sounded a lot less tentative than in their first editorial. "It's a shame that a cartoon intended to satirize exploitation of sex in America has been interpreted as one more example of exploitation," they began. The unsigned "Crank Case" was not foisted on them by "the guys"; it was drawn by two women. "Crank Case" didn't represent the artists' "policy" for women's liberation, the *Vortex* women explained, but instead "illustrated, in a reverse manner that women are exploited and exploit themselves." Besides, "The Crank Case was not a cartoon strip specifically to stimulate intellectual activity or provide guidelines for action. Cartoons cannot provide guidelines, they can either illustrate them or mock them. Ours was mocking."

Grant Canfield's "drawing was another image—another cartoon . . . Grant was illustrating what seemed to him a typical male reaction to the *words* women's liberation. The guy being shit on was the one who fears that

all women's liberation means is female chauvinism and male exploitation."
(His orgasm remains unexplained.) The short piece ends with what might
seem a supplication, but comes out more as a demand: "Don't write us
off—at least not yet. Vortex women."

So much remains unresolved: Is the transgressive necessarily progressive? Are there male and female modes of expression? Are images
significant, or are these "just" cartoons? Where does sex fit in Women's
Liberation? Quite probably the *Vortex* women had no clear answers. Three
different, if implicit, definitions of feminism underlie the three letters to
which they responded, and the somewhat incoherent politics of their issue
may suggest a fourth. But throughout the takeover and the subsequent
controversy, the *Vortex* women worked in a tradition that saw in the ugliest
representations of sex a potent weapon.

This may be the strand of the sexual revolution that is most difficult
to find sympathy for today—the relentless use of four-letter words, the
vulgarity, the frequent misogyny that weaves through the counterculture's
claiming of sex, both across the nation and in Lawrence. Today, too much
of this part of the sexual revolution looks like boys (and girls) scrawling
"FUCK" on bathroom walls, trying a little too hard to shock the grown-ups.
It is easier to accept the communitarian impulses and to extract from this
other strand a few pathbreaking works of art—poetry, literature,
comix—and leave the rest alone. But this use of sex as a weapon was a
crucial, fundamental aspect of the sexual revolution, and it cannot be
dismissed.

It can, however, be recontextualized. These words, these images, had
a different sort of power then. In their shock value, if nothing else, they
seemed to many to be powerful weapons in the struggle against a repressive
culture. That today this use seems more banal than shocking, its sexual
politics appalling, is testimony to how much has changed rather than to
their initial irrelevancy.

7

Sex and Liberation

In June 1970, one year after acts of resistance at the Stonewall Inn in New York City sparked the rise of the gay liberation movement, Lawrence saw the birth of its own Gay Liberation Front.[1] The seven men and women who founded the group were trying to create a revolutionary force out of what seemed a vacuum. Although the KU dean of men had noted (unhappily) in 1959 that Lawrence had become a "congregation point for homosexuals" in the region, Lawrence did not claim a vibrant gay culture. The university created a more socially progressive atmosphere than most small towns could boast, and KU and Haskell Indian Junior College offered a concentrated population of young but sexually mature adults; nonetheless, Lawrence was a small town. The relative anonymity and diversity that allowed or even fostered the growth of gay cultures in the nation's large cities simply did not exist in Lawrence. The closest gay bar was thirty miles away in Topeka; Kansas City's Liberty Memorial (an hour from Lawrence in the opposite direction) was the place one went to cruise. There were meeting places on campus—most famously the student union restrooms and the trophy room—but no coherent gay community and no real gathering spaces for gay men or lesbians. The events that took place on New York's Christopher Street in June 1969 could never have happened in Lawrence.

But in the summer of 1970 all of Lawrence was at war. The student union building was a charred ruin; sniper fire rang out in streets and alleys; tensions between blacks and whites, freaks and straights stayed at explosive levels day after day, week after week. Words like "revolution" and "oppression" and "liberation" had a different immediacy when people lay dead in the street. It was in this world that the Lawrence Gay Liberation Front (GLF) was founded.

The first public statements of the GLF make its origins quite clear. "COME OUT," began the full-page proclamation introducing the organization in *Vortex*. "The new sexuality is helping to free men and women from the restrictive roles and repressive institutions of Amerika. We are letting go of these securities in an effort to grab ahold of our lives and know who we are. Gay men and women are coming out into the open to help shape this new sexuality. We are being confronted by an uptight, authoritarian, racist, sexist Amerika. So the Gay Liberation Front joins other oppressed brothers and sisters of Amerika and the Third World to struggle against the nightmare and create one world of people living together."

The proclamation was signed, in language adapted from the "revolution": "POWER TO ALL REPRESSED AND OPPRESSED PEOPLE." A broadside announcing a Gay Liberation Front "OPEN rap session" made common cause even more explicit: "We assert our strong belief that gay liberation is not an end in itself, but merely one of similar means aimed toward ultimate, unconditional liberation; toward active respect for all men; and toward the freedom to love without fear."[2]

In claiming solidarity with the liberation struggles of all oppressed peoples, the Lawrence GLF (in what were sometimes heavily derivative or wholly borrowed statements), joined by significant segments of Lawrence's women's liberation movement, relied on a popularized Marxist analysis that traced oppression to capitalism, competition, and private property. "The disease called 'civilization,'" explained a *Vortex* article titled "Purple Power," "came into being when the tribal matriarchal societies were taken over by men. Intertribal sharing was supplanted by a common medium of exchange . . . competition overrode cooperation. MAN's worth became defined in what he possessed and the most sought prize was woman." Moving from Engels's analysis to a more contemporary framework, the author traced the results: the "assertion of cock privilege" and the rise of "continual competition" in which the losers were "women, the third world, the homosexuals." Capitalism, the author concluded, "is the enemy I must fight in myself and in you."[3]

In Lawrence, as elsewhere, such analysis fueled both the gay liberation and women's liberation movements. In general, these writings tell us less about Lawrence, less about "authentic" or autochthonous local movements, than about the ways in which ideas circulated through American communities. Read enough of "local" sources from this era, and you begin to notice the replication of phrases, sentences, even whole articles. Intellectual property rights were no more valued by many in the Movement than material ones. The larger point, however, is that many of those who entered the struggle were not seeking simply individual sexual freedom or civil rights. They meant to remake the world.

In emphasizing their larger revolutionary concerns, these activists were not minimizing the importance of sex. Sex was critical to their definitions of liberation. But sex was critical in very different ways to different groups, both in theory and in practice. Sex proved a particularly difficult issue around which to organize a pan-liberationist movement. No matter how much they claimed common visions of freedom, equality, and human dignity, early gay lib and women's lib groups often diverged on the role of sex in that Utopia—or in the struggle itself.

On the cusp of the 1970s in San Francisco, gay liberationists circulated a manifesto that celebrated the power and beauty of their nascent movement and explored its challenges. This document, which was explicitly for and about gay men, not lesbians, claimed solidarity with the women's liberation movement and warned of the critical division that existed over the issue of sex. "Sex for [women] has meant oppression," the manifesto's author, Carl Wittman, explained, and "a major part of their liberation is to play down sexual objectification and to develop other aspects of themselves which have been smothered for so long." For gay men, in contrast, "sexual objectification is a focus of our quest for freedom. It is precisely that which we are not supposed to share with each other." In attempting to forge the necessary coalition, Wittman argued, gay men needed to understand how sex had been a tool of women's oppression, and women's liberationists needed to accept the "open and prominent place that we put sex in our lives," even if it seemed "appall[ing]" or "disgust[ing]" because of their own experiences with sexualized oppression.[4]

While the division was never so absolute or so simple as Wittman's schema suggests, and was always (as he acknowledged) complicated by the experiences of those who were both female and homosexual, the role of sex was a fundamental point of divergence between the early liberation movements. In Lawrence, in the hundreds of thousands of words written and circulated as calls to liberation, the philosophical division was evident. Gay

177

men offered sex as a redemptive force. Women who did not specify their sexual orientation almost always located oppression in their inability to escape *being* sexualized by a white, male, capitalist culture. And self-identified lesbians explored both claims, articulating a paradox that unsettled many who meant to theorize the revolution.

In the end, however, all agreed that existing sexual codes—whether those of "traditional" American society or of the "sexual revolution"—were oppressive and unacceptable. The very public acts and claims of women's and gay liberationists challenged traditional mores, but they also interrupted and at least partially reoriented a sexual revolution that, in the late 1960s, looked to many like the same old thing, just more of it.

While the proclamations and manifestos of the gay liberation and women's liberation movements are critically important, the groups did not exist solely in the realm of discourse. Individuals attempted to implement a new, liberated sexuality, and groups fought to change the communities in which they lived. To understand the roles liberation movements played in the sexual revolution we must analyze their ideological claims together with the concrete and multifaceted struggles in which their members engaged.

—

While the Lawrence Gay Liberation Front embraced a philosophical agenda of global transformation and revolutionary change, its first actions were definitively local and more than a bit conservative. In the summer of 1970 it sought university sanction. The GLF's request to be recognized as a student organization, however contraindicated by its polemical language (and by the fact that it was a Lawrence organization, not simply a student association), was a politically savvy step for a group that hoped to make Lawrence "a place where gay people could relate out of their naturalness."[5] If any place in Kansas was likely to be socially progressive enough to accept gay liberation, it was the campus on Mt. Oread. After all, despite a somewhat checkered record on race relations, the KU administration had forced racial integration in the town's theaters by threatening to show first-run movies free at KU. And official status as a student group would offer resources otherwise unavailable: free space for meetings and events, access to student activity fees for funding, and, not least important, the legitimacy such status accorded in the eyes of the public.

When student members of the group approached KU administrators that summer, however, they discovered the limits of progressive action at a public institution. The very same revolutionary intensity that had helped inspire the GLF's founding made its recognition next to impossible. Even though a great many people in Lawrence believed (whether accurately or not) that the KU student union had been burned by Lawrence High School students, not KU students, and even though the armed confrontations on Lawrence's streets involved self-proclaimed "outlaws," most of whom were not (current) students, much of the state and, indeed, much of Lawrence blamed the university for the violence and unrest.

It was not public knowledge at the time, but in July the board of regents had voted to request the chancellor's resignation, despite his success in keeping the university open in the days following the double crisis of Kent State and Lawrence's own "days of rage." Chancellor Chalmers's job was spared when one of the regents changed his or her vote. But the chancellor was in a fragile position, and the regents made it clear that they did not want to see gay liberation on their campus. They also opposed funding for a university women's center.[6]

This is not, however, just a story of one man's moral backbone or lack thereof. This is a story of the difficulty and complexity of effecting social change in a democracy. Members of the KU administration, including at least one principled and powerful advocate for the GLF, were looking over their shoulders at the state legislature, whose members in turn were peering back at their constituents in Strong City and Tonganoxie, who, the legislators assumed, would not look favorably on rampant homosexuality at the state university to which they were expected to send their sons and daughters and tax dollars. It's not that Kansans were particularly conservative on this issue; the vast majority of Americans opposed homosexuality, let alone gay liberation.

With the university already beleaguered, the chancellor serving on sufferance, administration officials told the GLF that this was not the time to press its case. "When do we come out?" the group asked. "How long do we put ourselves down so that we don't upset someone?" Rejecting the plea for patience, the GLF applied to the student senate executive committee for recognition that August. The request was approved. On September 5, however, Chancellor Chalmers issued a news release: "Since we are not persuaded that student activity funds should be allocated whether to support or to oppose the sexual proclivities of students, particularly when they might lead to violation of state law, the University of Kansas declines to formally recognize the Lawrence Gay Liberation Front."[7]

As for sexual proclivities, student and other public funds were currently going to a "Human Sexuality Series" organized by the Commission on the Status of Women, to a group that promoted birth control, and to a group called "KU Singles." State law was another issue. According to the 1970 Kansas penal code, sodomy, defined as "oral or anal copulation between persons who are not husband and wife or consenting adult members of the opposite sex, or between a person and an animal" was a class B misdemeanor with a term of imprisonment of six months.[8] However, as the GLF pointed out, there were regulations in place that prohibited the use of public funds for illegal activities. Should the GLF be found in violation of those rules, the funds could be withdrawn. GLF spokesmen repeatedly explained that the group was educational: it meant to inform the larger public about homosexuality and to offer a venue in which gay men and lesbians could learn about homosexuality free of the prejudices of a society that labeled it sin or mental illness.

Virtually all concerned understood the university's position to be legally untenable. Jack Klinknett, the lawyer who was working with the GLF (he had just graduated from Kansas's Washburn Law School and was holding informal office hours in the KU student union) believed it was a transparent strategy: the administration was publicly holding the line against gay liberation, but in a way that could not stand up in court. That way, when its position was struck down, the university might present itself to potentially hostile alumni and state legislators as a victim of judicial activism. The GLF would thus gain official recognition and the public relations cost to the university would be minimized.[9]

This reading probably gave the administration credit for greater Machiavellian talent than it possessed. In fact, administration officials were divided on the issue, though all agreed that there would be political and budgetary costs in recognizing the GLF. Vice-Chancellor of Student Affairs William Balfour became a trusted ally and advisor to the group. Chancellor Chalmers, in contrast, continually reiterated his concerns about public funds and "sexual proclivities." In particularly tortured logic, he defended his vetoes of the student senate's actions on the grounds that the university should not be "involved in the sexual preference" of students. "We have been working for quite a few years within our colleges and universities," he explained, "to remove ourselves institutionally from involvement in the individual sexual proclivity of our students . . . I don't think we should get back into that arena."[10]

The members of the GLF could also be quite disingenuous. At times, it seemed their version of homosexuality had nothing at all to do with sex. But in one statement explaining why official standing was so important to the group, sex was put front and center, denying the rather awkward, though useful, claim that though homosexual acts were illegal there was no law against *being* homosexual. "Inseparable from the freedom to be homosexual," the Lawrence GLF wrote, " is the freedom to participate in homosexual activities. In a society that professes the freedom of the individual, moral and sexual legislation has no valid place. Therefore, to recognize our right to exist is to recognize our right to engage in homosexual acts."[11] This is the sort of language that gave university administrators nightmares—no matter what their personal beliefs about gay liberation.

Battles over recognition continued for over a year. Three times the student senate voted in favor of the GLF; three times the chancellor vetoed their action. The judiciary committee of the university senate failed to resolve the issue. But by this time the GLF was looking beyond the KU campus.[12]

In the spring of 1971 the attorney William Kunstler, fresh from his controversial and high-profile defense of the Chicago Seven—Abbie Hoffman, Jerry Rubin, Bobby Seale, and the others who were charged with disrupting the 1968 Democratic National Convention in Chicago—spoke at KU. One of the GLF members approached him, presenting the group's situation as a free speech case of great importance. And in July Kunstler agreed to represent the Lawrence Gay Liberation Front in a legal suit against KU.

The grounds for the suit were basic First Amendment arguments: denial of recognition was unconstitutional and would have "a forbidding and chilling effect on free expression and association."[13] The case was scheduled in the Topeka district courtroom of Judge Templar on December 15, 1971. Kunstler flew in the night before and met briefly with Jack Klinknett, the GLF's local lawyer. Judge Templar had made some noise about barring Kunstler from his courtroom, but both Klinknett and Kunstler considered it an empty threat. Kunstler intended to argue the case, and scarcely discussed his plans with Klinknett.

When Kunstler rose to address the court that morning, however, Judge Templar told him he was not eligible to practice law in the state of Kansas. Typically, judges allowed attorneys licensed in other states to argue cases, especially if they were working in tandem with locally licensed attorneys. But legally such outsiders appeared at the judge's pleasure. Judge Templar told Kunstler: "The court finds that your attitude toward the courts and judges is one of utter disdain . . . Your fame is notorious throughout the nation. You have gone all over this country deriding our judicial system . . . I will not let you appear in this case."[14]

Kunstler tried to placate the judge, pleading with him to "give me a chance, and judge for yourself. I am not an abrasive person. I pride myself as an attorney. I have not had trouble with anyone, except [Judge] Hoffman in the Chicago trial, which was a very unusual proceeding." When none of his arguments worked, Kunstler made a final appeal: "I'm begging your honor just to reconsider and let me argue my little case." Opposing counsel, KU's attorney Charles Oldfather, approached the bench and asked the judge to reconsider, but Templar again refused and ordered Kunstler to take a seat. Kunstler returned to the counsel table, but the judge told him to move to the spectator section. "I don't even want to sit in your court-room and face you after this decision," Kunstler said, but he sat where the judge told him, leaving the young, green, and woefully unprepared Jack Klinknett to argue the GLF's case. Klinknett himself characterized his presentation as "incompetent"; the *New York Times* reported that the case had been argued by a law student.[15]

While the GLF's case centered on First Amendment rights, the judge's decision turned heavily on concepts of sexual morality and normality. Concluding that "public school authorities" should be accorded "the widest authority in maintaining discipline and good order" in their institutions, Templar said: "When the announced objectives and purposes of the Lawrence Gay Liberation Front . . . are considered, it is not difficult to understand the concern of Chancellor Chalmers . . . and his conclusion that the school funds . . . should not be made available for the purpose of opposing or supporting the discussion of *bizarre sexual activities* for which the plaintiffs apparently seek formal and public approval" (italics added). Reporting Templar's characterization of their "activities," the GLF, whose members sorely needed a sense of humor at this point, asked: "Does he know about something we don't?" But it was in such words as "proclivities" and "bizarre" that the substance of the opposition was expressed.[16]

The case went, on appeal, all the way to the U.S. Supreme Court, which declined to consider it.[17] Meanwhile, the GLF continued to function in Lawrence, and KU officials quietly accorded it greater privileges, including an office in the student union and free access to space for meetings and dances.

The legal proceedings took up much of the energy and resources of the core members of the Gay Liberation Front. The most prominent activists were the most politically engaged, and their concerns are the ones most fully preserved in the historical record. At the same time, however, men and women began to "come out" into the charged atmosphere of a small town in Kansas that felt itself in the midst of a revolution. Most of them were never political in the sense that they wrote and published condemnations of capitalism or sued public institutions or picketed for gay liberation. Many saw the decision as essentially a private matter. But as men and women in Lawrence decided to avow their sexual orientation or to explore new sexual and/or romantic possibilities, they found a public system of support in place. Some took the first step in an anonymous phone call to the KU's human sexuality counseling line or to the town's volunteer counseling center, Headquarters.[18] Others began with tentative attendance at one of the meetings or seminars sponsored by the Women's Center or the GLF or the United Ecumenical Christian Ministries on campus, which had opened their doors to the GLF when it had few allies.[19] And many of these men and women soon found their way to the dances held by the Gay Liberation Front.

Despite its emphasis on institutional recognition, this gay liberation movement did not split over the issue of personal politics. From the beginning, the personal, the private, the intimate, was at the center of their liberationist understandings. Sex itself—represented as proud, healthy, joyful human contact—frequently appeared as the fundamental means to liberation. A Lawrence delegate to the first national gay lib convention, disappointed by the "big city chauvinism" he encountered ("[People] kept reacting strongly when they found out John Steven and I were from Kansas," he wrote without irony), unsettled by the rancor between white men, women, and "Third World brothers," found meaning in the personal. "I had met some caring people," his *Vortex* article on the convention ended, "especially Ralph from New York. We made love in strength and laughter, not shame."[20]

As the "Women and Men of the Lawrence Gay Liberation Front" wrote in yet another manifesto, "We are gay because we are privileged in the ability to love human beings of the same sex . . . To all our gay brothers and sisters we ask you to hold up your heads and look the world squarely in the eye as the gay people you are, . . . confident in the goodness of what you do, what you feel, who you are. Gay is beautiful when gay people make it that way."[21]

Dances were a key part of the strategy of "making" gay beautiful. In a town without established spaces for gays and lesbians, the irregularly scheduled dances were critically important. Open to all, men and women, town and gown, gay, straight, and otherwise, the dances held at the student union throughout the 1970s played a major role in creating and consolidating a gay culture and community in Lawrence.

These dances were intended to offer a space where people could "relate out of their naturalness." This meant not only freedom for men to dance with men and women with women without fear of harassment, but also freedom from the "restrictive roles" imposed by straight society. Because the dances were open, harassment remained a too-real possibility; at one of the first ones, in the spring of 1972, jeering spectators lined the balcony of the union ballroom. Toward the end of the evening four or five young men grabbed the cash box containing the evening's admission receipts, beat up the man who tried to stop them, and ran away with the money.[22]

In general, however, the dances fulfilled their purpose. Chuck Ortleb, who had come out during his senior year at KU and moved to New York (where he would publish a gay weekly, the New York *Native*) shortly after his graduation in 1971, came back to Lawrence for a gay lib dance in the fall of 1972. He wrote to the *University Daily Kansan* that he had "yet to see a dance with such intensity of 'good vibrations' in New York City, where the birth of the Gay movement took place," and praising the "warmth, ecstasy and liberation" expressed at that dance.[23]

These were somewhat calculated words of encouragement, but the dances did attract people. At first it was mainly students and a few townsfolk, but soon they were drawing from the whole region. A lesbian who was in high school in Kansas City in the mid-1970s remembers her first Lawrence dance: she was hanging out with a group of under-age kids at the Mall (the Liberty Memorial Park in Kansas City) when someone mentioned there was a dance going on in Lawrence. "Several hundred people were already there when we arrived, including many from Kansas City who would normally have been at the bars . . . People were dressed in everything from street clothes to high drag to gender-fuck . . . People we talked to had come in from Manhattan [Kansas], Wichita, Topeka, and even Omaha for this dance."[24]

While the GLF and its successor organizations regularly ran ads in the local papers with headlines like "We are out to let you love the one you want," advertising their speakers' bureau and rap groups and seminars and counseling service, it was the dances that transformed "homosexuality" from concept to reality, from ideology to flesh. Some of the GLF stalwarts believed that transformation was the best thing that could happen in Lawrence's nascent gay community. Events like the dances were a form of "street therapy," a therapy for once aimed not at "curing" homosexuality but at making gay beautiful. "A picket and a dance can do more for the vast majority of homosexuals than two years on a couch," asserted the GLF.[25]

The dances moved gay liberation from abstract concept (First Amendment rights), from words (speakers, seminars, rap groups), from private (what two people do in the privacy of the bedroom) to a very public, embodied fact. The men and women who gathered at the "HOT TO TROT! to the Penetrations" dance or who (a few years later) saw the Village People at the KU student union and then took over the local Sambo's restaurant for an early breakfast were not "asking" for "tolerance." They were not saying to straight society, "We are just like you, so please don't discriminate against us." They were simply enjoying who they were.

And this caused conflict. The KU administration continued to be pressured by a member of the board of regents for several years, and a psychiatrist at the famous Menninger Clinic, well known for his "work" with homosexuals, lobbied against the dances. Most telling are letters from Kansans—not students—who stumbled across the dances and were appalled. One man, who "happened" to be at the union on a date, followed the sound of music to the ballroom. For a while he and his date watched "men embracing men, caressing each other." "At first we thought it was funny," he wrote, "but after a short while it began to look really vulgar so we left."[26] Another young man took great care to establish his reasons for attending a gay dance. A girl had invited him to Lawrence for the dance, and he hadn't quite understood her intentions. Since they had a fight shortly after arriving, he spent most of the evening "sitting alone under the balconies in the twilight." Though he was "approached tentatively" a few times, he "naturally" declined invitations to dance and kept the conversations "superficial." But his solitary state offered ample opportunity for observation, and he provided a detailed description of what he saw.

"Hot pants and dresses on males were not uncommon," he wrote, "and some even wore hose. Their legs were not hairy, and so I assume they were shaved . . . A couple of the men who approached me used falsettos and an exaggerated shaking of the hips." Lesbian couples received little attention from this young man, who continued to describe the "feminine appearance" of men: "Much of the clothing was skin tight, and many men wore brassieres with padding, which they continually adjusted to prevent lopsidedness. A couple of people wore high heels."[27]

This letter is primarily descriptive, though the author does offer his opinion that the "purpose of the ball seemed to be public anonymity, a public show with individual anonymity." He doesn't call for any action, seeming convinced that such description as he provided was a self-evident case against the dances. Two men from the nearby town of Eudora, however, sought the assistance of the Menninger Clinic psychiatrist Harold Voth to end the dances after encountering one by chance in early 1975.

They had gone up to campus to see a late movie at the union, and had stopped to "peer" through the plate-glass door of the ballroom to see what band was making the "racquet." Though the room was too crowded for them to see the band, "it did not take long to ascertain what group had sponsored this dance. One only had to observe what was before his eyes." The letter continues: "Seated directly in front of us at the table near the door was a young man with a 'pixie' haircut, long false eyelashes, a tight body shirt, tight pants, make-up on his face, and swigging on a bottle which seemed to be wine. He was holding hands with his lover (masculine) while the intermittent talk between the two was interrupted only by the sweet nothings they whispered when not nibbling on each others ear. I suggested to [my friend] that the Gay Liberation organization must have sponsored this dance. He concurred."

These two men, instructing Dr. Voth to "use this letter in any way you deem fit," offered their "conclusions":

1. That there are a lot more homosexuals at the University than we thought.

2. That homosexuals from the vicinity, Topeka, Kansas City, etc. are coming to these dances sponsored by the "Gay Libs" to give them support and to socialize.

3. That the University of Kansas is promoting this species of perversion by allowing the homosexuals to have these dances on University property . . . This gives legitimacy to homosexuality in the eyes of stu-

dents who attend the University for if the University condones it why shouldn't they?

4. That this movement forbodes ill for the University and its students. It forbodes ill for the students in that young people at a formative stage are often seduced by these people and led into practicing this form of deviant behavior or to at least condone it.[28]

Dr. Voth approached the chancellor with this ammunition, and Chancellor Dykes had his staff set up a meeting to discuss the various complaints he'd received about the dances. Following the meeting, Vice-Chancellor Balfour notified the GLF's faculty advisor that the dances could continue ("no problem"), but that fall he also, under protest, informed the group that they could not hold a regional gay liberation conference on campus. The university counsel was adamant on the subject in a letter to Balfour: "I'm sure it has not escaped your attention that the conference is planned for the time when our appropriations bill will be coming up for consideration in the Legislature. I am seldom accused of prudishness or conservatism, but I can honestly say that I can hardly think of anything that could cause the University more difficulty than having a regional Gay Conference."[29]

The Gay Liberation Front and its varied programs could not have existed in Lawrence without the university. In the issue of gay liberation, as in so much else, the relatively cosmopolitan university served as a beachhead for change in its state and its region—as did other universities throughout the nation. At KU the GLF received significant institutional support, as well as the personal encouragement—and advocacy—of quite a few highly placed administrators and faculty members. At the same time, the group was refused official status and summarily denied permission to hold its planned conference on campus.

From the public record—the GLF's suit against the university, most particularly—the situation appears completely polarized: the GLF against the world, more or less. But behind the scenes the politics were much more complicated. It was hard to get around the fact that the university was a public institution, funded on a yearly basis by taxpayers. Ultimately, no matter how much a part of a national, liberal culture, the university was in and of its region as well, and its potential for promoting social change was compromised by the more conservative citizens of the state of Kansas. It is clear that many of those citizens disapproved of homosexuality and of gay liberation. Some of the opponents were at the university itself; the *Kansan* ran many letters from students debating the issue of homosexuality (though most called for "tolerance"), and while the chancellor's actions were politically understandable, his constant use of the term "proclivities" does not suggest open-mindedness on the subject.

But while some university officials declared themselves morally opposed to homosexuality, several others were actively supportive and most of those with any power were primarily concerned with the stability of the university. Gay liberation was a problem to them only to the extent that it threatened alumni giving or legislative appropriations. Otherwise they had no interest in the issue. The wall they erected was in most ways a façade, a false front with great political utility but with much less substance than it appeared to have.

Despite the university's waffling, Lawrence's gay and lesbian community was becoming more visible and more established. A group of committed activists did hard political work to make that possible. They set up newsletters and a library; they ran a speakers' bureau that sent GLF members to church groups and women's clubs and college and university classrooms throughout the region. They organized peer counseling and discussion groups and vetted the professional therapists who sought gay clients. GLF activists established a legal assistance fund, pushed a political agenda, made connections—and in 1972 all three of Douglas County's Democratic party caucuses passed a gay rights resolution.[30] Perhaps most important, the activists helped to organize the dances and seminars and celebrations for the burgeoning community of men and women who were coming out into what was still a very difficult world.

KU and Lawrence were relatively open for that place and time—but the stress is on the word "relatively." Gay men and lesbians faced very real discrimination and harassment in their daily lives, not only in the official proscriptions and barriers the GLF targeted in their suit against the university, nor even in the direct verbal or physical harassment offered by a tiny minority of Lawrence's citizens, but in the widespread assumption of a heterosexual norm, in the minutiae of daily life. One of the "senior yells" used at football games by KU's class of 1965 ended: "Fifteen Queers on the O.U. Team!"—and that was within the comparatively liberal boundaries of the university.[31] Despite the successes in forging public gay identities and in "opening the minds" of straights, some of Lawrence's gay activists grew frustrated with the strategy of promoting acceptance through education.

After four years of community-building work, one of the GLF's key members finally exploded during a long radio interview on Topeka's WIBW-FM.[32] The moderator, after having identified his four guests not only as gay but also as "people from Lawrence" (still code words even though the greatest antagonism between the citizens of the state and their university had ended), began the interview by noting that "most of the people that I know mostly look at the gay community from a negative stand-point." He seemed more put off by his guests' general critique of American life than by their homosexuality, but his basic—and prideful—ignorance of homosexuality was clearly irritating the men from Lawrence. "Do you call yourself queers?" he asked at one point. "I've steered away from the term 'queer'. . . . I thought it would offend you." And a bit later, after shifting the conversation to "the homosexuality part of it," the moderator interrupted the man who was describing the gay counseling service with: "Look at it from my stand-point. I don't know what you people do."

Richard, the most confrontational of the four, blew up. Cutting off the moderator's protestations, he spoke directly to "the gay people listening": "If you're in a situation that is intolerable, which I imagine it is, especially if you're living in this part of the country, then get out of it. If it means leaving your family, hurting people, then I don't care. Get out of it. Go to a place where there are other gay people who are intelligent, who are not living with guilt or pain, who refuse to put up with the kind of crap we get. Just leave it. It's not necessary. Go away from it. And quit worrying what straight people have to say . . . There is nothing wrong with deviating from this culture. This culture is aberrant—this culture is sick." One of the other men joined in: "Being fags who are open in . . . our identities . . . [we] don't identify with this culture and its observable aims because those aims are perverted. I cause no harm, and I never asked for the bullshit I've gotten. It came from the outside, from the social mentality."

The social mentality. The culture. No matter how hard they battled for political and legal and institutional rights, these men believed the problem was more fundamental, more tightly woven into the fabric of American society. They knew it to be a problem of culture. Thus the solutions they sought were cultural as well. Some members of Lawrence's gay and lesbian communities worked to change the culture, one step at a time, through education. After members of the GLF spoke to classes at Missouri Western College, the newsletter rejoiced: "A nearby seismograph recorded a ninth magnitude tremor caused by the opening of minds."[33] But much more fundamentally, many of the men and women who came out in the heady months and years following Stonewall sought to create a new culture for *themselves.*

Lawrence never split into the "political" and "cultural" factions that plagued the New York gay community. The GLF's most visible act—suing the university—was clearly political, and at least one university administrator considered the leaders he dealt with to be eminently "reasonable" men who understood the politics of compromise. The premises from which Lawrence's gay activists worked, however, were profoundly cultural. In a town where cultural revolutionaries greatly outnumbered those who were straightforwardly political, the most visible members of the gay liberation movement were self-identified freaks. Like their brothers and sisters in the counterculture, they meant to make a new world. The loudest and most compelling voices of Lawrence's gay liberation movement offered cultural liberation: a new realm of pride and freedom for those who possessed the "ability" to love members of their own sex.

—

The cultural revolutionaries of Lawrence's gay liberation movement publicly celebrated sex. Not only movement manifestos but also the poems and short stories and personal testimonies that filled Lawrence's several gay or lesbian publications tell of individual salvation through the redemptive power of sex. There is often a tone of earnest joy, as when "Mary" writes of what she has learned "from my loving," when finally "my mind was with my body was with my heart." And sex itself is powerfully present, as when "Lz. Shari" celebrates "jasmine wreathed women" who "dance holy sexual freedom," or when "Richard" writes of "Steven": "I smell him spread across the smouldering earth / I taste him in his seed I eat, in his ripetime / bursting he is flesh for food and food for flesh / core and skin."[34]

Neither such earnestness nor such earthy joy infused Lawrence's women's liberation movement. A few women, like those just quoted, did ground themselves in the pleasure and politics of lesbian sexuality, but in so doing they were—as they understood—challenging many of their movement sisters. In Lawrence, as elsewhere, the issue of lesbianism created schisms in an already fractured movement. [35]

Sexual freedom was not a consensus goal among women, even among those committed to liberation. Many, especially those who did not position themselves within the larger universe of radical politics, framed their concerns fairly tightly around the issue of gender equality. And while many of these women understood the current sexual organization of society to be a factor in, or a consequence of, women's oppression, the issue of sex, both hetero and homo, remained a controversial one in the polymorphous movement.

What appeared in Lawrence under the broad umbrella of women's liberation was wildly contradictory. Liberationist women were full participants in the use of sex as a weapon, in the proliferation of the vulgar, the scatological, the obscene. Some of these same women also loudly decried the exploitation of women in a sexualized commercial culture. Others sought to remake sexual relations through a renegotiation of gender roles. Many focused on women's right to control their own bodies. Some moved to a largely apolitical lesbian commune; others embraced lesbianism as politics; still others took up an aggressive notion of (hetero)sexual freedom. These are not simply different manifestations of a singular ideology; fundamental differences should not be obscured. However, when it came to sex, most women's liberation groups in Lawrence treated it as a problem, not a solution.

—

Some women, while not defining sex as a tool of liberation, believed that claiming their own sexual beings was one route to self-possession. It became an article of faith in many women's groups that the power they sought must be grounded in self-knowledge, and that this self-knowledge had a profoundly material base. As one of the more radical groups explained in a self-published "how-to" handout, "We believe that in learning to accept the care and knowledge of our own physical selves, we will be well on the road to self determination." These women, who "banded together to seriously consider some mutual questions concerning the care of their reproductive and fucking organs," repeatedly emphasized the "political implications of women being able to control their own bodies." At their first meeting, each had climbed up on the table and, with the "help of 5% courage and 95% curiosity," as well as plastic speculums ("one for each woman," they reassured their readers), they had begun "the process of awakening our consciousness to that area of self-knowledge and self-help between our navel-south."[36]

These women found their physical self-explorations "mind-blowing," and attempted to proselytize. But not all women felt equally liberated by such direct acknowledgment of their sexuality. A women's group in Lawrence hit a crisis point during the summer of 1970 after members decided to take off their clothes together. They had thought it was an important thing to do, but they discovered that the intimacy didn't have the effect they'd anticipated. When they came together for their next meeting it became clear that they were upset about the experience. (Someone tape-recorded that meeting and deposited the tape in the Kansas Collection at KU, specifying that it be sealed for twenty-five years.)[37] One of their number had become quite exhilarated when she stripped off her clothes, skipping around the room, wanting to run out on the porch. During the subsequent meeting several other women criticized her with great "honesty": "[She] pushes so hard for attention"; "I don't believe [she was] so happy." It was all "Look at me . . . Look at me . . ." But a member who hadn't been there interrupted. Maybe some of you are feeling guilty about the experience, she suggested, and are projecting that guilt toward the woman who had been the "most obviously nude."

Another woman, close to tears, confessed: "Until we started talking it felt ok. Now it's just the opposite. I would feel better off anywhere but the group now because of what happened last week." "Everybody said they were reassured enough about our group love that we could do it," a third woman said, somewhat plaintively, and a fourth asked, in a voice somewhere between concern and aggression, "Did anybody take their clothes off because they thought they had to?" The group tried to recast the discussion by acknowledging that they were all "in a state of very strong emotion . . . all a little nervous right now." But as they turned their focus to group dynamics, one woman said wistfully to another, "You looked so pure without your clothes on." And the other answered, rejecting that intimacy: "That's just because I'm so white."

As women sought strength and solidarity in the fundamental materiality of their bodies, not all found it. A reading for four voices compiled and directed by a woman from the dean of women's office in 1974 sounded more like a lament than a celebration:

> READER I : I know each of my sisters has sat
> locked in a still room
> with a mirror and a desk and a window, . . .
> I understand how long each of us was locked up
> with herself;

how each self became goddesslike,
in dreams,
compared to our *real* powerlessness.
READER 2: I thought I might be
the person I saw when I was alone.
READER 3: I thought I might be
the person a woman said she loved.
READER 4: I thought I might be
the rage that wanted to turn and kill my murderers.
READER 1: I thought I might be the shout and the explosion
that would destroy society
for making honest love between women
a crime.
But I am suspicious of
any woman who tells me she has seen her own face,
READER 2: knows what her voice sounds like,
READER 3: the shape of her body,
READER 4: or how her hands feel to themselves.

The piece had begun: "It is hard to be a woman; hard to be a lesbian; hard to be a heterosexual; hard to lie about important things. Almost impossible to respect yourself."[38]

—

Anger, not joy, gave shape to most of Lawrence's women's liberationist writings on sex. Sex appeared most often as a site of pain, a locus of oppression. Anger spilled out: strident or sarcastic, volcanic, oceanic. "I thought I might be the rage," one of the voices in the reading said. And a second: "I thought I might be the shout and the explosion that destroyed society."

The women who came to the revolution fighting for liberation did not so much celebrate the liberating force of making love as fight the exploitative power of sex. "A large part of our oppressions stem from the sexual exploitation of our bodies," stated one *Vortex* polemic. "Women's bodies are used as tools to sell everything from cars to magazines. As such, women are viewed as objects. It is difficult for a woman to walk down a street without being weighed, measured, and judged." This sexual exploitation reached from the anonymous city street and the newsstand into the intimacy of relationships: "Relationships with men often become strained and artificial because the man has been taught to regard the woman as a method of satisfying sexual drives rather than as an individual." The sexual revolution, the author claimed, had left women more exploited, not liberated. "We rationalize the constrictive Puritanical attitudes out, but instead of being offered more human and more fulfilling relationships, we are given the other side of the same bull-shit—the dehumanized role of the sex doll and the unpaid prostitute."[39]

Freedspeak, Lawrence High School's alternative newspaper, ran a series of articles to "try and point out the many ways women have been used, fucked over, in this society." In addition to being men's "housekeepers, baby-makers and ego-builders (just to name a few)," the introductory article asserted, "women are used to sell everything. The sexy woman's body sells shave cream, shampoo, cars, etc." Another article attempted to explode the "myth" that "women's lib followers" were "man-haters." Arguing that "all human beings are oppressed, not just women," the author explained: "If any feminists at all are 'man-haters' it is certainly only a few. These women 'hate' only certain individuals, such as Hugh Hefner, who makes his whole life exploiting women."[40] The greatest enemy the high school author could summon was a man who sexually objectified women.

In poetry and fiction, women authors moved from such analysis to fantasies of revenge. *The Lavender Luminary* twice published "True Story/A Fiction," in which:

> The corporate cock one day was hurrying on his way inflicting
> corporate punishment by committing
> corporate rape . . .

when

> he found a car with two lesbians and
> he harassed them to no end and
> they pulled out their double-labrys and
> killed him.[41]

And the radical *Oread Daily* retold a familiar tale: Cinderella, pregnant, bored, caught in the lie of happily ever after. One night,

> after the prince—now king—
> had taken his pleasure,

she slipped out
she escaped
with her child on her back
a rifle on her shoulder
leaving a piece of glass heel
in the throat of the king.[42]

Vortex, though it largely avoided the poetry and short stories that filled some of the other publications, did publish a tribute from the "Fucking Insane Sisters of Terrorism" to Valerie Salonas [sic], the "madwoman" who had shot and nearly killed Andy Warhol in 1968.[43] The headline was "HE ASKED ME TO EAT HIM"; the illustration, a woman posed with a skeleton, proclaimed: "He ASKED ME TO EAT HIM AND I DID." Though all these women believed oppression came in many forms, the most visceral anger attached to its sexualized expressions.

While fantasies of revenge abounded, only two (public) "terrorist" acts on behalf of women's liberation are recorded in Lawrence. One was committed by the Fucking Insane Sisters of Terrorism, who threw an offending issue of the *Kansan* into Potter Lake on campus. The other was the deed of a lone woman, who removed her shirt in public. The most celebrated and highly orchestrated act, the occupation of a campus building by "The February Sisters" in 1972, was definitely not terroristic. The Sisters immediately issued a press release insisting that their intentions were "non-violent [and] non-destructive," and they left an apple on each desk when they ended their brief occupation. No double labryses; no glass heels.

—

Moving beyond rhetoric, the concrete actions undertaken in the name of women's liberation varied greatly, as did the women who undertook them. However, concerns about sex and sexuality centered on women's ability to control their own bodies and to define the boundaries of sex for themselves. The liberation they sought was rarely identified with sexual freedom—in the conventional sense of the term. The concept of freedom circulating among these women was more complicated.

As a character in Margaret Atwood's dystopian novel *The Handmaid's Tale,* published in the mid-1980s, explained: "There is more than one kind of freedom. Freedom to and freedom from. In the days of anarchy it was freedom to. Now you are being given freedom from. Don't underrate it."

This cautionary fable of a right-wing fundamentalist Christian authoritarian state, in which women have no independent existence or public voice, posited the unwitting complicity of radical women's groups in destroying women's "freedom to." In attempts to "Take Back the Night" and end pornography's violence against women, these fictional feminists contributed to the anti-sex ascendency of the Christian right. In their suspicion of (hetero)sexuality and their demands to be freed *from* the oppression of a sexualized culture of violence and exploitation, they traded "Freedom to" for "Freedom from," and it was a bad bargain.[44]

Atwood's radical feminists were rooted in the rhetoric of the early women's liberation movement; while overdrawn, her "freedom from"/ "freedom to" dichotomy is useful as we analyze the public face of the movement. It's not that Lawrence's early feminists were anti-sex. Many if not most of these women practiced some version of sexual freedom in their own lives. There was no radical disjuncture between freedom from and freedom to in lived experience. And sex wasn't the central issue for most groups. The February Sisters did not say much at all about sex in the demands they addressed to the KU administration. They called for comprehensive women's health care, and they made it clear that it was unacceptable for health service doctors to subject patients to "morality lectures," but they did not discuss "sex." Their demands focused on such institutional issues as unfair employment practices and lack of equity in the distribution of scholarships, and they called for free day care, an affirmative action program directed by women appointed through the February Sisters, and a women's studies program. They were explicit: their action was "an expression of our frustration with the continuing sex-based inequities perpetrated by this university."[45] Gender inequity motivated them, not sexual revolution.

But women were beginning to complain about sexual exploitation, especially on campus. In the fall of 1970 there was a protest against "the alleged misuse of sex," as the *Kansan* called it, in the student paper's classified ads. The protests were prompted by two advertisements, one featuring a "young lady wrapped in a towel" and the other "a reclining woman with voluptuous curves."[46] Earlier the same month, women had complained in the *Kansan* about a "Waiver" being distributed to women in law school classes by their male colleagues: "I,_____, do hereby acknowledge that I am 18 years of age, or older, and do, further, hereby consent to the act-acts of sexual gratification that I will experience today. I, further, stipulate that I do this of my own free will and under no duress or coercion." The law school had long been notorious for such stunts. Since before World War II, when weather permitted, male law students had gathered to "girl watch," rating the passing women by holding up large cue cards bearing numbers from one to ten. As late as 1977 a student wrote to the *Kansan* to protest this continuing behavior: "Women are not cattle . . . packages of goods or brands of objects to be rated."[47]

Perhaps the most substantial public effort by women in Lawrence to redraw the boundaries of sexuality centered on rape. In 1972 the number of rapes reported in Lawrence increased by 271 percent over 1971, even as the overall crime rate decreased by 4.4 percent. In absolute numbers the change was somewhat less alarming—from four reported rapes in 1970 to seven in 1971 to twenty-six in 1972. At least eleven of those were committed by a single individual, who was eventually convicted of the crimes.

Pressed for an explanation of the growing number of rapes, Lieutenant Harrell of the Lawrence Police Department mentioned the abolition of the death penalty and said that crimes sometimes were an "indirect result of new freedom gained through activism." Pointing (wrongly and with absolutely no evidence) to the students at Haskell Indian Junior College, he noted: "They want to attend more taverns. They've often been drinking when they commit a crime." The signed *Kansan* editorial noted that "these seemingly simplistic explanations by a policeman for a complex and frightening issue indicate a need for an intense investigation by the police into the conditions that allow rape to occur so frequently in Lawrence."[48]

In the fall of 1972 Pat Henry, one of the women who had been sexually assaulted on campus the previous spring, established the Lawrence Community/University of Kansas Rape Victim Support Service (RVSS), an organization to provide peer support to rape victims and to change the ways medical personnel, police, and lawyers "reacted" to them.[49] While Henry did not make her own specific experiences public, some of the problems the organization was intended to address are evident in published sources. An article in the *Kansan* in 1970 entitled "Rapists and Molesters: Lone Women on Streets Provide Easy Target for Sex Offenders" offered a photograph of such a "lone woman" with the caption: "Even Today's Liberated Woman . . . can be helpless when all alone." The piece began: "Trees surrounded the single streetlight in the middle of the block and cast their shadows across the curbs and lawns. A lone woman was walking when a harsh voice broke the silence. She screamed, broke away and ran for the nearest house. She was lucky."[50]

As an increasingly vocal women's liberation movement met with some hostility in the tense atmosphere of late 1970, the implicit threat in this article was ominous, even if unintentional. But the article continued with advice from Dr. Schraeder, a psychiatrist at the student health center, who explained that "a woman sometimes plays a big part in provoking her attacker by the way she dresses, her actions and overall attitude and appearance." Many rapes, he noted, occurred when a woman accepted a ride with a strange man. "What is a woman's reasoning in getting picked up by a strange man?" he asked rhetorically. "I don't see as much of this as I used to, but I never could understand the flashily dressed woman that was surprised and even frigid when a man made a pass at her."

RVSS volunteers worked with women who had been raped, trying to make them understand that they had not—no matter what the KU psychiatrist said—"provoked" their attackers. And they tried to move Lawrence's police, courts, and medical personnel to see rape not as a relatively understandable act of sexual passion provoked by the "flashily dressed woman," but as a crime of violence. It was a complicated position, for in order to be effective they had to maintain and even strengthen relations with officials like the police detective who, in 1974, greeted them with, "Oh, you're here to talk about women who get their boxes knocked off." Through diplomacy and persistence, they built a network of support throughout Lawrence. By late 1975 Kathy Hoggard, one of the volunteers, was able to tell a *Kansan* reporter: "I suspect that in many places rape victims are still treated like damaged goods. But in Lawrence, a woman who is raped will be treated very well by the police." This public statement is supported by private RVSS notes and incident reports, which note that police detectives had been particularly "sensitive" or "helpful" in questioning rape victims.[51]

It has become common wisdom that rape is a crime of violence, not sex—to the extent that some seek to resexualize our concept of rape, fearing that in emphasizing generic violence we have lost the understanding of how sexual violence is different from other sorts of physical assault. In the 1970s, however, activists were working to destroy the assumption, held not only by the average citizen but by those with direct power and authority over rape victims, that rape was simply an extreme version of normal male sexual response. They meant to desexualize rape.

Their effort may not seem a part of the sexual revolution, but only if we conceive of the sexual revolution as "freedom to." If claiming the right to have sex outside the bonds of marriage was revolutionary, was it not equally revolutionary for women to assert control over their bodies, over their sexual beings, and to attempt to redraw the boundaries of sex, insisting that violence and exploitation not be accepted and even celebrated as "sexual freedom"? The twinned notions of freedom and exploitation shaped many feminists' understandings of the sexual revolution. And while many of these feminists may have found joy or fulfillment in sex, few of them saw (hetero)sex as a means to liberation despite the media's frequent use of the term "liberated" as a code word for sexually free or even "promiscuous."[52]

The shared term "liberation" bound the women's liberation movement and the (primarily male) gay liberation movement together in some intangible sense, despite the fact that parts of each movement were uncomfortable with—if not downright hostile to—the other. When it came to the role of sex in their respective movements, they worked from very different assumptions. In a very real way, however, they did compose a coherent, though complex, strand of the sexual revolution. For in their divergent struggles over the role of sex in liberation, both movements challenged the idea that women's saying "yes" to men instead of "no" was enough to constitute a revolution. In seeking liberation, they meant to change the world and to remake the place of sex in it.

8

~

Remaking Sex

Late in the spring of 1968 the new president of Barnard College, Martha Peterson, traveled from New York to her native Kansas, where she addressed the graduating class of Salina High School. It is likely she stopped off in Lawrence to visit her mother, who worked as a clerk in a local hardware store, and to see friends from her days as KU's dean of women. She returned as a minor celebrity, a woman whose picture had just been in *Time* magazine and whose name was bandied about by newspaper columnists and cultural critics throughout the country. It was not something she was pleased about. Dr. Peterson's unwelcome brush with fame overshadowed her local-girl-makes-good return to Kansas; even the Salina high school students wanted to hear about what national pundits had christened the "LeClair Affair."[1]

In Martha Peterson's first year as Barnard's president, right in the middle of a major fundraising campaign, she had been blindsided by an institutional scandal of national proportion. It had started with an article in the lifestyle section of the *New York Times:* "An Arrangement: Living Together for Convenience, Security, Sex." The piece was not meant as an exposé; the surrounding articles were "How to Duck the Hemline Issue" and "A Cook's Guide to the Shallot."[2] But this feature story, which offered a fairly sympathetic portrait of several unmarried student couples who lived together in New York City, included an interview with a Barnard sophomore who rather naively explained to a reporter how she had used loopholes in Barnard's strict housing regulations to live with her boyfriend in a

$100-a-month apartment on Riverside Drive. Not surprisingly, the article caught the attention of Barnard administrators, who had little trouble identifying "Susan" as Linda LeClair.[3]

LeClair was charged and brought before the college judiciary council—not for her sexual conduct, but for lying to Barnard about her housing arrangements. In a letter to the student newspaper she argued that the housing regulations discriminated on the basis of sex, for Columbia men had no such rules. Noting that "Barnard College was founded on the principle of equality between women and men," she asked: "If women are able, intelligent people, why must we be supervised and curfewed?"[4]

The student-faculty judiciary council deliberated for five hours. In the end, it found LeClair guilty of violating college regulations, but it also called for reform of the housing policy. The punishment the council members recommended for LeClair seemed like black humor to most people who had been to college: they barred her from the Barnard cafeteria. President Peterson refused to accept the council's decision. Drawing on her many years of experience as a dean of women, Peterson wrote to Linda: "It is my inescapable conclusion that no useful purpose can be served by your continued enrollment at Barnard College." Final dispensation, she stipulated, would depend on Linda's semester grades. But Linda dropped out of Barnard before the end of the semester.

Barnard administrators attempted to treat Linda's transgressions as a college matter, confined to the familial framework of *in loco parentis,* but her case became irrevocably public. The media were quick to take up a story that offered such potential for twinned moralism and salaciousness. And so Linda LeClair's conduct and her fate became the focus of what amounted to a national referendum on the sexual mores of the nation's youth. As *Life* magazine proclaimed, in virtually self-fulfilling prophecy: "A sexual anthropologist of some future century, analyzing the pill, the drive-in, the works of Harold Robbins, the Tween-Bra and all the other artifacts of the American Sexual Revolution, may consider the case of Linda LeClair and her boyfriend, Peter Behr, as a moment in which the morality of an era changed."[5]

While this drama was played out on a single campus, it was much more than a struggle over Barnard's housing regulations. In its public incarnations, the LeClair case became a synecdoche for the sexual (im)morality of youth, and the ensuing controversy showed in just how many different ways Americans understood what they were all calling "the sexual revolution." The strand of the revolution Peter and Linda represent appears modest compared to many claims of the women's and gay liberation movements, even more so compared to "the" counterculture's uses of sex as a weapon. These modest revolutionaries didn't use the word "fuck" in public writings and scarcely ever made claims about sexual freedom. But their claims and actions were no less revolutionary, no less a challenge to "traditional" sexual mores. This strand of the revolution, one that defined sex (in earnest tones) as *part* of a relationship between two human beings and that tended toward monogamous relationships and cohabitation, fundamentally challenged the dominant paradigm that located sex—and its control—in the *difference* between men and women. These revolutionaries claimed commonality; they sought freedom from strict male and female roles. They meant to remake sex by remaking gender.

—

After the LeClair story broke, Dr. Peterson's office received more than two hundred telephone calls (most demanding expulsion) and over one hundred letters; editorials ran in newspapers, large and small, throughout the country. The response was truly national, and overwhelmingly negative.[6] Francis Beamen of Needham, Massachusetts, suggested that Barnard should be renamed "BARNYARD"; Charles Orsinger of San Antonio wrote: "If you let Linda stay in college, I can finally prove to my wife with a front page news story about that bunch of glorified whores going to eastern colleges." A Presbyterian minister wrote from a small town in West Virginia: "Quite frankly, and quite bluntly, we had a name for girls like her when I was in school which began with w_____." And an attorney from New Rochelle ventured the opinion that "in all probability, [LeClair] is being educated beyond her intelligence." Mrs. M. J. Payne of Bellingham, Washington, accused President Peterson of contributing to the "moral decline of our country," despite Peterson's public opposition to LeClair's actions: "You are opening the way for thousands of students to live in open sinful, immoral living-together." Frank Hosic wrote from Cleveland: "Thank the Lord, I have no daughter attending Barnard who would be forced, even vicariously, to associate with—to put it bluntly—a reputed whore." An octogenarian from Los Angeles enclosed quotations about decadence and the fall of the Roman Empire from Will Durant's *The Story of Civilization*.

Newspaper editorials were no more measured in tone. The Benton Harbor, Michigan, *News-Palladium* opined that "chastity among women is an appropriate and reasonable moral characteristic to require of young ladies," explaining that "any promiscuous woman, even one who shares only the bed of the one man who won't tell, is a pathetic figure—either the butt of locker room jokes, or destined to get the shattering brushoff that ultimately comes to all trusting fools." And William F. Buckley, whose column appeared in newspapers across the nation, expressed no surprise "that the LeClairs of this world should multiply like rabbits, whose morals they imitate."[7]

Despite pervasive animal imagery (the term "alley cat" was also common) most of those who wrote to Peterson were attempting to come to terms with the changing morality of America's youth. Many letters were from parents who understood the symbolic import of the incident. As one writer from Illinois noted, "Parents all across this nation will be following this case." In detailing their disapproval, those who did not simply rant about "whoredom" structured their comments around concepts of public and private. Most of these were willing to acknowledge that "mistakes" could happen; many were willing to allow for a little "discreet" sex among the unmarried young. But for Linda and Peter to admit openly that they lived together and for LeClair to claim publicly the right to determine her own "private" life—those were something else entirely.[8]

The most striking thing about the letters to President Peterson is how often the word "flaunt" appears. Linda and Peter were "openly flaunting their disregard of moral codes"; they were "violating the laws of decency when they flaunt their derelictions in public"; they were "openly flaunting rules of civilized society." (Some writers obviously confused flaunting and flouting.) "Do not let Miss LeClair attend Barnard as long as she flaunts immorality in your face," one writer advised.

These letters show just how far apart two worlds had grown. Many of America's youth—even many who were quite conservative compared to the extremes of the counterculture—rejected a world in which sleeping with her boyfriend made a young woman a "whore." But that was only the first level of the divergence. The woman who wrote to Peterson that "it is time for these young people to put sex back in its proper place, instead of something to be flaunted" and Buckley, who in his column condemned the "delinquency of this pathetic little girl, so gluttonous for sex and publicity," were not listening to the young people they judged. Sex was not what Linda and Peter talked about. Sex was not mentioned. Security was, and "family." "Peter is my family," said Linda. "It's a very united married type of relationship—it's the most important one in each of our lives. And our lives are very much intertwined."[9]

Of course they had sex. They were young and in love. Their peer culture accepted sex in those circumstances. They had an apartment. Sex was a part of their "relationship" and they never suggested otherwise. But what they claimed was a partnership—a partnership that obviated the larger culture's insistence on the difference between men and women. Linda explicitly refused to accept the idea that men and women had different interests and needs. She was not concerned that she would lose "value" in the marriage market by having premarital sex, and she was not worried about her "reputation." In the universe of Linda LeClair and Peter Behr, the letter suggesting to Barnard's president that young women would "welcome a strong rule against living with men to protect them against doing that" made no sense.

Many people in the 1960s and 1970s struggled with questions of equality and difference in sophisticated and thoughtful ways. Neither Peter Behr nor Linda LeClair was especially gifted in that respect. What they argued was commonplace to them—a natural language and set of assumptions that nonetheless had revolutionary implications. It is when a set of assumptions becomes natural and unselfconscious, when a language appears in the private comments of a wide variety of people, that the assumptions and the language demand to be taken seriously.

The word "whore" and its correlates welled up in response to Linda LeClair's story—from lawyers and psychiatrists and housewives and even a minister and a self-described "hillbilly"; from California and New York and Texas and Ohio and Florida and Illinois and Colorado and South Carolina; from the cosmopolitan as well as from the provincial. Linda LeClair was a "whore" because she lived with her boyfriend. The ubiquity of the term reminds us how ugly, and how sexist, much of the mainstream culture was. The word "whore," repeatedly applied to a young woman in a long-term monogamous relationship, offers a critical context for understanding "the sexual revolution." No matter how extreme some strands of this revolution were, the beliefs the revolutionaries opposed were also extreme.

The unselfconscious and commonplace use of the word "whore" reveals deeply rooted assumptions that underlay discussions of "morality" and sexual "standards" in various segments of American society. But by 1968 the languages of sexual revolution had also become unselfconscious and commonplace. The word "fuck" seemed ubiquitous; the rhetoric of liberation circulated freely. And the language spoken by Linda LeClair and

Peter Behr, obviating a male-female dichotomy, claiming a common humanity, not only was on the lips of students at progressive institutions on the east and west coasts, but also was the unselfconscious language of many 18- and 19-year-old boys from rural Kansas.

—

In the fall of 1970 a group of students at the University of Kansas began working with the administration to create "a coed living situation." Coed dorms were nothing new at KU. The first such experiment took place in the summer of 1959, and all who went on record were quite pleased with the results. Another coed dorm was created during the summer of 1964, and the *Kansan* reported on it with tongue-in-cheek drama: "Peaceful co-existence came to KU this past summer, although university residence halls, not a summit conference, were the site of an experiment in human relations." Overall, the students were well satisfied, though a woman complained that it was awkward to go downstairs to the candy machine with her hair in curlers. Residents noted "improved manners" and praised the opportunity to "meet and date the opposite sex." In fact, 50 percent of them reported having dated other residents.[10]

The students who developed the proposal in 1970 would have been appalled at such reasoning. They very explicitly and insistently rejected "convenience in finding dates" as a justification for coed dorms. And while their choice of language was certainly strategic—you didn't want to remind administrators of S-E-X, though no one seriously thought they'd forget about it—these students were not facing opposition. By 1970 there were already three coed dorms on campus, one of which had opened in 1966. This proposed coed hall, however, was not to be like the other dorms. It would be a scholarship hall, a residence exclusively for graduates of Kansas high schools attending KU on scholarship. These halls were much smaller than the existing coed dorms. Most had fifty or fewer residents, and these students were expected to do housekeeping chores in the halls as a condition of financial aid. The administration was supportive of the coed plan but concerned about the future of the scholarship hall system in general. It had become increasingly difficult to recruit qualified students into a fairly old-fashioned system. "Chores" were not the same as paid jobs, and scholarship halls segregated these students from others and publicly defined them as Kansans who were "on scholarship." Students who lived in the halls tended to be quite committed to them, however, and had administrative backing.[11]

The proposal crafted by this group of committed scholarship hall residents was long on philosophy and short on details. In the several drafts that survive, one key point is made over and over: men and women need to get to know each other as human beings. These students sought to put male-female relationships on a "friendship basis" rather than a "dating basis," because, as they explained, dating was built around "previous expectations" about male and female roles, while "friendship" would allow men and women to transcend those limiting roles. "The coed living situation," this proposal claimed,

> would contribute to the development of each resident as a full human being. Opportunities to formulate a self-concept based upon what one really is, instead of upon standard roles, would be increased . . . If a woman desires more spontaneous and thorough interaction with a male than typical male-female situations might afford, she could benefit from a situation in which they both wash dishes together. The same advantage could hold true for a male. In other words, what we aim to accomplish is opportunities for interpersonal relationships based on friendship and cooperative efforts rather than on the male/female roles we usually play in dating situations . . . Residents will develop a real concern for what others think and do, . . . a human concern that transcends membership in one or the other sex. This would be a really challenging living situation, but it is in meeting this challenge that residents could grow.[12]

The authors—showing they were serious about this "challenge"—recommended a mandatory three-week-long orientation course for residents of the new coed hall.

In the previous spring semester the offices of the dean of men and the dean of women had conducted a survey of scholarship hall residents. Each person was asked to rate his or her level of interest in living in a coed dorm, to indicate whether or not it would be *possible* ("including parental reaction") to do so, and to state housing choices for the following year. The forms left plenty of space for open-ended responses.[13]

Because of the different approaches of the two deans, only the men's responses survive. Of the men, 75 percent—and this survey had a 100 percent response rate—said they were interested in living in a coed hall; 10 percent were neutral. Only 4.5 percent said they were "very uninterested," but those men were vehement. One bore down so hard as he registered his opposition he almost tore the paper. Another opponent wrote simply, "ugly girls." A few supporters left it at "interesting experiment," or "I'm curious. Why not?" Most, however, had more to say, and the consistency of language used to support—or attack—the plan is striking. This survey was conducted well before the proposal for a coed hall was drafted, so that document did not structure the survey responses.

"As a stereotypical answer," one man wrote, "I already am able to do all the roleplaying socially I need, and see communication now as an ultimate goal." A student who listed his classification as both "soph." and "4-F I Hope" said: "I believe that the segregation of the sexes is unnatural. I would like to associate with women on a basis other than dating roles. This tradition of segregation is discriminatory and promotes inequality of mankind." One man declared his desire to "get to know the opposite sex as they really are instead of [in] artificial situations such as dating." Another called coed living "more humane"; one of his hall-mates proclaimed the "present structured roles of the sexes" a "philosophical farce," and expressed his belief that coed living "would effectively destroy them." The most eloquent of the sophomores wrote: "[It would] allow them to meet and interact with one another in a situation relatively free of sexual overtones; that is, the participating individuals would be free to encounter one another as human beings, rather than having to play the traditional stereotyped male and female roles. I feel that coed living is the only feasible way to allow people to escape this stereotypical role behavior."

The most cogently stated argument against the plan came from a young man who insisted: "To say that it would be a puritanical brother sister relationship is ridiculous. First of all these people are not blood relatives and everyone knows what incest is . . . [You] can't ignore the sexual overtones involved in coed living; after all, sex is the basic motivation for your plan. (I didn't say lust, I said sex)." One of his compatriots in another hall thought the "brother sister" scenario less ridiculous, but for that very reason rejected the plan: "I do not believe that the brother-sister type of relationship which would probably develop is either desirable or beneficial." One thought it impossible, the other thought it undesirable, but both saw the purported goal of coed living as fostering nonsexual relationships between men and women.

The young men and women who favored coed living did not mean to dismiss sex or, for that matter, romance. But they believed there were other bases for involvement between the sexes. The critic who had no desire for a "brother-sister type of relationship" implied that his only interest in women was romantic or sexual. These students did not want to write off every member of the opposite sex to whom they were not sexually attracted. They believed men and women had much to share as "people." And for those who did become romantically and/or sexually involved, they reasoned, it was better to meet outside the artificial system of dating. Coed living, they believed, could provide a system of gender equality, in which men and women would share responsibilities, truly talk with one another, and break down the restrictive roles that impeded true intimacy.

—

No matter how adamant students were about their philosophical justifications, the issue of sex would not simply disappear. Some men and women clearly had sexual relationships in coed halls or dormitories—though possibly fewer in these supervised residences than in the off-campus apartments that by the early 1970s housed the majority of KU's students. But coed dorms—because they openly placed the sexes in such proximity—were especially vulnerable to charges of sexual misconduct.

In early December 1967, as fall-semester classes wound to a close, the *Kansan* ran a front-page article on "Hanky-Panky" in a coed dorm, McCollum Hall. Showing how much students were still caught between worlds, the writer used a term from the previous generation—PDA, or Public Display of Affection—to describe what was going on. Emery Goad, a senior from Junction City and president of the 1,000-resident dormitory, told a *Kansan* reporter that McCollum's executive board was taking action to crack down on PDA. This action was not initiated by the administration but by students themselves. According to Goad, "necking [had] become a popular pastime as the residents became better acquainted," and this "undue physical contact that's out of the ordinary" was embarrassing some residents. Thus the executive board had decided to "supervise . . . stairwells, the library, and the stereo room."[14] (While the dorm had been coed since 1966, men and women were not yet permitted in each other's rooms.)

This brief article in the student paper became a television news story about the "mass necking problem" at McCollum Hall, and parents tied up the dormitory switchboard with calls from around the state—most of them to daughters, not sons.[15] The story was picked up by the newspapers, and by television and radio stations throughout the Midwest. More calls flooded in. McCollum residents were outraged. One offered Goad ten dollars to resign as president. When that didn't work, male residents impeached him. The controversy—and the flood of letters it provoked—kept students reading the *Kansan* even as finals neared.

Some letters disputed the magnitude of the problem. Goad had estimated that about 10 percent of residents were involved; other dorm officers wrote to correct his figures. It was not fifty couples, but only ten, they insisted. A senior from Colby, Kansas, wrote that he had rushed home from class after reading the article, anticipating that he'd find fifty couples "lying around on the floor in the depths of passion." Instead, he encountered one couple, sitting quietly, reading the newspaper and holding hands. Despite his sarcasm, this writer also accepted "the PDA problem" as a framework, arguing that it was more like one percent of residents who behaved inappropriately—though with those, he noted, "the situation is more or less perpetual."[16]

One resident, a junior from New York City, rejected this framework entirely. Whether one couple or all 1,000 residents engaged in "undue physical contact" was irrelevant to him. PDA was not the problem. Writing as one who had been "curbed" in the crackdown, he described his crime. He and his girlfriend were watching television in the lounge. He had his arm around her shoulders. A staff assistant, "dressed in a mini-skirt no less," told them to "sit in a more appropriate position or go to a more appropriate place." He continued:

> I suppose the "more appropriate place" is the back seat of a car which everyone seems to enjoy very much. You have to display any kind of emotion in the back seat of a car because love, or anything that suggests love, is filthy, disgusting, and repulsive to others. What the residents' embarrassment is is really an overwhelming sense of guilt. They are so hung up in their pseudo-morality that any presentation of reality is unbearably traumatic . . . The proposed crackdown, encompassing all-night illumination of the lobby and constant supervision of the stairwells by McCollum storm troopers, strongly brings to mind Orwell's sexless society of 1984 . . . It is indeed alarming that a society which can blindly rationalize an immoral war and blatant discrimination cannot tolerate public displays of affection.[17]

With Goad's impeachment the controversy subsided, but this episode serves as a reminder that boundaries of sexual expression were at issue not only between the young and their elders but among the students themselves. This was, after all, only three years after the "Morality Survey" in which 91 percent of KU freshmen and seniors said premarital sex was morally unacceptable.[18]

While these students publicly squabbled over sexual behavior, the KU administration stayed out of the fight. In general the administration tried to downplay the issue of sex whenever possible. Just as the dean of women had informed parents in the late 1950s that senior keys for women were not about sexual freedom but about maturity and responsibility, these administrators portrayed new arrangements such as coed dorms as ways to encourage "mature and responsible relations between the sexes." In these comments, administrators share much with the "modest revolutionaries" quoted earlier. The defensive document prepared in 1969 as KU began to institute an open visitation policy (which allowed men and women free access to each other's rooms) both expressed confidence in the "maturity and responsibility of the younger generation" and explicitly rejected the "often repeated statement" that "the only thing two young people of the opposite sex are studying behind closed doors in the residence hall is anatomy." While not fully accepting the students' claims that such contact would destroy inequality and stifling sex roles, these administrators did assert that "the companionship of persons of the opposite sex is frequently conducive to serious academic work," and argued that open visitation would make life more "normal," and thus "more hospitable to both intellectual and personal growth."[19]

Acknowledging that "the problems that accompany relations between young men and women are well known to those who counsel them," these administrators nevertheless concluded that "the benefits of open-visitation in encouraging mature and responsible relationships between the sexes outweigh the potential risks of additional tragedy."[20] This is not precisely the same argument that the scholarship hall students were making. Students were unlikely to refer to sexual relationships as "tragedies." The administrators were still working primarily within the framework of "responsibility," which presumed that students would develop maturity by making their own decisions (and which gambled that those decisions would be the "right" ones when it came to sex).

Thus the administrators, responding to public concerns about the "risk" of sex, argued that increased freedom of contact between male and female students would not increase the incidence of "tragedy." This argument kept sex front and center even as they attempted to downplay the role of sex in their policies and plans. The scholarship hall students, in contrast, were trying to reposition sex in the context of male-female equality and multidimensional relationships, while at the same time endorsing the sort of sexual bonds that might grow in this new coed setting. As they attempted to craft associations between men and women that were not centered around or mediated through sexual attraction and prescribed sex roles, these students also intended to provide a new basis of honesty and equality for the sexual connections that did develop. The outcomes the two groups envisioned were not identical. Nonetheless, both the scholarship hall students and the student life administrators meant to change the nature of sexual relationships by changing the nature of interactions between the sexes.

———

Paradoxically, this attempt to remake sex by remaking gender roles received its fullest expression outside the boundaries of heterosexuality. As members of Lawrence's gay community formulated a philosophy and a call to action in the early 1970s, they targeted gender roles in language no less adamant than that used by those working within a heterosexual framework. Gay and lesbian activists argued that socially prescribed masculine and feminine roles not only created a gulf between men and women but circumscribed the potential of all human relationships. "We are gay because we reject strict role definitions for men and women," the "Women and Men of the Lawrence Gay Liberation Front" wrote in one of their first manifestos. "[We are gay] because we want to relate out of our total beings, whether that essence is at times called feminine or masculine by straight society." Addressing an imagined heterosexual "you," the authors insisted that the "hard work" required is "as much your responsibility as it [is] ours, for it is your liberation too. It is your liberation from restrictive role playing in human interaction. When the way you love people is not based upon conditioned behavior, but goes fully out to men and women from shared relationships, then you will begin to understand gay liberation. In effect you will cease being straight, but you will regain the full potential of your humanity."[21]

Once again, the revolutionary goal appears. These writers begin with the premise that true sexual freedom is not just more of the same. Freedom to engage in an act that is structured by inequality and limited by the restrictions of "masculinity" and "femininity" is not freedom at all. Sex, they argue, must be reinvented. Loving someone of the same sex is a start, but it is not sufficient. True freedom and fulfillment lie in transcending the sexual categories of male and female, choosing to love another person because of his or her humanity, not his or her sex. Freedom comes from creating oneself as a whole person, masculine and feminine. Freedom comes from "speaking in new voices, new words; it is liberation from the categories and myths" of heterosexual society's gendered love.

In *Lavender,* a film about lesbianism made in Lawrence in the 1970s and shown through the KU dean of women's office as part of its progressive program of education and counseling, two women discuss the need "for people to understand a real lesbian couple." This film attempts to naturalize the homoerotic by the most obvious means—endless shots of nature. The women run through the snow, embrace in sunshot images. But what it does much more effectively is domesticate lesbian love. At the heart of the film are the women in their apartment, cooking, eating, watching TV. The most naturalizing shot may be the one of the two side by side in their nightgowns, brushing their teeth. The voice-over throughout is predictably earnest, as the women reject the "stereotypes" of lesbians. The young lesbians they know are "intent on being women, loving women." "One of the exciting things about this kind of relationship is that we have the freedom to really create the relationship."[22]

Other challenges to gender roles were more explicit and more extreme. In a long, unsigned coming-out story published in *Vortex,* one gay man conflated object choice and gender identity into his definition of being "gay." "All my life," he wrote, "I've had to struggle against two labels in order to justify my existence in straight society": "Homosexual," and "Effeminate." Describing his "indoctrination" in "self-hate" by the "ogre SOCIETY," he began with the lesson that "there is nothing more sinful, sick, and *abnormal* than making love with a person of your own sex." But most of his personal testimony focused on the oppressive force of gender roles in his life. "To violate the rigid law for speech, demeanor, choice of work and play, and modes of interpersonal contact that were seemingly God-given to each of the sexes," he said about the second label, effeminacy, ". . . and thereby abandon the privileges and prerogatives of masculinity is [treated as] the vilest offense against 'Nature.'"[23]

His story was not so much about the difficulty of forbidden love or forbidden sex as of forbidden identity. He wrote of adolescent struggles, of "telling myself that it's really okay that I'm a homosexual because I'm not bothering anybody with it . . . telling myself that I was better than 'faggots' because I was masculine—i.e. acceptable." He detailed the lessons he had taught himself: to keep his voice low and on an even pitch, to sit "straight-front," with "legs spread like other males," even, after reading in a book that "'faggots' had limp wrists," "disciplining" himself to keep his "stiff."

Coming out, for this man, was not only about loving other men, but about accepting "faggotry": "I used to stereotype faggots as somebody who wears colorful clothes, has limp wrists, has a poodle, is an interior decorator, talks effeminately, is submissive, weak, passive. Till now I have been so afraid of that image." But his liberation lay in recognizing the power inherent in that identity: "It takes a lot of feminist strength to live that way in this culture."

"Gay is beautiful," he proclaimed, as he moved into exhortation. "Faggotry can be revolutionary." So, "if the MAN says I'm supposed to have stiff wrists, I let mine droop. If HE says somber work-shirts and blue jeans are correct, I'm going to wear a dress. If HE says don't lisp, I'm going to scream my lisp. Fuck 'em . . . Effeminacy is a word that says there is something wrong with being feminine if you're a man—but that word no longer has any meaning because there's *nothing wrong* with being Feminine. Feminine means being sensitive, autonomous, strong, and good."

As exhortation gave way to prescription, he circled back to an integrative vision and reintroduced the critical components of sex and love. By integrating the masculine and feminine, we become whole, he explained, and in our wholeness, we become "able to love anybody, regardless of sex." He concluded: "Become whole. Be Gay. Be Proud, honey."

This man's vision was at the extreme end of a continuum. "Faggotry" was not the outcome or the process most envisioned when they called for "a human concern that transcends membership in one or the other sex." But this man, along with others in Lawrence's Gay Liberation Front and like most of the KU scholarship hall students, engaged the revolution first by renegotiating gender. They were going to remake sex in the process of remaking gender. By the early 1970s these claims had become no more and no less than common wisdom.

———

In 1972, at 7 P.M. on a cold December night, Lawrence's public radio station aired a show entitled "The Dating Game."[24] It began with a series of on-the-street interviews—young men and women responding with varying degrees of discomfort to versions of the question "Do men and women have trouble relating in a dating situation?" The rest of the show was panel discussion. The five discussants, men and women ranging in age from 18 to 23, seemed to forget they were on the radio after a while. There was a lot of giggling, and sometimes everyone talked at once. But there was little disagreement. Everyone involved decried the "artificiality" of dating, complained about the difficulty of really "getting to know someone" in that atmosphere, insisted on the importance of "really talking." A woman criticized the "sexual aspect of dating . . . not viewed as a relationship between two people but between a male person and female person and that's so steeped in sexuality." One of the men responded with a story. He'd recently spent four or five hours "really talking" with a girl he liked. One of his friends just couldn't believe it: "You spent four hours together and you didn't do anything?" His answer: "Sure, we did a lot, but it was all verbal."

The group discussed the pros and cons of group versus couple dating, and then circled back to sex. We need to "get ourselves liberated enough from the whole sexual bag, sexual thing, so you meet people openly and honestly, just as people, without thinking of [them] as sexual objects," one man said, and a women concurred: "We've been talking all around that." Another man called it a shame that men and women "can't just be our-selves"; after all, he said, here we are, men and women talking together, with "no sexual overtones . . . [pause] . . . though we are talking about sex." And the group dissolved into laughter.

Like Peter Behr and Linda LeClair, like the KU scholarship hall students—and even, to some extent, like the gay liberation activists—these young adults in Lawrence, Kansas, were attempting to redefine both sex and sex roles. They insisted, with greater and lesser degrees of self-awareness, that sex should not be negotiated through dichotomous pairings of male and female. They sought sexual relationships grounded in the common humanity of the participants, not in the notions of sexual difference on which the ideological system that controlled (hetero)sex had been based.

The *Life* magazine article that proposed the LeClair affair as the defining moment of America's sexual revolution went on to characterize that "revolution" as "dull." "Love still makes the world go square," the author concluded, for the revolutionaries he interviewed subscribed to a philosophy "less indebted to *Playboy* than *Peanuts*, in which sex is not so much a pleasure as a warm puppy." To his amusement, one "California girl" had told him, "Besides being my lover, Bob is my best friend in all the world," and a young man had insisted, "We are not sleeping together, we are living together."[25]

For those to whom *Playboy* promised revolution, this attitude was undoubtedly tame. And in the context of the cultural revolution taking place among America's youth and documented in titillating detail by magazines like *Life,* these were modest revolutionaries indeed, seeming almost out of step with their generation. The earnest voices of these young people, calling for relationships based on friendship and equality and centered in the individuals' common humanity, tend to get lost in the cacophony, submerged in the spectacle offered by "Free Love." But this strand lies at the heart of it all. These people sought to remake sex, not just to free it. Thus the common wisdom stated by a 19-year-old college kid from rural Kansas may be the most truly revolutionary part of the "sexual revolution."

Epilogue

What is the legacy of the sexual revolution? We as a society do not agree, and that disagreement itself is one result of this revolution. In the last half of the twentieth century, a public consensus on what was "moral" and "legitimate" has been replaced by a multiplicity of voices. While that consensus was built on the division between public claims and private acts and was maintained by a culture that silenced the voices and denied the experiences of many Americans, it was powerful. It not only set limits on public discourse but was written into law and public policy, incorporated into psychological theory, taught to children in schools, enforced by peer groups. The sexual revolution did not destroy the beliefs central to this prerevolutionary public consensus. Polls reveal that large numbers of Americans still believe that sex is immoral except within marriage and that homosexuality is a sin. The rise of organizations like the Promise Keepers demonstrates the continuing strength of "traditional" values that include the subordination of women. But, because of the sexual revolution, these beliefs and values are contested. They do not mark the boundaries of public discourse; they are proclaimed by one set of voices among many.

As we continue to struggle over the legacy of revolution, however, it is important to remember that the revolution was not just about sex—that is, about what sexual acts are legitimate, what sexual images can be seen in public. It was also about concepts of rights and duties, citizenship, equality. The conflicts of the sexual revolution were, in part, over who could belong to America's civil society, whose voices could be heard. The greater inclusiveness of American society after World War II helped to undermine the public consensus about sexuality. The growing influence of a national culture and of the federal government, combined with the dislocations of war and the social and economic mobility of the postwar era, lessened the power of local elites and created spaces for new voices, new ways, new demands. The broadening base of America's public culture caused the sexual revolution every bit as much as did the demands of young people for sexual freedom.

And even the sexual freedom demanded by American youth was always about more than sex. Many countercultural figures used sex as a symbol of the larger freedoms they sought; others used sexual words and images as weapons against the society they hoped to destroy. In creating a public culture largely centered around sexual identity, orientation, and practice, some gay men and lesbians forged a claim to public rights. That position is not uncontested today, but whether one looks to domestic partnership laws or to Queer Nation, it is clear that the possibilities for acting in America's civil society have been transformed.

The sexual revolution also played a critical role in America's continuing negotiations over gender relations and sexual equality. A system that controlled sexual behavior partly by insisting on the differences between men and women shaped gender relations well beyond the bedroom. A system that equated a woman's "value" with her sexual "virtue" necessarily circumscribed women's sphere. The progress we have made toward gender equality in this nation is, to a great extent, possible because the sexual revolution weakened a sexual ideology that reinforced women's subordination in all realms of life.

The sexual revolution was created by the fundamental transformations of modern American society, and it in turn fundamentally shaped our contemporary notions of power, identity, diversity, and gender. Thus to reject the sexual revolution, incoherent and contradictory and mixed as its blessings are, is to reject much more than a narrow notion of sexual "freedom."

In evaluating the legacies of revolution, however, we must confront the crisis of AIDS. As we look back from the present to the late 1960s and early 1970s, the brave new world of sexual freedom heralded by revolutionaries seems no more than a moment of illusion. Penicillin had vanquished venereal disease; the Pill had put an end to the fear of pregnancy. Sex, freed from consequences, could be remade. But the human triumph over disease was fleeting. The younger brothers and sisters of the revolutionary cohort came of sexual age facing the new threat of genital herpes, which was soon dwarfed by the discovery of the sexually transmitted Human Immunodeficiency Virus and the potential deaths of millions, throughout the world, from AIDS.

The threat of AIDS has largely eliminated one possible trajectory of the sexual revolution. Those who have grown up knowing that "unsafe" sex can kill them will never wholeheartedly believe in the liberating power of sexual freedom, no matter what their sexual practices. And those, myself included, who have lost loved ones to AIDS cannot look back on the sexual revolution and its claims to sexual freedom without seeing the shadow of what was to come. AIDS cannot be ignored, but it is not the epitaph for revolution. If we view AIDS as the foreordained endpoint of sexual revolution, we fail to understand the full significance and possibility of that revolution.

In seeking the lessons of the sexual revolution, we need to begin with an understanding of what people were in revolt against. We need to remember the young gay man who was sent to the psychiatrist under threat of expulsion from college. We need to remember Linda LeClair, branded a whore in newspapers across the nation for the crime of living with her boyfriend. We need to tell stories that look past extreme claims and radical actions to the texture of everyday life in places like Kansas. We need to understand how thoroughly and inextricably a part of American life the sexual revolution was, and the extent to which it made our lives better. We need to untangle the strands, to analyze the revolution's failures, and to embrace its successes. We must understand the sexual revolution in all its complexity, for the lessons we draw from it will shape our future.

Abbreviations

Notes

Credits

Acknowledgments

Index

Abbreviations

AJPH	*American Journal of Public Health*
BMC	*Bulletin of the Menninger Clinic*
BOH	Board of Health, Lawrence–Douglas County, Kansas
CSA	Council of Social Agencies files, KC
CSL	Community Service League, KC
DCHDA	Lawrence–Douglas County Health Department Archives
DOM	Dean of Men's files, KUA
DOW	Dean of Women's files, KUA
GL	Gay Liberation files, KUA
JCSP	*Journal of College Student Personnel*
JNAWDAC	*Journal of the National Association of Women Deans and Counselors*
JW	*Lawrence Daily Journal World*
KC	Kansas Collection, University of Kansas Libraries
KFP	*Kansas Free Press*
KUA	University of Kansas Archives
KUSDSJ	*The Kansas University Students for a Democratic Society Journal*
NACURH	*National Association of College and University Residence Halls Review*
NASPA	National Association of Student Personnel Administrators

Abbreviations

P&D	Dean of Men's Problems and Discipline files, KUA
PHC	Public Health Committee of Lawrence–Douglas County Board of Health
RVSS	Rape Victim Support Service
SRL	Spencer Research Library, University of Kansas
UDK	*University Daily Kansan*
WSPA	Women's Studies Program Archives, KU

Notes

Introduction

1. See "David Susskind," *Mademoiselle*, Oct. 1963, 112.

2. Paul Nathanson, *Over the Rainbow: The Wizard of Oz as a Secular Myth of America* (Albany: State University of New York Press, 1991), 157. CBS TV began annual broadcast of the film in 1956. Nathanson estimates that it was seen in 436 million homes between that date and 1985.

3. On another university town see Mary Ann Wynkoop, "Dissent in the Heartland: The Student Protest Movement at Indiana University, Bloomington, Indiana, 1965–1970" (Ph.D. diss., Indiana University, 1992).

4. The key historical synthesis on the history of sexuality in America is Estelle Freedman and John D'Emilio, *Intimate Matters* (New York: Harper and Row, 1988). Works on the post–World War II sexual revolution include Linda Grant, *Sexing the Millennium: Women and the Sexual Revolution* (New York: Grove Press, 1994); Barbara Ehrenreich et al., *Re-making Love: The Feminization of Sex* (New York: Doubleday, 1986); Steven Seidman, *Romantic Longings: Love in America, 1830–1980* (New York: Routledge, 1991); and John Heidenry, *What Wild Ecstasy: The Rise and Fall of the Sexual Revolution* (New York: Simon and Schuster, 1997). Though I begin my analysis in World War II, the roots of the revolution can be traced further back. Works on the "first" sexual revolution in the early twentieth century and on American communities that did not subscribe to the sexual ortho-doxies of the age include George Chauncey, *Gay New York: Gender, Urban Culture, and the Makings of the Gay Male World, 1890–1940* (New York: Basic Books, 1994); Paula Fass, *The Damned and the Beautiful: American Youth in the 1920s* (New York: Oxford University Press, 1977); Kathy Peiss, *Cheap Amusements: Working Women and Leisure in Turn-of-the-Century New York* (Philadelphia: Temple University Press, 1986); and Kevin White, *The First Sexual Revolution: The Emergence of Male Heterosexuality in Modern America* (New York: New York University Press, 1993).

5. John Sinclair, *Guitar Army: Street Writings/Prison Writings* (New York: Douglas, 1972), 69.

1. Before the Revolution

1. "Sunday's Calm Is Broken By Clash," *JW*, Dec. 8, 1941; *Sixteenth Census of the United States, 1940,* vol. II, pt. 3, 158.

2. Richard Polenberg, *War and Society: The United States, 1941–54* (Philadelphia: Lippincott, 1972), 139.

3. See Paula Fass, *Outside In: Minorities and the Transformation of American Education* (New York: Oxford University Press, 1989).

4. See John Costello, *Virtue under Fire: How World War II Changed Our Social and Sexual Attitudes* (Boston: Little, Brown, 1985); Polenberg, *War and Society,* ch. 5; Beth Bailey and David Farber, *The First Strange Place: The Alchemy of Race and Sex in WWII Hawaii* (New York: Free Press, 1992).

5. David Dary, *Lawrence: An Informal History* (Lawrence: Allen Books, 1982), 336; Albert Castel, *William Clarke Quantrill: His Life and Times* (New York: Frederick Fell, 1962).

6. *Sixteenth Census,* vol. II, pt. 3, table 31.

7. Ibid. As neither Haskell students nor KU students counted as permanent residents, in 1940 only 47 people fell outside the census categories "white" or "Negro." For more on race see Clifford S. Griffin, *The University of Kansas: A History* (Lawrence: University of Kansas Press, 1974), 626–628.

8. The *JW* estimated that in 1939 each student spent $443.50 for tuition, room, and board and the university benefited every resident of Lawrence by $214.87. Dary, *Lawrence,* 315, 327.

9. "Make Comment on Munitions Plant," *JW*, March 26, 1942; "May Use 25,000 at Eudora Plant," *JW*, April 16, 1942; "Sunflower Plant Boundaries Fixed," *JW*, May 9, 1942.

10. "Make Comment," *JW*.

11. "These Douglas County Citizens Gave Their Lives in World War II," *JW*, May 30, 1946. "Women in Vital Role at S.O.W.," *JW*, Aug. 16, 1944; "Tells of SOW's Working Program," *JW*, July 26, 1944; "Half of Lawrence Workers Are at the Powder Plant," *JW*, Jan. 4, 1944.

12. Robert Smith Bader, *Prohibition in Kansas: A History* (Lawrence: University Press of Kansas, 1986).

13. "Munitions Plant—Good or Evil?" *JW*, April 27, 1942.

14. "Lawrence and the War Effort," *JW*, March 29, 1945; "First Published Views of Sunflower Ordnance Works," *JW*, Sept. 27, 1945; "Tells of SOW's Working Program."

15. "A Short Walk to Next Beer Joint," *JW*, April 7, 1943; "Three Raids on the Wonder Bar," *JW*, April 24, 1943; "Sheriff Tour No Pleasure Cruise," *JW*, April 21, 1943.

16. "Make a Liquor Raid," *JW*, April 10, 1943; "Baptists Call for Check on

Liquor and Vice at Camps," *JW*, Sept. 15, 1943. The sheriff vowed to use "stern measures" to protect the town from "organized vice." "Will Use Stern Measures," *JW*, June 2, 1942.

17. "Health Unit Plan Is up for Action," *JW*, April 3, 1942.

18. See Nancy K. Bristow, *Making Men Moral: Social Engineering during the Great War* (New York: New York University Press, 1996); "Army Cracks Down on Vice That Still Preys on Soldiers," *Newsweek,* Aug. 31, 1942, 27; Philip Soffer, "'Victory Girls': Defining and Controlling Female Sexuality during World War II" (seminar paper, University of California at Berkeley, 1995), 19.

19. Allan M. Brandt, *No Magic Bullet: A Social History of Venereal Disease in the United States since 1880* (New York: Oxford University Press, 1985). Well before Pearl Harbor, Lawrence's health department offered Wassermann tests and treatment for syphilis and gonorrhea, as did the university's student health service. The Kansas City *Journal-Post* reported on Dec. 2, 1937, that the Wassermann tests were offered through the KU health service, and that "prim sorority girls asked for it in a matter of fact manner." An agreement among the branches of the military and public health agencies in 1939 provided for information-sharing between military and civilian authorities when "contact" took place between "enlisted men" and "infected civilians." See "Army Cracks Down"; Brandt, *No Magic Bullet,* 161–162; Soffer, "Victory Girls," 14–16.

20. "Named Dr. Chambers," *JW*, May 12, 1942; Director's Report, Aug. 1942, and Minutes, BOH, Oct. 1942, DCHDA.

21. "What Does an Octogenarian Think About? Let Dr. Chambers Tell You," *Outlook,* June 16, 1949, DCHDA.

22. Appendix to 1942–45 notebook, DCHDA; monthly board meeting minutes.

23. Minutes, BOH, April 14, 1943, DCHDA. A Lawrence Girl Scout official told the *Journal World* that "statistics show[ed]" the average age of "delinquency" for girls had fallen two full years since Pearl Harbor. Delinquency, here, meant sexual activity. See "Home as Controlling Factor in Child's Life Emphasized by Speakers," *JW*, April 10, 1943, 5; "Reports Given on Emporia Meeting," *JW*, April 15, 1943, 9.

24. "Rapid Rise in Teen-Age Crime Is Traced to Wartime Tension," *Newsweek,* Nov. 9, 1942, 27–29; "VD among the Amateurs," *Time*, March 29, 1943, 46; Brandt, *No Magic Bullet,* illustration 18, n.p.

25. "Not Out of Line," *JW*, May 15, 1943.

26. Ibid.; Minutes, BOH, Feb. 10, 1943, DCHDA.

27. Brandt, *No Magic Bullet,* 166–170; Soffer, "Victory Girls," 24.

28. Soffer, "Victory Girls," 25–27; Minutes, BOH, Oct. 14, 1942, DCHDA. "Contact reporting," or interviewing patients' past sexual partners, was deemed the most efficient way of intercepting the "amateurs" who, studies showed, accounted for the majority of venereal infections.

29. Brandt, *No Magic Bullet,* 164–170. At the beginning of mobilization, men found to have VD during their draft physicals were rejected. As manpower concerns became more pressing—by early 1942—they were inducted and treated before being sent for training. At least 170,000 men were treated for syphilis under this program.

30. David J. Langum, *Crossing Over the Line: Legislating Morality and the Mann Act* (Chicago: University of Chicago Press, 1994). Director's Report, April 12, 1944, DCHDA.

31. "Octogenarian," *Outlook.* Director's Report, March 14, 1945, and Director's Monthly Report, June 13, 1945, DCHDA.

32. Minutes, BOH, Sept. 1945, DCHDA. "S.O.W. Employees Now Down to 2,485 Total," *JW,* Jan. 12, 1946. Of the remaining employees, 302 were women. VD statistics in monthly Minutes and Director's Reports, DCHDA.

33. Before the war the largest population of young men and women in Lawrence was the students at KU. In the academic year 1938–39, the *UDK* reported, 1,006 students went to the health service for Wassermann tests. Only two men and one woman were found to be infected, but that such a high number of students chose to be tested is intriguing. The author of the article noted that none of the three had become infected at KU, and that "they are not expelled or in any way made to feel that their reputation is ruined." Ruth Saunders, "Less than Three out of 1,000 Are Syphilis Victims," *UDK,* May 3, 1939.

34. On class see William M. Tuttle Jr., *Daddy's Gone to War* (New York: Oxford University Press, 1993).

35. "Virtue under Fire" is the title of John Costello's book, cited earlier.

36. Clarence Briener, address to Council of Social Agencies (handwritten notes from his talk), Oct. 10, 1944, 29, CSA.

37. KU also provided training for almost 39,000 civilian war workers through the Engineering, Science, and Management War Training Program; see V. R. Cordozier, *Colleges and Universities in World War II* (Westport, Conn.: Praeger, 1993), 168–179. The KU registrar, Laurence Woodruff, justified college deferments in a radio program, "Exploring Your University," Oct. 4, 1943; text in KUA.

38. Marge Stockton to Mayor Russell, Feb. 8, 1943, CSL.

39. Woodruff, "Exploring Your University."

40. Marge Stockton to Blanch Maloney, Feb. 7, 1943, CSL.

41. Ibid.

42. See, in CSL: "Community Service League" (no author, n.d., but seems to be final report by Stockton); Marge S. Stockton, "For the Journal World—Sept. 23, 1942"; "To Chairman and committee personnel of Community Service League," memo from M. S. Stockton, July 30, 1942; document without heading or date that appears to be minutes from CSL organizational meeting; Stockton to Mayor Russell, Feb. 8, 1943.

43. Marge Stockton to Vice Admiral A. S. Carpender, Sept. 15, 1945, CSL. This is a reply to his letter of thanks. Emphasizing the local, she writes that Lawrence was proud to have run the center "without leadership or financial aid from outside our own community."

44. Stockton to Maloney, Feb. 7, 1943.

45. *Kansas Vital Statistics* and "Divorces and Annulments by County," 1955, KC.

46. Notes from Council of Social Agencies meeting, May 22, 1945, CSA.

47. *Sixteenth Census of the United States, 1940,* vol. II, pt. 3; *Seventeenth Census of Population, 1950,* vol II, pt. 16; *Eighteenth Census of Population: 1960,* vol. I, pt. 18; Dary, *Lawrence,* 344; Enrollment Statistics, 1866–1957/58, KUA.

48. Dary, *Lawrence,* 348.

49. Ibid., 315–316, 353; Enrollment Statistics, KUA.

50. Peter Guralnick, *Last Train to Memphis: The Rise of Elvis Presley* (New York: Little, Brown, 1994), 279, 337–338.

51. "This, Too, Will Pass," *JW,* May 24, 1956; "Bad Night for Judy," *JW,* April 10, 1956.

52. "County Heads Are Lauded, Criticized," *JW,* Feb. 27, 1946; "Ban Is Lifted on Beer and Dancing," *JW,* Sept. 19, 1946.

53. "County Heads," and "Ban Is Lifted," *JW.*

54. See Freedman and D'Emilio, *Intimate Matters,* 197; Roland Marchand, *Advertising the American Dream* (Berkeley: University of California Press, 1985); Robert Westbrook, "I Want a Girl, Just like the Girl That Married Harry James: American Women and the Problem of Political Obligation in World War II," *American Quarterly* 42 (Dec. 1990); Gary M. Valant, *Classic Vintage Nose Art* (Ann Arbor: Lowe and B. Hould, 1997).

55. Kenneth C. Davis, *Two-Bit Culture: The Paperbacking of America* (Boston: Houghton Mifflin, 1984), esp. 134–141; Lillian Faderman, *Odd Girls and Twilight Lovers: A History of Lesbian Life in Twentieth Century America* (New York: Columbia University Press, 1991), 146–148; Mary Jane Aldrich-Moodie, "Lesbian Libido: Its Use and Abuse in Pulp Novels of the 1950s and 1960s" (Senior thesis, Barnard College, 1990).

56. Heidenry, *What Wild Ecstasy,* 59–61; Barbara Ehrenreich, *The Hearts of Men: American Dreams and the Flight from Commitment* (New York: Anchor, 1983), 42–51; Joanne Meyerowitz, "Women, Cheesecake, and Borderline Material: Responses to Girlie Pictures in the Mid-Twentieth Century U.S.," *Journal of Women's History* 8 (Fall 1996): 9–35.

57. Freedman and D'Emilio, *Intimate Matters,* 282–284. Meyerowitz, "Cheesecake"; Margaret Culkin Banning, "Filth on the Newsstands," *Reader's Digest,* Oct. 1952, quoted by Meyerowitz, 23.

58. Freedman and D'Emilio, *Intimate Matters,* 282–284.

59. Accounts of this campaign, including "Objectionable Literature Survey—PTA Juvenile Protection Committee," are in Parent-Teacher Association records, KC.

60. Editorial by Arden Booth, KLWN radio, n.d., Parent-Teacher Association records, KC.

2. Sex and the Therapeutic Culture

1. Accounts of panty raids drawn from: "Manners and Morals: Girls! Girls! Girls!" *Time,* May 26, 1952, 27; *Chicago Sun Times,* May 23, 1952, untitled clipping in AEO records, Box 1, folder 2, Northwestern University Archives; "Men Students Raid Women's Dorms," (newspaper clipping without further source included), "Panty Raids" (dean's memo), May 30, 1952, and "Trouble Report," KU Police Dept., May 20, 1952, all in P&D, 1951/52; Bob Steward, "7 Women's Houses Invaded by 1,500 Raiding Students," *UDK,* May 21, 1952, 1; "Murphy Speaks Up to Halt Raiding," *JW,* May 21, 1952; "Romeos, Juliets—But No Balcony," *JW,* May 21, 1952.

2. "Manners and Morals," *Time.*

3. "The Rites of Spring," *Time,* May 11, 1953, 82.

4. On the tradition of student riots, see Helen Lefkowitz Horowitz, *Campus Life* (New York: Knopf, 1987); on sexuality and college youth, see Fass, *The Damned and the Beautiful.*

5. On fears about juvenile delinquency, see James Gilbert, *A Cycle of Outrage: America's Reaction to the Juvenile Delinquent in the 1950s* (New York: Oxford, 1986); William Graebner, *Coming of Age in Buffalo: Youth and Authority in the Postwar Era* (Philadelphia: Temple University Press, 1990).

6. Everett Hunt, "The Dean and the Psychiatrist," *Mental Hygiene* 27 (April 1953): 180. Kate Hevner Mueller, "The Role of the Counselor in Sex Behavior and Standards," *JNAWDAC* 5 (Jan. 1963): 4. Mueller is the editor of the Journal, and was a professor of higher education at Indiana University, where KU's dean of women from 1956 on earned her Ph.D.

7. This description is based on seven documents, including dean's memos and letters from three psychiatrists to the dean, found in P&D, 1947. I have changed or omitted all names of those who appear in the disciplinary files (with the exception of this first name, which the student did not use). I have also omitted certain details that might identify individuals. All quotations from psychiatrists come from letters to university officials, not from patient files or case notes, and none is marked "confidential." I also identify the cases I discuss here only by year and file subject category. University officials and medical personnel are identified by their real names.

8. This exchange of four letters is found in the dean's academic department files for 1947, KUA.

9. This description is drawn from a memo in P&D, 1952.

10. This account is drawn from a file of 13 letters written in the summer of 1921, from the instructor to the chancellor and dean, from the dean to the instructor, and from a former student to the dean. The file is in box 2/9/1, filed under 1922, KUA.

11. The timing and significance of the "medicalization" of homosexuality are subjects of debate. I am not arguing that the postwar triumph of therapeutic understandings at a heartland university was a new or sudden development in the history of medical studies of "sexual deviance," or that the psychiatric definitions shaped either homosexual identity or individuals' perceptions of their sexual experiences. However, the shift from "moral" to "psychiatric" frameworks marks a major change in the institutional management of discovered cases of male homosexuality. See George Chauncey, "Christian Brotherhood or Sexual Perversion? Homosexual Identities and the Construction of Sexual Boundaries in the World War One Era," *Journal of Social History* 19 (Winter 1985): 189–212; Estelle Freedman, "'Uncontrolled Desires': The Response to the Sexual Psychopath, 1920–1960," *Journal of American History* 74 (June 1987): 83–106; Jennifer Terry, "Siting Homosexuality: A History of Surveillance and the Production of Deviant Subjects (1935–1950)" (Ph.D. diss., University of California—Santa Cruz, 1992).

12. Michel Foucault, *The History of Sexuality: An Introduction* (New York: Random House, 1978). Letter from Henry Werner to Chancellor Lindley, Oct. 20, 1938, DOM. (Don Henry is not a pseudonym.)

13. Harry Stack Sullivan, "Psychiatry and the National Defense," *Psychiatry* 4 (May 1941): 202, quoted in Allan Berube, *Coming Out Under Fire: The History of Gay Men and Women in World War Two* (New York: Free Press, 1990), 11.

14. The Editors, "Explanatory Note," *BMC* 5 (Sept. 1941): 129–130; this was a special issue on psychiatry and the armed forces developed from a series of seminars held by the Menninger Clinic in June 1941. William C. Menninger, M.D., and Edward D. Greenwood, M.D., "The Psychiatrist in Relation to the Examining Boards," ibid., 136; Karl A. Menninger, M.D., "Civilian Morale in Time of War and Preparation for War," ibid., 188. On psychiatric screening, see Berube, *Coming Out,* and Leisa D. Meyer, *Creating G.I. Jane: Sexuality and Power in the Women's Army Corps during World War II* (New York: Columbia University Press, 1996).

15. Robert P. Knight, M.D., "Recognizing the Psychoneurotic Registrant," ibid., 161–166. Robert P. Knight, M.D., and Douglass W. Orr, M.D., "Psychiatric Problems of the Armed Forces in Training and Combat," ibid., 176–180.

16. Lt. Colonel William C. Menninger, "The Medical Psychiatrist," *BMC* 7 (July 1943): 129–136. Harry Stack Sullivan, the man who, with Menninger, was most responsible for the role psychiatrists played in the war, made a similar point: "It is the Army's business first and foremost to win the war . . . The war calls on psychiatry to be practical." Quoted in Ellen Herman, *The Romance of American*

Psychology: Political Culture in the Age of Experts (Berkeley: University of California Press, 1995), 95.

17. Menninger quoted in Herman, *Romance of American Psychology,* 118.

18. Sigmund Gundle, M.D., and Alan Kraft, M.D., "Mental Health Programs in American Colleges and Universities," *BMC* 20 (March 1956): 57–69.

19. Interview with Dr. Raymond Schwegler, Lawrence, June 1990.

20. Dr. Dana Farnsworth, quoted in the *Proceedings of the Thirty-Fourth Conference of the National Association of Student Personnel Administrators,* Colorado Springs, April 1952. This was not a prepared statement but a response to a question in the midst of a long discussion of the respective roles of deans and psychiatrists in cases of sexual deviance.

21. Sherwyn M. Woods and Seymour L. Halleck, "Psychiatric Evaluation of Unacceptable Behavior in a University Community," *JCSP* 5 (March 1964): 141. A total of 111 men and 13 women were referred for treatment.

22. Milton E. Hahn and Byron H. Atkinson, "The Sexually Deviate Student," *School and Society* 82 (Sept. 17, 1955): 85–87.

23. See Kathryn Nemeth Tuttle, "What Became of the Dean of Women? Changing Roles for Women Administrators in American Higher Education" (Ph.D. diss., University of Kansas, 1996).

24. Cases of unwed pregnancy occasionally appear in the dean of men's files—usually because the woman's parents have become involved and there is disagreement between parties about what to be done. In one case (P&D, 1957–1958) the male student provided a list of five other men he believed had had sexual intercourse with the woman and insisted that his parentage could not be proved. Her father, noting the strategy of "defaming the female" in a letter to the dean, threatened court action. He wrote: "I did not realize that nowadays a moral offense could be condoned. It would seem that all the miscreant has to do is to confess and be forgiven. While this may greatly restore the confidence and self-esteem of the well-educated delinquent, there yet remain slight drawbacks. For one, it is still rather difficult to wash away the seduction and degradation of a teen age girl." The letter ends: "An attractive girl, socially unsuccessful. A lovely voice, too loud perhaps; from lack of confidence. Lonely. Wistful. Wanted attention. She got it. And there was no crime?" Note the confluence of moral and psychological analysis in the father's letter.

In another case (P&D, 1950–1951) the dean also recorded allegations that the woman might have been "involved" with other men. This young woman, pregnant by a man who (in the dean's words) had "lost interest immediately" after the one time "the actual insertion of organs occurred," had attempted suicide. Both sets of parents became involved, the woman's parents urging marriage, the man's resisting it. (Though the dean never mentioned race in his notes, letters from the two families reveal that both fathers were ministers of African-American churches.) The deans of men and women worked to facilitate a brief marriage, which was followed by divorce, so that the young woman would "have the security of a name for her youngster." The young man (an outstanding student) was not required to furnish "any continued support" for the child. The dean referred to the man's situation as "in difficulties"; there was no discussion of further disciplinary action, despite the strongly worded urgings of the woman's parents. A newspaper clipping records the young man's death from polio the following year. P&D, 1950–1951.

231

25. This account is constructed from several files in P&D, 1959. Included are dean's handwritten notes, including charts and diagrams, incident reports from the KU police department, "defendant's statements" to the police, students' handwritten accounts for the dean, dean's notes from meetings with other students and their parents, and official memos on the disposition of cases.

26. Memo from Robert Edwards, M.D., Psychiatrist, KU Health Services, to Martha Peterson, Dean of Women, Oct. 31, 1955.

27. These cases are in P&D, 1955, 1961, and 1956.

28. P&D, 1962.

29. P&D, 1960.

30. *Proceedings*, NASPA, 1952, 31, 51, 71.

31. Ibid., 63.

32. Dean Everett Hunt of Swarthmore College noted that the dean "is, in the eyes of the constituency of the college, the upholder of the traditional mores of the communities which send their students to the college, and, on a somewhat low and cynical level perhaps, he is at least expected to provide a certain cloak of respectability to the college to see that those official mores are publicly paid tribute to, and so far as he can to see that they are obeyed." Ibid., 53. "Other standards" quote, ibid., 63. The compromise position is suggested in Hunt, "The Dean and the Psychiatrist," 183.

33. Benjamin H. Glover, M.D., "Observations on Homosexuality among University Students," *Journal of Nervous and Mental Disease* 113 (May 1951): 377–387.

34. Letter "To Whom It May Concern," from Cpl. William Cranston, May 26, 1952, in P&D, 1951–1952.

35. Letter from Dean Laurence Woodruff to Cpl. William Cranston, June 2, 1952, P&D, 1951–1952.

3. Responsible Sex

1. "Feminist Perspective" radio show, n.d. [1974]; KUA; Leslie J. Reagan, *When Abortion Was a Crime: Women, Medicine, and Law in the United States, 1867–1973* (Berkeley: University of California Press, 1997). On youth and sex in this era, see Wini Brienes, *Young, White, and Miserable: Growing Up Female in the Fifties*

(Boston: Beacon, 1992); Susan J. Douglas, *Where the Girls Are: Growing Up Female with the Mass Media* (New York: Random House, 1994); John Modell, *Into One's Own: From Youth to Adulthood in the United States, 1920–1975* (Berkeley: University of California Press, 1989).

2. Alfred Kinsey, *Sexual Behavior in the Human Female* (Philadelphia: Saunders, 1953), 315. Elizabeth Woodward, "Sub-deb: Bargain Buys," *Ladies' Home Journal,* May 1942, 8; Gay Head, "Boy Dates Girl," *Senior Scholastic,* 1945, 28.

3. Alfred Kinsey, Wardell B. Pomeroy, and Clyde E. Martin, *Sexual Behavior in the Human Male* (Philadelphia: Saunders, 1948), 364; oral history conducted by Ben Grant for "History of Sexuality in America" course, Barnard College, Spring 1991; Elaine Tyler May, *Homeward Bound: American Families in the Cold War Era* (New York: Basic Books, 1988).

4. Nora Johnson, "Sex and the College Girl," *Atlantic,* Nov. 1959, 57–58.

5. "Students: Moods and Mores," *Time,* Nov. 18, 1966, 95–98, in Student Protests files, 1919/20–1968/69, KUA.

6. On the concern about fostering democratic citizenship, see Herman, *Romance of American Psychology,* and Erik Scott Peterson, "Psychological Frontiers: Politics, Culture, and the Redefinition of Democratic Freedom" (Ph.D. diss., University of Minnesota, 1996). On the emphasis on "maturity," see Ehrenreich, *Hearts of Men.*

7. "Enrollment Statistics, 1940/41–1957/58," KUA. When the dean of men was asked in 1950 to provide a list of "Negro students" for a "Negro Student Association," he replied that there was no such list, but suggested the writers go through student files, noting that they probably could pick out "the majority of the negro students . . . from the church affiliation and by other criteria." Letter, Aug. 23, 1950, in "Negro Students" file, Dean of Men papers, 1952–53, KUA.

8. Tuttle, "Dean of Women," 328–329.

9. An administration committee on foreign students was formed in 1946 to work with the growing number of international students. Letter from Donald Alderson (dean) to E. O. Stone, Sept. 29, 1949, KUA.

10. Laurence C. Woodruff, "Opinions from the Hill," *JW,* March 11, 1963; Council on Student Affairs, no title, Jan. 11, 1966, in Council on Student Affairs, 1966/67, KUA.

11. Donald A. Strickland, "In Loco Parentis—Legal Mots and Student Morals," *JCSP* 6 (Nov. 1965): 339. Tuttle, in "Dean of Women," quotes David Ambler (vice chancellor for student affairs at KU beginning in 1977): "We had all these first generation people, all this diversity, just a lot of nurturing academically and socially that was needed in American higher education" (329). Jo Ann Fley, in "Campus Regulations: Are Girls Different?" *JNAWDAC* 31 (Spring 1968): 118, notes: "The diversity of the student population makes the writing of common standards of expected behavior extremely difficult."

12. William G. Craig, "The Student Personnel Profession: An Instrument of National Goals," *JCSP* 3 (June 1963): 162.

13. Gwen Barstow, "Forty Years of Growth: Student Affairs at the University of Kansas," manuscript, n.d., 13. Annual Report, June 30, 1958, KUA.

14. Woodruff, "Opinions." Council on Student Affairs, Jan. 11, 1966. On gender and controversy in the student personnel profession see Tuttle, "Dean of Women."

15. Barstow, "Forty Years," 4; Council on Student Affairs, Jan. 11, 1966. The personnel committee included the deans of men and women, registrar, director of health services, dean of the university, director of the guidance bureau, and director of housing. It was chaired by the dean of students.

16. This account is drawn from the AWS handbooks and "Wise Words for Women" in KUA, and from Kathryn Kretschmer (Tuttle), "The Nice Girl's Handbook: A Guide to Proper Behavior for Young Ladies at the University of Kansas, 1930–1970," furnished by its author.

17. Quotations from *The Haskell Handbook,* which bears no date but is definitely from the 1950s, and "Haskell Institute," *KFP,* Dec. 18, 1965, 1–2; this article makes it clear that these rules were still in effect in 1965, when the high school had been completely phased out and all students were in postsecondary programs.

18. Interview with Emily Taylor, Lawrence, June 1992. For student actions in disciplinary cases see DOW 53/0 Box 1. For example, the privileges of everyone who lived in the Gamma Phi Beta house were revoked for 10 days because two incidents, in which women had not turned in their keys on time, were not reported through disciplinary channels. Both women were in early, and had forgotten to return their keys until the next morning. Both women had their keys taken away for one month. Case from Oct. 20, 1961.

19. Fass, *The Damned and the Beautiful,* 144.

20. "Rules not meant to curb morals," *UDK,* n.d. [Feb. 1966?], clipping file, KUA; Letter to "Parents of Senior Women" from Emily Taylor, fall semester 1966, in DOW, 1956/57–70/71. Parents could withhold permission from their daughters. Some letters of protest from parents are contained in this file, though it seems that few refused permission. Taylor interview.

21. Letter to Emily Taylor from Helen Gibson Throop, Jan. 11, 1961, in DOW.

22. Lee Byrd, "Student Freedom Movement Gains Momentum at Meeting," *UDK,* Nov. 12, 1965; illustration by Richard Geary.

23. Kirkpatrick Sale, *SDS* (New York: Random House, 1973), 193; Todd Gitlin, *The Sixties: Years of Hope, Days of Rage* (New York: Bantam, 1987); James Miller, *Democracy Is in the Streets: From Port Huron to the Siege of Chicago* (New York: Simon and Schuster, 1987).

24. Byrd, "Student Freedom Movement."

25. Douglas Rossinow, in "Breakthrough: White Youth Radicalism in Austin, Texas 1956–1973" (Ph.D. diss., Johns Hopkins University, 1994), 7, argues that "existentialism was a basic frame of reference in the emergence of the new left"; James Miller *(Democracy)* and Todd Gitlin *(The Sixties)* also discuss the role of existentialism. For a contemporary statement of existential principles in student personnel work see W. Max Wise, "Existentialism and Guidance Personnel Work," *JNAWDAC* 25 (Jan. 1962): 161–165.

26. John Garlinghouse, "In Loco Deus," *KUSDSJ,* issue 2, Dec. 1965, 1–2.

27. Byrd, "Student Freedom Movement"; Mrs. Donald Emmons, "Student Responsibility," *KUSDSJ,* issue 2, 3.

28. University Party, "White Paper on Student Rights," March 1966, 5, in Student Protests files, 1965/66, KUA. "Rules not meant to curb morals," *UDK.* Dorm hours became an issue and were changed at Haskell Indian Junior College in 1971—much later than at KU. Presented in the Haskell student newspaper as a debate among students, this movement for change also employed the concept of "responsibility": "responsibility" is the only word in a full-page "Opinion Poll" to appear in boldface—suggesting an editorial position. "Never before has Haskell been known to give its students responsibility," said Robert Jackson, Yavajai-Apache, from Clarksdale, Ariz. "This may be the reason for the high percentage of people being dismissed from their jobs after they leave Haskell. So far Haskell has had such an intense paternalistic atmosphere that the students are cramped by rules and regulations." Arlene Gardipe, Flathead, Arlee, Mont., insisted: "This is a Junior College, not a BIA babysitting service," and Raymond Taylor, Cherokee, Whittier, N.C., said that open hours "would show that we are young adults with a responsibility to perform not only for ourselves, but for our teachers and parents." The opposition centered much more around the possible consequences of alcohol abuse and absence from classes than around sexual conduct: Rose Mae Lee, Navajo, Shiprock, N.M., worried that "some drunk might get killed, or murder someone," while Liz Francis, Chinle, Ariz., supported reform but still objected: "Who knows if a student might freeze to death from here to the Inn? I mean if he passes out along the way . . . Secondly, I'm afraid if we're given this privilege there might be an increase of absentees." "Opinion Poll," *Indian Leader,* Dec. 3, 1971, 3.

29. Eric Morgenthaler, "Questions Given to Surface," *UDK,* Feb. 25, 1966; "Text of Questions Handed Provost by Student Group," *UDK,* Feb. 25, 1966; "Policy Probe Gets Answers," *UDK,* March 1, 1966; "SDS Dissatisfied with Query Result," *UDK,* March 2, 1966; Provost Sees Loaded Queries," n.d. [mid-March 1966]; "Students Want to Know . . ," pt. 1, Feb. 25, 1966; pt. 2, March 11, 1966; all in Student Protests files, KUA. See also UPI, "KU Students Seek Rule Definition," *Wichita Eagle and Beacon,* Feb. 27, 1966, which was forwarded to Surface by a student's mother.

30. See *The E.P.E. 15-Minute Report for College and University Trustees* (Edi-

torial Projects for Education, Baltimore), May 29, 1968, report on "Legal Relationships Between Colleges and Students," in Balfour papers, KUA. *In loco parentis* issues were not fully settled by 1966: the Student Protests files contain a national survey of organized student protests from the 1967/68 academic year; the second most prevalent issue, after Vietnam, was women's hours, with 289 institutions reporting protests. Richard E. Petersen, "The Scope of Organized Student Protest in 1967–68" (Princeton: Educational Testing Service, 1968).

31. Council on Student Affairs, no title, n.d. [Jan. 1966]; letter from Harold R. Fatzer, attorney general of Kansas, to Hubert Brighton, secretary, state board of regents, Feb. 15, 1956, this copy stamped with date Feb. 21, 1966; both in "Council on Student Affairs" file, KUA. Strickland, in "In Loco Parentis," argued that the "delegation of general morals to the college . . . distracts institutions of higher learning from their main purpose and subverts their morale and dignity." Even when "there is genuine pressure of public opinion that the college 'do something' about student morals, the college ought to realize that acknowledgment of these claims is a badge of social incompetency, much as the willingness of the legal or medical professions to supervise the morals of their clients and patients would be a mark of incompetency."

32. My account comes from transcripts of the AWS convention, reports from AWS officers, and *UDK* coverage; documents and clippings in "AWS Regulations Convention, 1965/66," KUA. Hayden document in Student Protests files, KUA.

33. Thanks to Allan Brandt for helping to clarify this point.

34. "AWS Regulations Convention" (transcript), pt. 1, n.d., 1, 3. Two transcripts of the convention are in this file; neither is quite complete and the pagination is confused. I use the page number as it appears, without trying to specify to which transcript it belongs.

35. Ibid., 1, 12.

36. Ibid., 16; ibid., combination of 2 and 8, which are clearly the same speech, but transcribed slightly differently; ibid., 8.

37. AWS Regulations Convention, pt. 2, March 22, 1966, 1, 14, 15.

38. Elizabeth Rhodes, "Student Opinion Varies," *UDK*, clipping, n.d. [probably March 17, 1966].

39. "Men Air Reserved Yes to No Closing Proposal," *UDK*, clipping, n.d. [March 1966], KUA. This article begins: "Do KU men want KU women to be equal?"

40. "The Relationship of Rules to Mental Health: A Statement from the Mental Health Clinic Staff," Council on Student Affairs, 1966/67, KUA. Not all university mental health personnel agreed with such assessments. Alex Braiman, M.D., of the University of Rochester, described the conflicts in Oedipal terms: "Rather than expressions of a desire for freedom and adulthood," student demands "can be viewed as an attempt to return the university to the parental role. The

debate over whether the university should or should not serve 'in loco parentis' is meaningless when viewed psychodynamically. Parents are inevitably sought out or created by the student in fantasy." "Riotous Behavior in the College: A Psychosocial View," *Journal of the American College Health Association* (Feb. 1966): 152.

41. This is discussed in "The 1966 AWS Regulations Convention," by Cathy Beagle, convention chairman, in AWS Regulations Convention, KUA, and in four

articles by Elizabeth Rhodes, *UDK*, March 1966.

42. Letter from Chancellor Wescoe to Cynthia Hardin, May 20, 1966, Chancellor's files, Students—Women's Regulations, KUA.

43. "White Paper on Student Rights," 1. For more evidence of support from portions of the administration, see the memo from the Mental Health Clinic Staff.

44. Chancellor's Office, Correspondence, 1965/66, KUA. The chancellor was politic and polite in his responses, but generally made it clear he supported the student resolutions.

45. Letters from Mr. and Mrs. Melford Monsees to Mrs. John Hughes, Chairman, Kansas Alpha Advisory Board, Pi Beta Phi, cc Chancellor Wescoe, April 1966; Jackie (Mrs. John H.) Tietze, Shawnee Mission, Kan., to Dr. Wescoe, March 1966; Mrs. Perry Fleagle, Wichita, Kan., to Dr. Wescoe, April 18, 1966. In Chancellor's Office, Student Correspondence, 1965/66, KUA.

46. Chancellor Wescoe to Jan B. French, corresponding secretary of Gamma Phi Beta Alumni Chapter, April 19, 1966, ibid. Taylor quoted in the *Kansas City Star,* May 13, 1973; my source is Kretschmer, "The Nice Girl's Handbook."

4. Prescribing the Pill

1. Several "Pill" posters are in a collection of posters in KC.

2. Estimates on usage vary; these are from Elizabeth Rose Siegel Watkins, in "On the Pill: A Social History of Oral Contraceptives in America, 1950–1970" (Ph.D. diss., Harvard University, 1996), 130–131, and are derived from estimates of G. D. Searle & Company (1963), the Population Council (1966), and the Advisory Committee on Obstetrics and Gynecology, Food and Drug Administration (1969).

3. Bernard Asbell, in *The Pill: A Biography of the Drug That Changed the World* (New York: Random House, 1995), discusses Roman Catholic responses.

4. Pearl S. Buck, "The Pill and the Teen-Age Girl," *Reader's Digest* 92 (April 1968): 111, quoted in Watkins, "On the Pill," 138.

5. Vicki Phillips, "Politics Plays Role in Birth Control," *UDK,* Jan. 8, 1970, 6. See also *Senate and House Journals: Proceedings of the Legislature of the State of Kansas* (Topeka: State Printer, 1963), quote from *Senate Journal,* 204.

6. Minutes, BOH, May 13, 1963, 1955–1965 Records, DCHDA.

7. Donald Harting and Leslie Corsa, "The American Public Health Associa-

tion and the Population Problem," *AJPH* 59 (Oct. 1969): 1927–29. For a history of population control initiatives see James Reed, *From Private Vice to Public Virtue* (New York: Basic Books, 1978).

8. Johnson quoted in Reed, *From Private Vice,* 304. Clinton, letter to the editor, *JW,* Jan. 4, 1965.

9. Leslie Corsa, "Public Health Programs in Family Planning," *AJPH* 56 (Jan. 1966, supplement); Reed, *From Private Vice,* 378; Watkins, "On the Pill," 141–142. For statistics on federal funding see "Family Planning Services," Hearing before the Subcommittee on Public Health and Welfare of the Committee on Interstate and Foreign Commerce, House of Representatives, serial no. 91–70 (Washington: GPO, 1970), 190–193.

10. See James Reed, "Public Policy on Human Reproduction and the Historian," *Journal of Social History* 19 (Spring 1985): 383–398.

11. Linda Gordon, *Woman's Body, Woman's Right: A Social History of Birth Control in America* (New York: Grossman, 1976); Watkins, "On the Pill," 150–151.

12. Mary Calderone, "Health Education for Responsible Parenthood: Preliminary Considerations," *AJPH* (Jan. 1964): 1735–40. On the politics of this era see Allen J. Matusow, *The Unraveling of America* (New York: Harper and Row, 1984); Bruce J. Schulman, *Lyndon Johnson and American Liberalism* (New York: St. Martin's, 1995).

13. "Should Birth Control Be Available to Unmarried Women?" *Good Housekeeping,* Feb. 1967, 14. *Senate and House Journals: Proceedings of the Legislature of the State of Kansas* (Topeka: Robert R. Sanders, State Printer, 1965), (Senate) 260, 277; (House) 404–405. "Memo RE: Family Planning," from Marvin E. Larson, State Director of Social Welfare, June 29, 1965, in DCHDA.

14. Corsa, "Public Health Programs," 3. On Clinton, two memos are especially relevant: "Lawrence-Douglas County Health Department," June 21, 1965, and "General Information on Health Department," April 1969, both in DCHDA.

15. Telephone interview with Dr. Richard Hermes, Lawrence, July 1992; Phillips, "Politics Plays Role." "Medical Estimates in City Conflict on Use of Enovid," *JW,* Aug. 8, 1962, Health Dept. scrapbook, DCHDA.

16. U.S. Census, 1960, 18–164, table 33, 18–222, table 78. The median income for Lawrence's 501 "non-white" families was $3,832.

17. In 1961 there were 2,986 undergraduate women, of whom 10.2% were married. There were also 3,425 women in graduate programs, of whom 13.9% were married. The percentages of married students would decline through the decade, with enrollments rising rapidly. Letter from Director of Admissions to Director of Dormitories, 3 April 1962, University of Kansas, DOW, Box 1, folder 61/62; "University of Kansas Housing Survey for Spring 1961," DOW, folder 1956/57–1970/71; Admissions and Records Enrollment Statistics, 14/0/1; all in KUA.

18. "Birth Control Now Is Becoming a Fact of Life," *JW*, Aug. 5, 1967.

19. This account is based on telephone interviews with Mary Lou Wright, former president of Douglas County Planned Parenthood, Dec. 1992; Sandra Wolf, former social worker with Planned Parenthood, Dec. 1992; Richard Hermes, M.D., Lawrence physician, July 1992; Minutes, BOH, Dec. 12, 1966; and articles from the Lawrence *Journal World* in the scrapbooks, DCHDA. Quotation from "Planned Parent Group Will Ask for New Clinic," *JW*, Dec. 10, 1966, in scrapbooks, DCHDA.

20. Minutes, Dec. 12, 1966, BOH, DCHDA.

21. Melanie Morgan, "Conflicts Cause Birth of Parenthood Clinic," *Sunday Outlook, JW*, Jan. 15, 1967, in scrapbook, DCHDA.

22. Schwegler interview; Hermes interview; Griffin, *University of Kansas*, 621. Schwegler retired from his position as director in 1973, at the age of 65, but remained on staff as a physician well into the 1980s.

23. Will Hardesty, "Birth Control Practices Debated," *UDK*, Nov. 4, 1966.

24. Letters to the editor: Lee Ellis, *UDK*, Nov. 8, 1966; Dennis J. Nauman, *UDK*, Nov. 14, 1966.

25. Letters to the editor: James Prentice, *UDK*, Nov. 10, 1966; Robert Hugh Gerner, *UDK*, Nov. 14, 1966; James Prentice, *UDK*, Nov. 16, 1966.

26. J. Gary Brown, letter to the editor, *UDK*, Nov. 14, 1966.

27. Mr. and Mrs. James Cooley, Mr. and Mrs. Angus Wright, Richard Lobdell, and John Mason, letter to the editor, *UDK*, Nov. 10, 1966.

28. "Should Birth Control Be Available?" *Good Housekeeping*, 14.

29. Willard Dalrymple, M.D., "A Doctor Speaks of College Students and Sex," *Journal of the American College Health Association* 15 (Feb. 1967): 286.

30. W. Roy Mason Jr., M.D., "Problems of Married College Students: Health Education Implications," ibid., 14 (April 1966): 273–274. Frances K. Harding, M.D., "The College Unmarried Population Explosion," *Journal of School Health* 35 (Dec. 1965): 450–457.

31. "Associated Women Students Survey for 'Roles of Women' Committee," 1964, KUA; "Survey of Women's Morals Grew from Study at Michigan State," *UDK*, May 4, 1964; Lee Stone, "Senior, Freshman Women Vote Same on Sex," *UDK*, May 4, 1964.

32. Unsigned, letter to the editor, *UDK*, Nov. 30, 1967; "'Free Love' Panelist Bargains on St. Paul," *UDK*, Nov. 29, 1967; "Panel Will Discuss Free Love Tonight," *UDK*, Nov. 28, 1967. The Campus Crusade for Christ was very active at KU in the 1960s. Material from this group is in KC; newspaper accounts include Dan Austin, "Humanists Discuss Basis for Sex Ethic," *UDK*, Sept. 30, 1966; Monte Mace, "In 'Crusade for Christ' Speech: Braun Lays Sex on Line," *UDK*, Dec. 6, 1967.

33. Lawrence High School *Freedspeak*, n.d., issue no. 2. The series in the *UDK* began on Nov. 16, 1966; Dr. Clark quoted in Barbara Phillips and Eric Morgen-

thaler, "Pills Hard to Get In Lawrence," *UDK*, Nov. 17, 1966. See Judy Browder, "Women's Decade of History," WSPA.

34. Phillips and Morgenthaler, "The Pill and How to Get It," *UDK*, Nov. 18, 1966.

35. Schwegler interview.

36. Statistics on the health department's birth control clinic are in DCHDA; the records begin in 1968.

37. Toby MacIntosh, "Low Cost Public Health Is Goal," *JW*, Feb. 8, 1973. "Contraception Clinic Is Not Planned at KU," *UDK*, Sept. 17, 1970; Clinton and Hermes interviews. Interview with Kathryn Kretschmer (Tuttle), Lawrence, July 1992.

38. "Over-Interest Closes County Clinic," *UDK*, Feb. 3, 1970; "Birth Control Clinic Closes," *UDK*, Feb. 5, 1970; Wright (Sherman) interview.

39. The student request was in conjunction with the Commission on the Status of Women at KU sponsored by the dean of women's office. Information here is from "February Sisters Position Statement on a Health Care Program for Women," Addendum II, in Lorna Zimmer personal files, Lawrence, Kan.; "Women—February First Movement," WSPA; Browder, "Women's Decade"; "Campus Problems for Consideration," Council on Student Affairs files, KUA.

40. Taylor interview; Julie Thatcher, "Dean Taylor Discusses Sex, the Pill and the New Morality," *UDK*, Jan. 9, 1970; "Birth Control" (chart) in DOW 53/0/1, 1970. ZPG records in KUA and in KC.

41. There was at least one woman physician in Lawrence, and she had been quoted in the *UDK* refusing to prescribe contraceptives to unmarried women. But in this controversy the divisions that appeared publicly were strictly along gender lines.

42. Sources include Browder, "Women's Decade"; copies of *Vortex* and *Lavender Luminary*, KUA; interviews with John Moritz, Ken Irby, Christine Leonard, Mary Coral, Jim Cooley, Emily Taylor.

43. This account is compiled from documents issued by the February Sisters, WSPA, Lorna Zimmer's files, and Student Activities—Women's Movement files, KUA; Margaret Greer, "The February Sisters History," typescript, WSPA; interview with Mary Coral and Jim Cooley, Lawrence, Dec. 1992; transcript from reunion of Lawrence feminists and February Sisters, WSPA; personal notes from February Sisters 20-year commemoration, KU, Dec. 1992; and assorted newspaper accounts. Robin Morgan said of the event: "While I'm flattered to be called an outside agitator, it's absurd. What happens is that the women in a community are oppressed and know they are oppressed. All I have done is connect these women with the knowledge they already have." Judy Henry, "February Sisters," *UDK*, n.d. [Feb. 1972], WSPA.

44. "February Sisters Position Statement on a Health Care Program for

Women," in Zimmer files. Portions of the American College Health Association's "Position Statement on Population and Family Planning," 1970, appear as Addendum III. Another document, "Health Services for Women: What Should the University Provide?" by the Project on the Status and Education of Women of the Association of American Colleges, June 1972, in the file, "Health Services for Women," DOW, cites the Lawrence situation in several places.

240

45. "February Sisters Position Statement," 6–7.

46. Judy Henry, "Groups Urge Birth Control," *UDK*, April 4, 1972. Browder, "Women's Decade," and transcript of "February Sisters Panel Discussion," 1987, statement by Mary Coral, in WSPA. Feminist opposition to ZPG is strongly stated in *Birth Control Handbook: Medicine for the People* (Montreal: Montreal Health Press, 1973), which was used by a Women's Self Help Clinic in Lawrence in 1973, WSPA.

47. David Garrow, *Liberty and Sexuality* (New York: Macmillan, 1994), 541; Jim Kendall, "Women Urged to Utilize Watkins," *UDK*, Aug. 23, 1973. The Supreme Court case, *Eisenstadt v. Baird*, was heard in Nov. 1971 but not decided until March 1972.

48. Statistics are from DCHDA.

49. This account is compiled from the minutes of PHC and BOH meetings, in DCHDA; articles in the *UDK* and *JW*; interviews with Petey Cerf (by telephone, June 1992), Dale Clinton (Lawrence, July 1992), and Raymond Schwegler. Lyman quoted in "Birth Control Funding Possible," *JW*, Sept. 27, 1972.

50. Minutes, Sept. 11, 1972, PHC, DCHDA; the minutes were taken by Dr. Clinton. "State Drops Birth Control Funding Here," *JW*, Sept. 22, 1972; "Birth Control Funding Possible"; Tim Pryor, "Health Agency Says Changes Due," *JW*, Jan. 10, 1973; Toby MacIntosh, "Policy on Pills Is Controversial," *JW*, Feb. 9, 1973.

51. This account is compiled from articles in *JW* and *UDK*; interviews with Cerf, Clinton, and Schwegler; and PHC and BOH minutes.

52. Mrs. Raymond Cerf, letter to the editor, *JW*, Sept. 25, 1972, and *UDK*, Oct. 19, 1972.

53. "Medical Estimates in City Conflict"; "Dr. Clinton Claims Enovid Great Drug, Asks No Panic," *JW*, Aug. 6, 1962; "Dr. Clinton Speaks Out on Enovid," *JW*, June 18, 1964. Barbara Seaman, *The Doctors' Case Against the Pill* (New York: Peter H. Wyden, 1969); Dr. Dale Clinton, letter to the editor, *JW*, Jan. 16, 1970.

54. Robert E. Markush and Daniel G. Seigel, "Oral Contraceptives and Mortality Trends from Thromboembolism in the United States," *AJPH* 59 (March 1969): 418–433; popular articles questioning the safety of the Pill include "Perils of the Pill," *Newsweek*, May 13, 1968, 66; Dr. Louis Lasagna, "If Not the Pill—What?" *Vogue*, Oct. 15, 1969, 102–103; "Birth Control: An Up-to-Date Summary of Contraceptive Methods," *Good Housekeeping*, Jan. 1967, 144–145; Morton Mintz, "The Golden Pill: We Can't Yet Be Sure It's Safe," *New Republic*, March 2, 1968, 18–20; Clinton's comments in Minutes, Oct. 30, 1972, PHC, DCHDA.

55. "Addendum to the Minutes of the Lawrence–Douglas County Public Health Committee for Meeting held Dec. 12, 1972," with Minutes, PHC, DCHDA; Toby MacIntosh, "Health Services Debated," *JW*, Dec. 12, 1972; Cerf and Clinton interviews.

56. MacIntosh, "Policy on Pills Is Controversial."

57. "County Health Controversy," Feb. 1973, Penn House document in scrapbook, DCHDA. Margaret Wedge, "Penn House—Grass Roots in Action," student paper, in KC. Carolyn S. Black, letter to the editor, *JW*, March 10, 1973. Cerf, in interview, cited the support of the League of Women Voters. The League maintained observers on the Board of Heath, and in 1965 had made a comprehensive study of the Lawrence–Douglas County Health Department. Records are in KC.

58. "Dr. Clinton Quitting," *JW*, March 8, 1973.

59. Toby MacIntosh, "Doctors at Health Meeting Offer Support for Clinton," *JW*, March 13, 1973; Minutes, March 12, 1973, PHC, DCHDA.

60. Minutes, March 12, 1973, PHC, DCHDA; MacIntosh, "Doctors Offer Support." Schwegler quoted in "Health Department Sets New Hours for Clinics," *JW*, May 2, 1973.

61. "Two Women Chosen for Positions with County Health Department," *JW*, May 22, 1973; "Physician Joins Department Here," *JW*, July 3, 1973; "A Woman's Touch," *JW*, Aug. 13, 1973, clippings in scrapbooks, DCHDA.

62. Statistics from DCHDA.

63. "County Providing Free Pills," *JW*, June 14 [1969 or 1970], DCHDA.

64. Kretschmer interview.

5. Revolutionary Intent

1. See David Farber, *The Age of Great Dreams* (New York: Hill and Wang, 1994); Terry Anderson, *The Movement and the Sixties: Protest in America from Greensboro to Wounded Knee* (New York: Oxford University Press, 1995).

2. Farber, *Age of Great Dreams*, 167; a version of Reagan's stump speech is in Gitlin, *The Sixties*, 217.

3. Reagan quoted in Anderson, *The Movement*, 327.

4. Letter from "Krazy," *Oread Daily*, July 15, 1970, 1.

5. David Ohle, Roger Martin, and Susan Brosseau, eds., *Cows Are Freaky When They Look at You: An Oral History of the Kaw Valley Hemp Pickers* (Wichita: Watermark Press, 1991), preface.

6. Bob (go nuts) Hole, "Daze Gone By," *Vortex*, Feb. 4–17, 1970, 5, 17.

7. Interview with Kenneth Irby, John Moritz, and Joe Van Zant, Lawrence, 1990.

8. Dick Russell, "A Visit to Kansas Hippieland," Topeka *Capital-Journal*, March 17, 1968, 3M. Some members of this group came to Atchison, Kan., at the

invitation of an "Atchison girl" who spent the summer of 1967 in the Haight-Ash-bury.

9. KC has copies of *Grist, Tansy,* and the *Kansas Free Press.* Laird Wilcox, editor of the *Free Press,* compiled a major collection of materials from extremist groups, which is deposited at KU as the Wilcox Collection. Copies of *Vortex, Screw, Reconstruction,* and the *Oread Daily* (also known as the *O.D.)* are in KUA and KC. Other information comes from the "Women's Decade of History" and "Movement Events" chronologies, assembled by Judy Browder and others, in KUA and WSPA, and interviews with Irby, Mortiz, Van Zant, Ed Grier, Mary Coral, Christine Leonard, Jim Cooley, Sam Anderson, Max Rife, Paul Steuwe, and many others.

10. *Cows Are Freaky,* despite the editors' use of pseudonyms and clear warning that it is "truth and fiction, fiction and truth," offers the most powerful and hardest-edged picture of those times in Lawrence; Preface. "Clinton Scoffs at 'Pot' Killers," *JW,* June 26, 1970, clipping, DCHDA.

11. "A Hemp Rope Around Our Neck," *Vortex,* Nov. 18–31, 1970; "Dear Azzhole" (letter from "Gunfreak") and "A Family Affair," *Vortex,* Dec. 1970. *Cows Are Freaky,* preface, 132–133; Joanna Wiebe, "Student Be-In Is a 'Success,'" *UDK,* April 26, 1968; *Oread Daily Review* (unpaginated "book" on Lawrence), n.d. [1971], KUA; tape of Hoffman's speech, April 1970 (RH MS 189), KC; "Outlaws," *Oread Daily* 5, no. 15 (n.d.), Student Protests files, KUA.

12. U.S. Census Data, 1960 and 1970; Griffin, *University of Kansas,* 628. Griffin discusses African-American students and university policy.

13. Griffin, *University of Kansas,* 629; "Movement Events," KUA. On the CRC's sit-in see *KFP,* March 22, 1965. On the struggles over race see Rusty L. Monhollon, "Away from the Dream: The Roots of Black Power in Lawrence, Kansas, 1960–1970" (M.A. thesis, University of Kansas, 1994).

14. U.S. Census, 1970, Kansas 18–87, 18–97; *Oread Daily Review;* interviews with Max Rife and Paul Steuwe, Lawrence, July 1992; files on Penn House, including Wedge, "Penn House," KC.

15. U.S. Census, 1970, 18–87, 18–339; "Contemporary Indian Affairs Class Polls Indian Affairs and Feelings," *Indian Leader,* May 11, 1973; interview with Prof. Daniel Wildcat, Haskell Indian Nations University, Lawrence, Nov. 1996.

16. This account is largely from the *Oread Daily Review,* supplemented by articles in *JW, Vortex,* and *Harambee* (KU's Black Student Union newspaper); "Movement Events"; interviews with Rife and Steuwe, with Peggy and Virgil Cooper, owners of the Rock Chalk Café (Lawrence, July 1992), and with Moritz, Coral, and Cooley; Valerie Mindel, "The Great Sheriff Race of 1970," *Kansas Alumni,* Jan. 1985, 25–30; and George Kimball, "This Little Yippie Ran for Sheriff," *The Realist,* Jan.–Feb. 1971, 15–19. See Michael Paul Fisher, "The Turbulent Years: The University of Kansas, 1960–1975" (Ph.D. diss., University of Kansas, 1979); Monhollon, "Away from the Dream."

17. Anderson, *The Movement*, 350–351.

18. Editorial, "Highly Commendable," *JW*, May 7, 1970.

19. Jane Lee, "No 'Abortion Mill' Seen Here under Altered Policy," *JW*, June 26, 1970. The *JW* editorial is quoted in another editorial, "More Trouble on Mount Oread," *Independence Daily Reporter*, April 7, 1970, Student Protests files, 1970–1990/91, KUA. Underlined in the file copy are the words: "Thank God for the Board of Regents' guidance and control over our state institutions of higher learning in keeping them from falling under the complete control of the malcontents among students and faculty."

20. The *Oread Daily Review* quotes the *Los Angeles Times* in its account of these events.

6. Sex as a Weapon

1. Eileen Wilcox, "Report," *KFP*, July 17, 1965.

2. Alice Echols, *Daring to Be Bad: Radical Feminism in America, 1967–1975* (Minneapolis: University of Minnesota Press, 1989), 28–37. While Carmichael's joke may have been intended as self-parody, it illuminated existing tensions and took on a life of its own in subsequent tellings.

3. Poem by John Sieler, in *Asterisk*, Jan. 8, 1969, quoted in Anderson, *The Movement*, 256. Herb Williams, "Naked," and photos by sylvester rising, *Vortex*, Nov. 18–Dec. 2, 1969, 17. On the ethics of the counterculture see Timothy Miller, *The Hippies and American Values* (Knoxville: University of Tennessee Press, 1991). Miller is a professor of religion at KU.

4. Sinclair, *Guitar Army*, 67–68.

5. Ibid., 69.

6. David Farber, *Chicago '68* (Chicago: University of Chicago Press, 1988), 218.

7. Quotations from ibid., 17, 53, 37.

8. Gitlin, *The Sixties*, 214.

9. Griffin, *University of Kansas*, 640–641; issues of *Sour Owl, Bitter Bird,* and *Squat* in KUA; dean's reprimand in P&D, 1956; "This Is Humor?" *JW*, May 16, 1956.

10. *The Screw*, Nov. 8, 1967 (issue 4). "Black American Club Plans Program," *UDK*, Feb. 10, 1970.

11. This image is probably from Ed Sanders's *Fuck You: A Magazine of the Arts.*

12. *The Screw*, Nov. 15, 1967; "Our Omaha Report," *The Screw*, March 15, 1968, 11. "Win with Cyn," *Harambee*, May 1970. "Revolutionary Poetry," *Harambee*, n.d. [1970, issue 3].

13. This account is compiled from "Printers Hold Walkout," *UDK*, Feb. 18,

1970; "Paper Not Obscene," *UDK,* Feb. 26, 1970; "BSU Confiscates UDK's," *UDK,* Feb. 24, 1970; "Controversy Continues," *UDK,* Feb. 25, 1970; Monhollon, "Away from the Dream"; and issues of *Harambee* (n.d., 1970).

14. Azrael, in *Vortex,* clipping, n.d. [1971?].

15. *KFP* ran an editorial entitled "'Fuck The Draft,'" which began: "To many of us this doesn't sound like a bad idea." But it excoriated Kimball for his actions: "Not only did George Kimball get himself into a lot of trouble but he also discredited the entire peace movement. . . If he wants to heap dung upon his own head he should be free to do so. But when he deliberately drags other people into the consequences of his incredibly stupid behavior he should be subject to the just wrath of his peers."

16. "Street Trials—a Reminder," *Vortex,* Dec. 17, 1968–Jan. 6, 1969. Cover, "S.F.P. Peddling Smut?"; no title, *Students Free Press,* vol. 1, no. 3, n.d. [1970].

17. Quoted in Anderson, *The Movement,* 111. See Kenneth Cmiel, "The Politics of Civility," in David Farber, ed., *The Sixties: From Memory to History* (Chapel Hill: University of North Carolina Press, 1994), 263–290.

18. "Don't Talk to Pigs!" *River City Headhunter,* n.d. [1970], KC. This was the "Official Publication of the Lawrence Chapter of the WHITE PANTHER PARTY."

19. Copies of *Grist* in KC and KUA. Malanga photo in *Grist* #9, 1966. This section is based on the following sources: George Kimball, "This Little Yippie Ran for Sheriff," *The Realist,* Jan.—Feb. 1971, 15–19; Valerie Mindel, "The Great Sheriff Race of 1970," *Kansas Alumni,* Jan. 1985, 25–30; Ohle et al., eds., *Cows Are Freaky; Oread Daily Review;* Lawrence Police Dept. records and files; "Yippie J-P Slips Past Voters," *Kansas City Star,* Nov. 5, 1970; Bob Velsir, "New Justice Plans Power Explosion," *UDK,* Nov. 6, 1970; "We Need a Two-Fisted Sheriff," *Vortex,* June 24, 1970, 10, 15; "Hemp High in the Saddle," *Free Press of Louisville,* Sept. 3, 1970 ("political hay" quote); Lee Byrd, "SPU Joins Viet Nam Protest," *UDK,* Oct. 18, 1965.

20. George Kimball, *Only Skin Deep* (New York: Ophelia Press, 1968), 94.

21. Ohle et al., eds., *Cows Are Freaky,* 25.

22. Timothy Miller, *The Hippies,* 27. "Alice?" and "dope history—lawrence: Daze Gone By," in *Vortex,* Feb. 4–17, 1970, 5–6.

23. "Concerned Citizens Ask to Meet with Ray Wells," *Lawrence Outlook,* July 28, 1969, clipping in Police Dept. files; Mrs. Carol Taylor, "Dandelions Not Illegal" (letter to the editor), *JW,* June 29, 1970.

24. Quotations from Anderson, *The Movement,* 286, and "Alice?"

25. Contributor's Notes, *Grist,* 1966.

26. Carolyn McMaster, (clipping, title missing), *JW,* Sept. 9, 1987.

27. S. Clay Wilson, Cover, *The Screw,* Nov. 18, 1966.

28. Sinclair quoted in Gitlin, *The Sixties,* 372. Robin Morgan refers to this statement in "Goodbye to All That," first published in *Rat,* Feb. 9, 1970.

29. Peck, *Uncovering the Sixties*, 212–213; Echols, *Daring to Be Bad*, 248. Lawrence's own story on clitoral orgasm—a condensed version of Anna Koedt's now-classic essay "The Myth of the Vaginal Orgasm"—appeared as "A Fucking Myth!" *Vortex*, Sept. 16–19, 1970.

30. suzi (all other members listed, also by first name only, immediately below this name), "Here We Are," *Vortex*, n.d. [March 18–31, 1970]. The next few paragraphs describe this "Women's Issue."

31. This image appeared fairly often in underground papers, though with slightly different details or framing material.

32. Delbert Petrick, "Dear Editors"; this and the quotations in the following paragraphs are from *Vortex*, April 1–14, 1970.

7. Sex and Liberation

1. See John D'Emilio, *Making Trouble: Essays on Gay History, Politics, and the University* (New York: Routledge, 1992) and *Sexual Politics, Sexual Communities* (Chicago: University of Chicago Press, 1984); Barry Adam, *The Rise of a Gay and Lesbian Movement* (Boston: Twayne, 1987); Toby Marotta, *The Politics of Homosexuality* (Boston: Houghton Mifflin, 1981); Laud Humphreys, *Out of the Closets* (Englewood Cliffs, N.J.: Prentice-Hall, 1972); Brett Bemyn, ed., *Creating a Place for Ourselves: Lesbian, Gay, and Bisexual Community Histories* (New York: Routledge, 1997).

2. "Come Out," *Vortex*, Sept. 2–14, 1970. "Lawrence Gay Liberation Front" announcement, n.d., in GL.

3. "Purple Power," *Vortex*, July–Aug. 1970, 4.

4. Carl Wittman, "A Gay Manifesto," rpt. in Mark Blasius and Shane Phelan, *We Are Everywhere* (New York: Routledge, 1997), 380–388.

5. "Come Out," *Vortex*. On gay history in relation to U.S. universities see John D'Emilio, *Making Trouble: Essays on Gay History, Politics, and the University* (New York: Routledge, 1992).

6. Phillip Brownlee, "Barred from Justice," *UDK*, Oct. 30, 1995; "Dear Fellow Christians," letter from UMHE Campus Pastors at Lawrence, July 29, 1970, Campus Ministry Archives; "Come Out," *Vortex*.

7. "Come Out," *Vortex*. News Bureau Release, Sept. 5, 1970, GL.

8. Kansas Penal Code, effective July 1, 1970, rpt. in David D. Barney, ed., *Gay and Lesbian History at the University of Kansas*, developed by the Student Assistance Center, KU, 1992.

9. Interview with Jack Klinknett, Lawrence, June 2, 1990. Klinknett had been one of approximately 125 students arrested for participating in the 1965 civil rights sit-in at KU.

10. Interview, William Balfour, Lawrence, Oct. 1996. Jan Kessinger, "Student

Senate Approves $600 to Gay Lib Front," *UDK*, Sept. 30, 1971. The GLF, in a document rating various Lawrence and KU therapists, counselors, and officials, gave Balfour its only "excellent" ranking. Other individuals were designated "damagingly-Jesus freak untogether" (a social worker); "generally trying but rather questionable" (Headquarters); "forget it" (dean of men); and "most generally very helpful" (dean of women); from "Resource and Refferal [sic] Persons," GL.

11. Lawrence Gay Liberation For the Preservation of Individual Rights, n.t., n.d., GL.

12. This account is compiled from documents in GL, including legal documents, personal and official correspondence, and position papers; dozens of articles in *UDK*, *JW*, and *Up Front* (the newsletter of Lawrence Gay Liberation, Inc.); clippings from newspapers throughout the state; Klinknett and Balfour interviews; and Brownlee, "Barred from Justice."

13. "KU's Gay Libbers File Federal Suit," *Topeka Capital Journal*, Dec. 14, 1971.

14. Lew Ferguson, "Topeka Court Bans Kunstler from Representing KU Gays," Wichita *Eagle*, Jan. 28, 1972; Robert H. Clark, "Kunstler Barred from U.S. Court," *Kansas City Star*, Jan. 27, 1972.

15. Ferguson, "Topeka Court"; "Topeka Judge Bars Kunstler," *JW*, Jan. 27, 1972; Clark, "Kunstler Barred." Kunstler told the press that Oldfather's appeal "took a lot of courage"; Oldfather said he spoke as a member of the legal profession, not a representative of KU: "I may be fired tomorrow . . . [but] I guess there are times . . . when a man must stand and speak and this is one of those times." Clark, "Kunstler Barred"; "Kunstler Barred from Courtroom," *Parson's Sun*, Jan. 27, 1972; "Kunstler Incurs a Judge's Wrath," *New York Times*, Jan. 28, 1972, clipping, KUA.

16. "Legal News," *Lawrence GLF News*, March 10, 1972, 1 (issue no. 1).

17. Kunstler was allowed to argue before the 10th Circuit Court of Appeals in Denver, and he made a case that the "lives of homosexuals have been made a 'living hell' because of general ignorance." "Kunstler Requests Court Order KU Gay Lib Okay," *JW*, Nov. 17, 1972.

18. Headquarters opened on Dec. 16, 1969, and was initially funded through the First Methodist Church. It was a community center for peer counseling and support, and attempted at first to focus on high school students. Thirty-five high school student volunteers worked as its staff, and a local pharmacist helped with drug issues. It received an average of 74 calls a month in 1971; 1,457 a month in 1973; and more than 1,600 a month in 1974. Douglas M. McEnery, "A Study for the Selection of Paraprofessional Counselors for Crisis Intervention Services: Headquarters" (M.A. thesis, University of Kansas, 1976); "Headquarters Deals with Various Issues," *UDK*, Feb. 9, 1970, 3; interview with Ric Silber, Lawrence, July 1992.

19. Many of the human sexuality seminars, sponsored by the Commission on

the Status of Women in conjunction with the dean of women's office, focused on or included gay and lesbian issues. The records of the Campus Ministries document their material and emotional support of the GLF.

20. "Purple Gaze," *Vortex,* Halloween, 1970. Lawrence sent 13 of the 125 people who attended the conference in Minneapolis, which was sponsored by Free, the Minneapolis-area gay liberation group. The Lawrence group maintained a fairly close connection with Jack Baker, the gay activist who was president of the University of Minnesota student body. According to this account of the conference, about 90% of the attendees were "freaks"—a reminder of the overlap of categories of identity.

21. The Women and Men of the Lawrence Gay Liberation Front, "On Our Own," *Vortex* 4, no. 2 [1971].

22. "Gay Liberation Front Emergency Position Paper," handed out on campus April 28, 1972, in GL; "Gays Present Requests to Balfour," *UDK,* April 28, 1972.

23. Chuck Ortleb, letter to the Editor, *UDK,* Sept. 25, 1972.

24. Ruth Lichtwardt, "A Stroll Down Gayhawk Lane," in Barney, ed., *Gay and Lesbian History.*

25. Henry A. Bubb, a member of the KU Board of Regents, sent a copy of the "love the one you want" ad to Chancellor Nichols with a note: "The ad below appeared in the University Daily Kansan, Sept. 5, 1972. Do you approve of this use of the Student Union?" GL. No title, no date [Aug. 1971?], announcement of open rap session at the KU student union, GL. Most of this statement is taken, word for word, from the Chicago Gay Liberation Front's "A Leaflet for the American Medical Association" (1970), which was used in challenging the American Psychiatric Association's classification of homosexuality as a mental illness. The Kansas group does not acknowledge the document's source. "Leaflet" is in Blasius and Phelan, *We Are Everywhere,* 394–395.

26. Undated document signed by Jim Conley describing dance in Oct. 1974, GL.

27. Undated document signed by William Bradley Jr. describing dance in April 1974, GL.

28. Letter from Robert Carlson and Herbert B. Mosher to Dr. Harold Voth, Feb. 28, 1975, GL. A copy was received in the office of KU's executive vice-chancellor on July 7, 1975.

29. Balfour to Prof. Michael Storms, Sept. 19, 1975, GL. Sources on the proposed conference include the GLF's original announcement and a series of letters and memos written between Oct. 12 and Oct. 25, 1975. Quotation from a memo from the university counsel to Executive Vice-Chancellor Shankel and Vice-Chancellor Balfour, Oct. 23, 1975, GL.

30. "We Did It!" *Gay Liberation News,* April 26 [1972].

31. "Senior Drinking Chant," no. 4 in *Class of '65—Senior Yells,* KUA.

32. The interview was transcribed as "Don't Touch That Dial," in *Wheat Dreams,* issue # 1 [1973 or 1974]. All quotations from this interview are from this document, 6–9; 14–16.

33. "LGLF Liberates St. Joseph Mo.," *Gay Liberation News,* April 26 [1972], 1.

34. Mary, "Gay is Good. Gay is Natural. Let it Go, Let it Go . . . ," *Vortex,* March 1, 1971; Lz. Shari, untitled, *Lavender Luminary,* Feb. 1975; Richard, "Feb. 4, 1974," *Wheat Dreams,* n.d. [1973 or 1974].

35. See Echols, *Daring to Be Bad,* 210–220.

36. "Handout Session One, Women's Self Help Clinic," Judy Browder files, Student Activities: Women's Movement, 1970–1985, KUA.

37. "A Lawrence Women's Liberation Group Meeting," audiotape, July 1970, KC.

38. "Readers' Theater for Human Sexuality Seminar on Same-Sex Relationships," compiled and directed by Jan Sanders, 1974, in Sexuality Workshops, Spring 1974, Zimmer personal files.

39. "Down the Drain . . . ," *Vortex,* July 8–21, 1970.

40. "Women Women Women Women," *Freedspeak,* n.d. [1970]; "Feminist and the Fuzz," *Freedspeak,* n.d. [1970].

41. Lz. Jesse, "True Story/A Fiction," *Lavender Luminary,* Feb. 1975.

42. "Cinderella has escaped," *Oread Daily,* Sept. 9, [197?].

43. This full-page tribute reprinted most of Solanas's 1967 "S.C.U.M. Manifesto," with commentary. Her name was misspelled consistently. "He Asked Me to Eat Him," *Vortex,* July–Aug. 1970.

44. Margaret Atwood, *The Handmaid's Tale* (ca. 1985; New York: Ballantine/Random House, 1989), 33.

45. "A Statement of Action," Feb. 4, 1972, WSPA. The February Sisters' demands were sent to the chancellor and read over the phone to members of the press. On the Sisters see Chapter 4.

46. Both ads had been appearing in the *Kansan* for two years. The male business and advertising managers acknowledged that "women are more misused in advertising because men's attitudes toward them are deeply rooted and condoned," and pledged, as the article's headline proclaimed: "Sex Advertising Goes for Good." The *Kansan* did not solicit sex-oriented advertisements locally, they said: many ads originated in New York and could not be altered. Cheryl Mehan, "Sex Advertising Goes for Good," *UDK,* Oct. 29, 1970.

47. "Coed Slams Sex Waiver," *UDK,* Oct. 7, 1970. "Who's to Judge?" *UDK,* April 18, 1977. On Sept. 16, 1971, the *UDK* ran an AP feature entitled "Women Nix Girl Watching."

48. Barbara Spurlock, "Local Rape Rate" (signed editorial), *UDK,* April 9, 1973; other sources include Betty Haegelin, "Concern over Rape Continues Despite

Arrest," *UDK,* Aug. 30, 1974; "Ottawa Graduate Charged in Rapes," *UDK,* June 11, 1974; Martin Zimmerman, "Rape Victims Said to Get Fair Deal from Local Police, Court System," *UDK,* Dec. 2, 1976.

49. "Douglas County Rape Victim Support Service History," July 10, 1976, RVSS archives (the organization's name changed slightly over time); interviews with Sara Jane Russell and Diane Duffy, Lawrence, Dec. 1992; assorted documents, including "Presentation Given by Kathy Hoggard and Polly Pettit . . . to the Conference of the American Association of State Colleges and Universities," Dec. 16, 1975; "Police Procedure," n.d.; "Hospital Procedures and Information," June 8, 1976; "Workshop," Jan. 1975; Cynthia A. Robinson, "How You Can Create a Rape Counseling Service: Some Legal Aspects," n.d.; a film the group made, *No Pat Answers,* and various "incident reports" from the early 1970s (names of women and identifying information were never included), all in RVSS archives.

50. Jan Goodison, "Rapists and Molesters: Lone Women on Streets Provide Easy Target for Sex Offenders," *UDK,* Oct. 6, 1970.

51. Russell interview; the detective's attitude, she emphasized, had not been widely shared. Zimmerman, "Rape Victims"; incident reports, RVSS Archives.

52. See Fred R. Shapiro, "Historical Notes on the Vocabulary of the Women's Movement," *American Speech* 60 (Spring 1985): 3–16.

8. Remaking Sex

1. Lee Stone, "Insistent Coed Caused a Crisis," Salina *Journal,* May 24, 1968; "Students: Linda the Light Housekeeper," *Time,* April 26, 1968, 51.

2. Judy Klemsrud, "An Arrangement: Living Together for Convenience, Security, Sex," *New York Times,* March 4, 1968.

3. My account is compiled from the many newspaper clippings in the Le-Clair files, Barnard College Archives, esp. series from the *New York Post,* April 17–18, 1968, and the *New York Daily News,* April 12–20, 1968. I am indebted to Amy Ceccarelli for telling me of the LeClair files; and see her "Women, the New Left, and Women's Liberation: A Case Study of Barnard College, 1968–70" (Senior thesis, Barnard College, 1991).

4. Linda LeClair, letter to the editor, *Barnard Bulletin,* March 13, 1968.

5. William A. McWhirter, "'The Arrangement' at College," *Life,* May 31, 1968, 56. This article is part of a special section on student sexuality.

6. All letters quoted are in the LeClair files.

7. Editorial, "And Now Another Constitutional Right," Benton Harbor *News-Palladium,* April 19, 1968; William F. Buckley, "Is the Moral Code Dead?" *Los Angeles Times,* April 29, 1968; both in the LeClair files. Despite Buckley's comments, LeClair was not pregnant, though she and Peter Behr expressed a desire to have children together someday.

8. On the redefinitions of public and private in this case, see my article "Sexual Revolution(s)," in Farber, *The Sixties.*

9. Quoted in Jean Crofton, "Barnard's Linda Has No Regrets," *New York Post,* April 17, 1968.

10. "Co-ed Dorms Get Hearty Approval," *UDK,* Oct. 23, 1964.

11. See memo "To Scholarship Hall Residents" from Vice-Chancellor Balfour, Feb. 23, 1971, in Housing: Scholarship Halls files, KUA.

12. "Coeducational Living System, University of Kansas Scholarship Hall System, Preliminary Proposal," Dec. 1970 (several drafts) in Coed Papers file, Housing: Scholarship Halls files, KUA.

13. The surveys, dated March 12, 1970, are in Coed Survey file, Housing: Scholarship Halls files, KUA.

14. "Hanky-Panky in McCollum Causes Embarrassment for the Residents," *UDK,* Dec. 6, 1967.

15. "Hall, Parents React to McCollum PDA Claim," *UDK,* Dec. 8, 1967.

16. McCollum Hall officers, letter to the editor, *UDK,* Dec. 8, 1967; James Zeller, letter to the editor, *UDK,* Dec. 11, 1967.

17. Walter F. Riker, letter to the editor, *UDK,* Dec. 8, 1967.

18. "Associated Women Students Survey."

19. "Working Paper on Open Houses," March 11, 1969, in DOW chronological files, 1968–69. Much of the language used is adopted from a leaflet by the Coordinated Ministries at Indiana University, "10 Questions & Answers on Visitation Privileges at I.U." (University Archives, Indiana University). KU's dean of women had done her graduate work there.

20. Ibid.

21. "On Our Own," *Vortex.*

22. *Lavender,* produced and directed by Colleen Monahan, KUA.

23. "Gay is Good . . . Real Good," *Vortex,* April 5, 1971, 6–7.

24. "The Dating Game," radio show, Dec. 4, 1972, B. Murr, K. Guthrie, M. Laflin, M. Biddle, H. Young, M. Ward, participants, audiotape in KUA.

25. McWhirter, "The Arrangement."

Credits

Quotation on p. ix from "She of the Shining Eyes" by Lawrence Ferlinghetti, first published in *Tansy,* vol. 2 (1970); copyright © 1999 by Lawrence Ferlinghetti, reprinted by permission of New Directions Publishing Corp. and John Moritz.

1. Duke D'Ambra Collection, Kansas Collection, University of Kansas Libraries
2. University Archives, University of Kansas Libraries
3. Duke D'Ambra Collection, Kansas Collection, University of Kansas Libraries
4. University Archives, University of Kansas Libraries
5. University Archives, University of Kansas Libraries
6. University Archives, University of Kansas Libraries
7. Duke D'Ambra Collection, Kansas Collection, University of Kansas Libraries
8. University Archives, University of Kansas Libraries
9. University Archives, University of Kansas Libraries
10. University Archives, University of Kansas Libraries
11. *Ladies Home Journal,* January 1968
12. Lawrence *Journal World* Collection, Kansas Collection, University of Kansas Libraries
13. University Archives, University of Kansas Libraries
14. Lawrence *Journal World* Collection, Kansas Collection, University of Kansas Libraries
15. University Archives, University of Kansas Libraries
16. University Archives, University of Kansas Libraries
17. Lawrence *Journal World* photograph, University Archives, University of Kansas Libraries
18. Lawrence *Journal World* photograph, University Archives, University of Kansas Libraries
19. *Vortex,* Women's Liberation Issue, 1970, in KU Archives
20. *Oread Daily Review,* 1970, in KU Archives
21. University Archives, University of Kansas Libraries
22. University Archives, University of Kansas Libraries

Acknowledgments

My first contact with Lawrence, Kansas, was in a TV movie of the 1980s, *The Day After,* which portrayed the aftermath of nuclear war in this heartland town. *The Day After* was a major media event in the Cold War years of Ronald Reagan's first presidential term. Psychologists and counselors offered advice on dealing with the anxiety it was sure to provoke; debates raged over whether or not children should watch. I was a graduate student in Chicago then, and my reaction to the film was predictably provincial and, in retrospect, pretty funny. Why, I asked, didn't they make a movie about someplace important?

I gradually came to believe that understanding social change in America demands that we look beyond the "important" places, and as a result I spent almost a decade studying the town I had once so cavalierly dismissed. The process was rewarding not only intellectually but personally. Today some of my best friends and favorite places are in Kansas.

Writing history grounded in a specific location depends profoundly on the generosity of the people who inhabit it, and I am pleased to have an opportunity to thank them. This book would never have existed without the extraordinary professional knowledge of the University of Kansas archivist Ned Kehde. He handed me the files that first convinced me this project was worth doing, and over the years he and his fellow archivist Barry Bunch gave me the kind of advice and assistance most researchers can only dream of. Dozens of people shared their memories with me, dug old photographs and papers out of dusty boxes, offered me new leads or new ways of understanding the history I was writing. I owe an enormous debt to them, and I hope they will see their influence in the pages of this book. I am grateful to the staffs of the Spencer Research Library and the Douglas County Public Health Department, and to the Board of Education, the Lawrence Police Department, Headquarters, and Rape Victims Support Services for their invaluable help. Kathleen Whalen, my research assistant during the summer and fall of 1992, was both meticulous and creative in her work.

Acknowledgments

Several friends and colleagues in Kansas deserve special thanks. Ann Schofield's friendship and scholarly interest made the project not only better but much more fun, and her hospitality is unsurpassed. Bill and Kathy Tuttle made me welcome in countless ways, including the summer Kathy lent her house to my family so I could do research in Lawrence. Their scholarship influenced the book, and their friendship was crucial to its completion. Stanley Lombardo helped me understand how to look at the landscape of Kansas, and rode a bicycle across the state with me—twice. Mary Jane Kelley and Chester Pach, though no longer in Lawrence, are forever entwined with that place in my memory. Mary Jane's perpetual confidence that "the wind will be behind us on the way back" kept me going more often than she knew.

I have been fortunate to receive support from several institutions for my research. The Ann Whitney Olin Junior Fellowship at Barnard College funded my overlapping projects on Hawai'i and Kansas between 1991 and 1994. I received an NEH summer stipend in 1995, as well as a Barnard College faculty research grant. I completed this book as a visiting scholar at the Feminist Research Institute, University of New Mexico, before joining the faculty of the American Studies department at UNM, and I am grateful to the institute and to its directors, Louise Lamphere and Jane Slaughter.

I have also benefited greatly from conversations with colleagues, students, and nonacademic audiences as I have presented portions of my work in seminars, conferences, classrooms, and public lectures. "Sex in Kansas" was sometimes a strange topic in New York, Honolulu, or Jakarta, but the challenge of communicating its significance sharpened my thinking and the astute questions I encountered in distant places shaped my analysis in important ways. I am especially grateful to Barry Shank and the Gender Seminar at the University of Kansas, to Atina Grossmann and the Women and Society Seminar at Columbia University, to Chester Pach and the Contemporary History Institute at Ohio University, and to Melani Budianta at the University of Indonesia, as well as to the University of Kansas Medical School, the Barnard Center for Research on Women, the departments of history at the University of Hawaii–Manoa, the University of Hawaii–Hilo, and the University of New Mexico, the law faculty of Universitas Tarumanagara (Indonesia), and the Wyandotte (Kansas) County Historical Society and Museum for invitations to discuss my work.

Four people went well beyond the calls of duty, collegiality, friendship, or even marriage in helping me with this book. My editor, Joyce Seltzer, did everything I hoped she would do when I signed an advance contract. Michael Sherry read the entire manuscript with care and asked questions that forced me to rethink some fundamental premises. I am immensely grateful for his encouragement and engagement with this project. Lisa Tiersten's many talents affected the book on every level from general outline to word choice, and her friendship has meant the world to me. David Farber, as always, pushed me to think harder and take more chances. He lived this work with me, and I appreciate what that means—and how lucky I am—more each time.

Over the past decade and a half, as my family and I have moved around the country, our lives have been enriched by several wonderful communities of friends. I will always be grateful for the shared good times. And once again, I thank my (growing) family—Richard Bailey and Esther Rodrigo, Susan Bailey and Kurt Friederichs, Sheryl Bailey and Scott Hamiel, and Don and Nancy Farber—for their love, support, and enthusiasm. My deepest gratitude is to the two people who are most important in my life: to Max, who continues to delight and amaze me, and to David, with all my love.

Index

Abington Bookstore, 164
abortion, 15, 63, 77, 151
Adamson, Linda, 101
administration, KU, 81–82, 85–88, 96–97, 102–104, 117, 127, 152, 159, 178, 179; and birth control, 124–125; and coed dorms, 205–206, 210–211; and February Sisters, 128–130, 196; and GLF, 178–183, 185, 187–188; and homosexuality, 50–54, 62–66, 175; and sex control, 50–56, 62–70, 74, 75, 88–91, 94–97, 101–104; and student life, 47, 82–83, 86–87, 104, 211
administration, LHS, 149–150
administrations, university, 70–71, 85; as allies to students, 7–8, 102–104; and authority, 8, 44, 47–50, 52, 82; Barnard College, 200–202, 204; and sex control, 45–54, 60–61, 67–68, 71, 73, 75, 80, 82–83
African Americans, 16, 17, 109, 110, 138–141, 154–155; in Lawrence, 6, 19, 111, 143, 147–150, 159, 160–161
Afro House, 148, 152
AIDS, 11, 217–218
Alex (pseud.), 63–66
Alpert, Jane, 169–170
American College Health Association, 128
American Journal of Public Health, 132
American Medical Association, 6, 110, 145
American Psychiatric Association, 1, 58, 60
American Public Health Association, 108
American Public Welfare Association, 110
androgyny, 10
anti-Semitism, 36, 115

Asian Americans, 17
Associated Women Students (AWS), 88; rules convention, 90–91, 97–103, 119; letters protesting, 102–103
attorney general, Kansas, 96–97, 161, 165
Atwood, Margaret, 195–196
authority, 36, 55, 114, 125; adult, 46, 76, 119, 136; cultural, 30, 33, 36, 38, 39, 44, 126; dean v. psychiatrist, 49–50, 52, 61, 62, 67–68, 70–71; male, 131, 134–135; moral, 36, 63, 70, 71, 73; new sites, 14, 48; of university, 92, 95, 47–50, 82, 95–97, 103
Azrael, 162

baby boom, 39, 84
Balfour, William, 180
Barnard College, 200–202, 204
bars, 5, 22, 30, 35, 36, 40–41, 63, 66, 148, 175, 184
Beat poets, 1, 4
Behr, Peter, 201, 203, 204, 214
be-in, 146
Bell, Betsy, 112, 114
Bert Nash Clinic, 67
Big Eat, 146, 150
birth control, 15, 77, 136, 105–106, 109–118, 128; availability of, 110, 111, 114, 116, 121, 126, 129; disapproval of single women's use, 110; and eugenics movement, 109; information about, 108, 112, 113, 114, 124; and law, 107–108, 111, 112, 121; techniques, 76–77, 112, 123. *See also* Pill
Black American Club, LHS, 159
Black Student Union: KU, 146, 148, 149–150, 160–162; LHS, 148, 149–150

257

Index

Board of Health, Lawrence–Douglas County, 24, 28, 29, 130–135
bodies, women's, 156, 191–193, 194; examining own, 10; right to control own, 7, 107, 117, 120–121, 195–199
Boston University, 134
Brown, J. Gary, 168
Buck, Pearl S., 106
Buckley, William F., 203
Bulletin of the Menninger Clinic, 57
business community (Lawrence), 4, 21, 167

Campus Crusade for Christ, 6, 120
Canfield, Grant, 171, 173
Carmichael, Stokely, 154–155
Cerf, Petey, 131–134
Chalmers, Lawrence, 128, 179, 182
Chamber of Commerce, Lawrence, 20, 39
Chambers, Harry, 24–25, 27–29, 37, 44
churches, in Lawrence, 6, 37, 40, 41, 112, 113, 148
Citizens for Decent Literature, 42
civil rights, 9, 14, 15, 80, 128, 141, 177
Civil Rights Act of 1964, 96
Civil Rights Council, KU, 147–148
Civil Rights Movement, 139–140, 154–155; in Lawrence, 147–149
civil society, and inclusiveness, 16–17, 48, 216–217
class, social, 11, 14, 19–23, 26, 27, 30–32, 38, 46, 66, 77–78, 84, 113, 123, 131, 133
Clinton, Dale, 108–110, 114–115, 121, 122–123, 130–135
cohabitation, 2, 10, 11, 96, 118, 137, 200–205, 215, 218
Cold War, 13, 46, 47, 50, 58, 85, 87, 104
College Personnel Association, 86
colleges. *See* universities
Collins, Vanessa, 159
comics, 42–43
coming out, in Lawrence, 183–185, 188, 212
comix, 168–169, 170–174
Commission on National Goals, Kennedy's, 86
Commission on the Status of Women, KU, 127, 180

Community Service League, 32, 33, 34–36
conflict: counterculture in Lawrence, 143–144, 146, 151–153, 167; gender, 132–135, 151, 154–155, 169–174; generational, 46, 138, 141, 151; race, 154–155
Congress, U.S., 42, 56, 58
Congress of Racial Equality (CORE), 140, 147; in Lawrence, 144–145
consciousness-raising groups, 127, 192
consumer culture, 39–41
Council of Social Agencies, 31, 37
Council on Student Affairs, KU, 96–97, 101, 124
counterculture, 1, 2, 9, 141–142, 155–158, 203, 217; Lawrence, 117, 125–127, 150–151, 155–160, 162–174, 179; description of Lawrence, 143–146; images of Lawrence, 167, 169; and gay liberation in Lawrence, 189
Cows Are Freaky When They Look at You, 145, 164
"Crank Case, The," 171–173
Cranston, William, 74
curfews, 78, 79, 150. *See also* parietals

dances, 22–23, 35, 40–41; "cultural," 64; GLF, 183–187
Dark Command, 18
dating, 10, 101, 207–208, 213–214; system, 77–78
"Dating Game, The," 213
Days of Rage, Lawrence, 149–151, 179
Defense Planning Committee, Lawrence, 33
defense workers, 15, 18, 32; fears about (Lawrence), 20–23, 27, 31
democracy: and limits of social change, 180–181; participatory, 92, 140
Democratic National Convention (1968), 139, 157–158, 170, 181
Department of Health, Education, and Welfare, 109, 130
deviance, sexual, 6, 8, 60, 61, 62, 68, 70, 71, 75, 96; in military, 57–59. *See also* misconduct; transgression
"discovered-behavior," 69
divorce, 37
Doctors' Case Against the Pill, The, 132

dormitories, coed, 10, 205–211; proposal, 206; survey, 206–208

Dorn, Ed, 145

double standard, sexual, 10, 11, 79, 95–97, 159

Douglas County Family Planning Association, 112–114, 115, 122–124, 131

Dowdell, Rick "Tiger," 152

drugs, 141, 143–146, 153, 157, 165, 166–167

Dykes, Archie, 187

Ed Sullivan Show, 39–40

elites, 125; local, 6, 14, 30, 31–39, 217; and loss of authority, 38–39, 44; youth, 136

Emmons, Mrs. Donald, 94

existentialism, 50, 92–94, 102, 116–117

exploitation: male, 174; sexual, 155, 193–194, 196, 199

February Sisters, 127–130, 131, 195, 196

federal government, 6, 18; and birth control, 107, 108, 109–110, 130, 131, 134; expanded role, 13–15, 36, 83, 148; in WWII, 23–24

Feminine Mystique, The (Friedan), 10

femininity, 211–212, 213

feminism, 127–129, 131, 155, 159, 169–174, 191–199, 213

Fred (pseud.), 63–65

freedom, sexual, 109, 117, 119, 126, 195–196, 199, 217–218; demands for, 101, 104, 136; individual, 177; and Pill, 105–107; and women, 10, 190

free love, 2, 10, 120, 137, 215

free speech, 15, 137; movement, 63

Fucking Insane Sisters of Terrorism, 195

"fuck trials," 162, 166

Gallalee, John, 46

Garland, Judy, 40

Garlinghouse, John, 93

Garrett, William, 152

gay culture, 10, 175, 211

Gay Liberation Front (GLF), Lawrence, 175, 176–183, 189–190; dances, 183–187; letters protesting dances, 185–187; manifestos, 176, 177, 183–184, 211; and public education, 188, 189–190; radio interview, 189–190; requests KU recognition, 178–183; and role of sex, 183–184; sues KU, 181–183, 187, 188, 190

gay liberation movement, 1, 3, 9–10, 137, 175–191, 199, 214; in Lawrence, 175–177, 178–191; role of sex, 177–178, 181

gender, 15; difference, 100, 217; equality, 8, 91, 96, 98, 103–104, 126–127, 190, 196, 202, 204, 205–208, 210, 217; relation to sex, 202–211; roles, 10, 71–72, 76, 137, 211, 212; and sexual misconduct, 63; and Student Responsibility Movement, 93, 94; transcending, 212–215

G.I. Bill, 38, 49, 83, 84

Ginsberg, Allen, 145, 164

Gitlin, Todd, 92, 158

Glover, Benjamin H., 71–72

Goad, Emery, 208–209

Great Society, 7, 107, 109

Grist, 145, 164, 168

Gundle, Sigmund, 51–52, 59, 60

Haight-Ashbury, 3, 125, 145, 146

handbooks, student, 79; Haskell, 89; KU, 88–89, 96

Handmaid's Tale, The (Atwood), 195–196

Harambee, 160–162

Harrell, Vernon, 68, 197

Harvard University, 92

Haskell Indian Junior College, 19, 89, 111, 149, 175, 197. *See also* students, Haskell

Haskell Institute. *See* Haskell Indian Junior College

Hawkins, Bill (pseud.), 63, 65

Hayden, Tom, 97, 155

Headquarters, 183

healthcare, women's, 114, 123, 128, 129, 130, 134, 191, 196

Hefner, Hugh, 3, 194

Henry, Don, 56

Henry, Pat, 197

Index

herpes, genital, 218
heterosexuality: cases (KU), 68–69; relationships, 200–211, 214
Higher Education Act of 1965, 84
high school education, 17; universal, 6, 38, 47
Hill, Phil, 165–166
hippies, 138. *See also* counterculture
Hispanics, 17, 149
Hoffman, Abbie, 141, 146, 158, 162, 181
Hoggard, Kathy, 198
Holcombe, Susan (pseud.), 68–69
homosexuality, 2; cases (KU), 50–54, 63–67; as "danger," 52, 53, 54, 58, 60, 65, 66; medicalization of, 55; as mental illness, 1, 8–9, 51, 54, 55, 60, 61, 70, 71–73, 180, 218; and military, 18, 55, 57–59; opposition to, 179, 185–188; and psychotherapy, 70–73, 188; as sin, 3, 8–9, 55, 180, 216; and street therapy, 185. *See also* Gay Liberation Front; gay liberation movement
Human Sexuality Series, 180

identity, 6–7; categories of, 44; counterculture, 145, 158; gay, 212–213; generational, 158; sexual, 9, 58, 71–72, 160, 167–174, 217
In Defense of the Nation, 24
Indiana University, 45
in loco parentis, 7–8, 78, 80–83, 85, 92, 95, 97–104, 122, 201

Jackson State College, 141
John Steven, 183
Johnson, Lyndon Baines, 107, 138–139
Journal of the American College Health Association, 118
Journal of College Student Personnel, 85
Journal of the National Association of Women Deans and Counselors, 48
Journal of School Health, 118
Joy of Sex, The, 1
juvenile delinquency, 1, 25–26, 42–43, 47
Juvenile Protection Committee, Lawrence, 43

Kansas City Women's Liberation Group, 172
Kansas Department of Social Welfare, 110
Kansas River Baptist Convention, 23
Kansas State Department of Health, 130–131
Kansas University Students for a Democratic Society Journal, 93
Kaw Valley Hemp Pickers, 145, 146, 168
Kent, Kay, 134–135
Kent State, 179
Kimball, George, 162, 163–166
Kinsey, Alfred, 2, 3, 46, 48, 77, 137
Klinknett, Jack, 180, 181–182
Korean War, 39, 45, 46, 74
Kunstler, William, 181–182

Lavender, 212
law: and birth control, 107–108, 111, 112; and homosexuality, 179–180; and obscenity, 160–161; and order, 139; rape, 10; and sex, 96; state, 95; and university, 8, 104
Lawrence: demographics, 4–5, 19, 21, 38, 111, 148, 149; history of, pre-WWII, 18–20; overview of "60s," 142–153; and race relations, 147–149, 178; relation to Kansas, 4–5
Lawrence Country Club, 41
Lawrence High School (LHS), 121, 148, 149–150, 159, 162, 164, 179. *See also* students, LHS
Lawrence Liberation Front, 151
Lawrence Memorial Hospital, 113
Lawrence Ministerial Alliance, 113
law school, KU, and waiver, 196
League of Women Voters, Lawrence, 133
LeClair, Linda, 200–205, 214, 218; letters about, 202–203, 204
lesbians, 62–63, 127, 178, 190, 193, 212; commune, 191
letter to parents, *O.D.,* 142
Levine, Ginny, M.D., 134–135
liberation movements, 8, 176–177
Liberty Memorial (Kansas City), 175, 184
liquor, 21–23, 30, 40–41, 81
local, relation to national, 5–7, 14–16,

25–26, 33–34, 36, 38, 40, 43–44, 127, 131, 135, 137, 142, 144, 176–177

Lz. Shari, 190

market economy, 33, 38, 41

marriage, 166; rate, 18, 37

Martin Luther King Jr., 139, 140

masculinity, 11, 72, 211–212, 213

mass media, 1, 5–7, 11, 17, 33, 37, 45, 137, 208; film, 18, 147; magazines, 42–43, 46, 47, 72, 80–81, 110, 117, 118, 132, 143, 145, 159, 200, 214–215; newspapers, 202–203; paperbacks, 41–43; radio, 13, 40; TV, 1, 40, 138, 139, 140, 143, 146; during WWII, 25–26

May Act, 24

McCollum Hall, 208–209

Menninger, William C., 57, 58

Menninger Clinic, 56–57, 59, 185, 186

Men's Christian Alliance, 41

mental health clinics, 59, 118; KU, 51–53, 65, 67, 101–102

middle-class culture, 13–14, 30, 76, 80, 89; white, 17, 85, 161

Midwestern Association of College and University Psychiatrists and Clinical Psychologists, 71

military, 16, 23; and homosexuality, 55, 57–59; and psychiatry, 49–50, 55, 56–60; training, 14, 32; and V.D., 27, 28

Miller, Keith, 160

Miller, Vern, 166

ministries, KU, 120, 125

Minutemen, 6, 145

misconduct, sexual, 75, 208–209. *See also* deviance; transgression

Missouri Western College, 189

mobility: geographic, 6, 15–16, 24, 33, 46, 84, 137; social, 6, 46, 84, 137, 217

Morality Survey, AWS, 119, 121, 210

Morgan, Robin, 127–128, 170

Moritz, John, 164

Mott, Dr., 25

Movement, the, 140, 169; role of sex in, 155

Murphy, Franklin D., 147

"Myth of the Vaginal Orgasm, The" 10

Nathanson, Paul, 4

National Association of Parents and Teachers, 42

National Association of Student Personnel Administrators, 60, 70

national culture, 5–6, 13, 15, 17, 36, 39, 132, 217

National Defense Act of 1958, 84

National Guard, 45, 141, 150, 151

National Highway Defense Act, 39

National Institute of Mental Health, 58

National Organization for Decent Literature, 42

National Organization for Women (NOW), 10, 126, 127, 171

National Venereal Disease Control Act, 24

Native Americans, 17, 19, 89, 149

New Left, 92, 97, 155

Notre Dame University, 81

NOW, 10, 126, 127, 171

obscenity, 15, 42–44, 160–161

Office of Economic Opportunity, 109, 148

Ohio State University, 118

Oldfather, Charles, 182

Open End, 1

Operation Newsstand, 42

Oral (pseud.), 50–52, 55, 62

Ortleb, Chuck, 184

panty raids, 45–48, 73–74, 81, 82

Paretsky, Sara, 100–101

parietals, 1, 2, 8, 75, 78–79, 80, 89–104, 119, 201, 210–211

parking, 69, 75, 79, 209

PDA (public display of affection), 208–209

Penn House, 133, 148, 160

Peter (pseud.), 68–69

Peterson, Martha, 200–202

physicians: Lawrence, 132–135, 151; military, 32; prescribe Pill, 1, 106, 111, 112, 114, 116, 118, 121–123, 126, 134–135, 196

Pill, 3, 7, 8, 217; and African Americans, 109–110; availability of, 121–122, 125, 135; and counterculture, 126;

Index

Pill (*continued*)
    dangers of, 111, 132; letters to editor about, 116–117, 120–121; and married women, 106, 111–112, 129; moral framework, 110, 115–119, 125, 126, 129, 131; and population control, 7, 107, 108–109, 112–115, 125, 126, 129, 131, 135, 137; and promiscuity, 106–107, 117–119, 122, 135; side effects, 105, 122; and single women, 1, 106–107, 111–112, 115–118, 120–122, 125, 129, 135; struggles over, in Lawrence, 112–115, 130–135; symbolize revolution, 106; *UDK* series, 121–122; use statistics, 105, 111, 122–123, 130, 134

Pincus, Gregory Goodwin, 3

pinup girls, 41

Plamondon, Genie, 170–171

Planned Parenthood, 112, 113, 114, 115, 123, 131

Playboy, 1, 3, 42, 158, 170, 215

poetry, 144, 145, 155–156, 164, 174, 190, 192–193, 194, 195; revolutionary, 160–162

poets, with Lawrence connections, 145, 164

police, 171; KU, 68–69; Lawrence, 29, 31, 45, 63, 65, 66, 67, 68–69, 75, 95, 149–153, 166, 197–198; Sunflower, Kansas, 67; white, 140, 141, 152

popular culture, 17, 39–40; sexualization of, 40–44, 76

Potter Lake, 146, 196

poverty, 148, 110, 111, 130, 133

pregnancy, 8, 48, 62, 75, 96, 101; fear of, 11, 76–77, 105, 117, 135, 217; teen, 11; unwanted, 109, 124, 151

premarital sex, 2, 3, 68, 76, 77, 116, 117–119, 210, 216

Presley, Elvis, 17, 39–40

Princeton University, 46, 81, 118

promiscuity, 7, 72, 135, 137, 154, 155, 199; and Pill, 106–107, 117–119, 122; women's alleged, 65; WWII rumors, 25–26

Promise Keepers, 216

prostitution, during WWII, 21, 22, 25–26

protest: antiwar, 138–139, 141, 150–151, 163; counterculture, 150–151; KU, 91–94, 97–98, 102, 179; racial, 147–150; student, 2, 80–83; women, 127–129

psychiatry: at KU, 50–53, 54, 55, 62, 65, 67, 101–102, 218; lobby against gay liberation, 185, 186–187; military, 49–50, 55, 56–60; and rape (KU), 198; and universities, 49–50, 59–61, 70–73, 118

psychotherapeutic system, 50, 54, 55, 61, 62–63, 67–68, 69, 70–73, 75, 83, 114

public health department: Lawrence, 23, 32, 108–111, 113–114, 121–123, 130–135; U.S., 10, 14–15, 108, 110

Putnam, Jon, 101

Quantrill, William Clarke, 18

race, 136, 139–140, 142; in Lawrence, 142, 147–149

rape, 10, 64–65, 79, 100, 137, 197–199

Rape Victim Support Services, 197–198

Ray, Johnny, 40

Reagan, Ronald, 139, 141

recreation, in WWII, 18, 20, 32

religion, 11, 48, 106, 107, 115, 120, 196; and birth control, 112

reputation: women's, 11, 77, 99, 117–118, 120; university's, 62, 66, 71, 151, 161, 179–180, 187

respectability, 9, 11, 14, 27, 28, 30, 32, 38, 39, 43, 71, 76–78, 88, 89, 126, 141; definitions of, 17, 43–44

responsibility, 9, 70, 83, 96, 98, 101–102, 104, 210; foster in youth, 50, 87, 90; language of, 92–93; universities', 8

revolution: in Lawrence, 142–153; as metaphor, 2. *See also* sexual revolution

revolutionaries: cultural, 155, 157–158, 190, 215; political, 140, 155, 158, 190

Richard, 189, 190

Rock Chalk Café, 144, 150, 152, 163

Rubin, Jerry, 158, 181

rules, about sexual behavior, 76–80

safety, women's, 10, 78, 79, 99–100

sanchez, sonia, 160

Sanders, Ed, 144, 145, 167

Schlosser, Patricia, M.D., 107

scholarship halls, KU, 205–208, 214

School and Society, 61, 65, 118

school board, Lawrence, 149–150

Schraeder, Dr., 189

Schwegler, Raymond, 59, 115–117, 124, 129, 130–131, 133

science, and sex, 48–49, 54, 72

Screw, The, 158–160

S.C.U.M., 127

Seale, Bobby, 181

Seaman, Barbara, 132

senior key system, 90–91, 101, 103

senior yell, KU, 188

servicemen: in Lawrence, 31–32; and sexual experience, 37; Lawrence center for, 34–36

sex: as problem, 191–193; philosophy, 156; role in liberation movements, 177–178; stages of intimacy, 77–78, 79; as weapon, 155–158, 160, 174

sex control, 44, 60–61, 81, 82, 91–93, 95; ideological system of, 76–78; institutional, 7–8; at KU, 55, 62–63, 69–70, 75, 95–96, 99, 101, 103–104; postwar, 40–44; structural system of, 78–80, 82; universities and, 47–50, 73; in WWII, 17–18, 30, 33

Sexual Behavior in the Human Female (Kinsey), 77, 82

sexual containment, 66

sexual mores, pre-revolutionary, 11, 76–80

sexual revolution: calls for, 136; and danger, 2; legacies of, 3, 11, 216–218; modest, 10, 215; portrayals of, 3, 5; prehistory, 44; strands of, 11, 137, 199, 202, 214–215, 218; unintended, 3, 7–8, 14, 107, 125, 135, 137. *See also* revolution

Simmons, John, 112, 115

Sinclair, John, 9, 151, 156–157, 169

60 Minutes, 146

Smith College, 81

Solanas, Valerie, 195

Squat, 159

Stars and Stripes, 74

state legislature, Kansas, 4, 20, 107, 108, 110, 112, 179–181, 187

Stockton, Frank, 20, 33, 36

Stockton, Marge, 32–36, 38, 44

Stonewall, 175, 190

student health service: KU, 24, 59, 115–116, 122, 124–125, 129, 196, 197; other universities, 118

Student Nonviolent Coordinating Committee, 140, 154–155

Student Responsibility Movement, 91–98, 116, 117, 124, 145

students, Haskell, 89, 90, 149, 197. *See also* Native Americans

students, high school, 6, 38, 184

students, KU, 18, 32, 75, 179; and antiwar protest, 151; attitudes about sex, 119–120; and birth control, 115–125; and coed dorms, 205–211; diversity of, 39, 84; and drugs, 166–167; and GLF, 178–183; *in loco parentis* struggle, 81–104; military trainees, 31; and Pill, 115–118; punishments, 52, 65–66, 74, 89–90, 96; radicalism of, 143

students, LHS, 149–150; African American, 143, 148, 159; and *Students Free Press,* 162

students, university, 1, 6, 7–8, 38, 44, 46–47, 74, 78–104, 139–141; centrality of, 87; and democratic citizenship, 50, 83, 137; diversity of, 49, 84–85; and drugs, 166–167; and protests, 150–151; and psychotherapy, 71–73

Students for a Democratic Society (SDS), 6, 92, 103; at KU, 91–94, 95, 124, 140, 145, 158

Summer of Love, 1, 3, 125, 137

Sunflower Ordnance Works, 20–23, 31, 32, 33, 36, 38

Supreme Court, Kansas, 95

Supreme Court, U.S., 7, 15, 129, 182

Surface, James, 95–96

Swarthmore College, 47, 70

Tansy, 145, 164

taxpayers, 4, 62, 81, 96, 103, 108, 109, 110, 151, 161, 179–181, 187

Index

Taylor, Emily, 62–63, 91, 94, 103–104, 124, 127

Templar, Judge, 181–182

transgression: sexual, 8, 30, 44, 49, 58, 60, 61, 62–70, 71, 136–137; heterosexual, 55, 65, 67, 68–69, 74; homosexual, 50–55, 62, 63–67, 71–73; images, 171–174, 217; language, 160–165, 202, 204, 217; and youth, 48–49

underground newspapers, 11, 26, 37, 142, 145, 151, 155–156, 169, 170, 176–177; in Lawrence, 158–162, 167–169, 176–177; lesbian and gay, 190

United Campus Christian Fellowship, 112

United Ecumenical Christian Ministries, KU, 183

universities: enrollments, 49, 83–84; mental health clinics, 59; mission, 84–86, 87; postwar, 49–50, 82–85; and protests, 140–141, 150–151; social landscape, 80; in WWII, 15

University of Alabama, 45, 46

University of California, Berkeley, 141, 146, 163

University of California, Los Angeles, 61, 65

University of Kansas, 4, 111, 153; Annual Report 1958, 86; and birth control, 115–118, 127–129, 132; description of, 19; enrollment, 38, 39, 83–84; and gay liberation movement, 178–183, 187, 188, 190; history of, 20, 147–148; and *in loco parentis,* 75, 81–104; and mental health, 59; panty raids, 45–46; and sexual misconduct, 62–70. *See also* administration, KU; students, KU

University of Michigan, 79

University of Minnesota, 115

University of Missouri, 45

University of Oklahoma, 45

University of Wisconsin, 61, 71, 81

University Party (KU), 94, 102

USO, 34, 36; in Hawaii, 35

venereal disease, 31–32, 40, 48, 217; fears of, 10; in Lawrence, 25, 26–30; in WWI, 23–24; in WWII, 14, 18, 23–30, 37; rates, 30; treatment, 29

Victory Girls, 18, 25–26

Vietnam war, 80, 92, 93, 128, 136, 138, 140, 142

vigilante groups, Lawrence, 152, 167

Village People, The, 185

violence, 140–141, 145–146; in Lawrence, 149–153, 162, 165, 167, 175–176, 188, 198–199

virginity, 77, 217; at KU, 119; technical, 11, 78

Voth, Harold, 186–187

War on Poverty, 109

Watkins Hospital. *See* student health service, KU

Weathermen, 158

Wescoe, W. Clarke, 103–104

Westminster Choir College, 46

White House, 150, 153, 169

White Panther Party, 163, 169, 171

whites, 109, 138; and civil rights movement, 139–140, 154–155; in Lawrence, 19, 32, 149, 152, 160–161; in military, 16; "trash," 167

Wilcox, Eileen, 154–155

Wilson, S. Clay, 168, 170, 171

WITCH, 127, 171, 173

Wittman, Carl, 177

Wizard of Oz, The, 4, 18

women's issue, *Vortex,* 169–174; letters to editor, 172–174

women's liberation movement, 9–10, 11, 169–174, 176, 199; in Lawrence, 107, 126–127, 170–174, 191–199; and lesbianism, 190–191; role of sex in, 177–178, 190–199

Woodruff, Jeanette, 35

Woodruff, Laurence, 60, 86

World War II, 4, 8, 38, 49, 115, 138, 146, 197, 217; death toll, 21; fears about sexual morality, 25–29; in Lawrence, 13–18; and psychiatry, 55, 56–60; and sexual behavior, 30–31; and social change, 13–18, 26, 29, 30–31, 33, 36, 39, 44; venereal disease, 23–30, 40

Yippies, 157–158, 160, 165
youth culture, 6, 49, 76, 78, 121, 125–126, 140, 203, 215; and counterculture, 141, 157–158; fears about, 47–48, 104, 136, 141, 201–203
"Youth in Crisis," 26

Zero Population Growth, 6, 124, 129